Second Edition

READ *Write!*

BREAKING DOWN A TEXT AND BUILDING UP AN ESSAY

Selena Stewart-Alexander
Patrice K. Johnson
Caitlin S. Stanford Kintner

Kendall Hunt
publishing company

D0144736

Cover image © Shutterstock, Inc.

Kendall Hunt
publishing company

www.kendallhunt.com
Send all inquiries to:
4050 Westmark Drive
Dubuque, IA 52004-1840

Printed in the United States of America

Contents

Readings List

Acknowledgements

To begin, it is important to acknowledge our contributing student and professional writers. Our deep appreciate goes out to the following people: Louis Cruz, Angela Miskell, Rhonda Lee, Christian Ramirez, Karelly Hernandez, Kenasia M. Johnson, Jennifer Loredo, David Ramirez, Stephen M. Kintner, Michelle Stewart-Thomas, Tasneem Basha, Jane Stanford, Kenny Wiley, Kerry L. Stanford, Nelda Contreras, Virginia Morris, Malik Alexander, Katherine Husted, Mayra Amador, and Lamarcus Warren.

Dedication

Selena

Being able to do what I love for a living is an honor that I thank my Creator for every day. For I know that not everyone can say that about his/her vocation. Besides thanking my Lord and Savior Jesus Christ for allowing me to help students improve their reading and writing skills as a professor and author, I would also like to acknowledge my family and friends who graciously allowed me to put their work in this book. Lastly, I thank my two coauthors for their friendship and for signing up to collaborate again for the benefit of our students.

Patrice

First, I would like to dedicate this book to my students who have given me the inspiration to publish educational material. I would also like to dedicate this book to my family Kevin, Kenasia, Tyson, and Mari for supporting me during this project and encouraging me along the way. Also, I would like to dedicate this book to my late parents Verse and Mary Franklin. My passion for teaching comes from their guidance and encouragement. I have the pleasure once again of dedicating this book to my coauthors. The passion we have for students' success is unique, and I am proud to be on a team with astute individuals such as you. Finally, I would like to thank God for once again giving me the opportunity to serve students

Caitlin

As always, this book is dedicated to my students. I hope you find it a useful tool in your college journey. I would also like to dedicate the new edition of this book to my people—my husband, Stephen, my daughter, Rylin Tatiana, my parents, Karen and Kerry, and my coauthors, Selena and Patrice.

Preface: The Reading and Writing Connection

Have you ever heard the riddle: Which came first—the chicken or the egg? Some say the chicken while others say the egg. What do you say?

A riddle that involves academics is the following: Do students improve their reading skills by writing, or do they improve their writing skills by reading? While the answer to the former question about the chicken and egg dilemma is still being debated, the answer to the latter question about reading and writing is actually circular, meaning they work together.

Reading   Writing

The graphic illustrates that reading and writing work together to improve the skills you need in both to be successful in college and in life. In other words, in order to improve your reading skills, you must write more, and in order to improve your writing skills, you must read more.

HOW WILL READING IMPROVE YOUR WRITING SKILLS?

When you read more, you improve your writing in various ways. The first way is that you expose yourself to a variety of writing styles based on what you read that you can use when you write. For example, when you read novels, you learn how to draw your reader in by using literary devices like foreshadowing, how to create characters that act and behave in believable ways, how to build suspense, and how to craft a well-written story that keeps your reader's interest and has a point. For example, if you read a passage about how someone overcame his/her fear of public speaking so that he/she could pass a speech class, the point would be that despite being afraid, an individual can still be successful.

When you read the newspaper or an article on the Internet, you learn how to put the most important information first, how language is used to inform, persuade, and entertain, and how to answer the reporter's questions: who, what, when, where, why, and how.

Also, by reading, you will learn to identify signal words that introduce organizational patterns, like simple listing, definition, comparison-contrast, and cause and effect, that you can use in your own writing. These patterns help to clarify the author's message because they provide a road map for how the information in a particular paragraph fits into an article, section, essay, or chapter.

Besides being exposed to different writing styles through reading, you expand your vocabulary through context clues or actually looking up unknown words in a dictionary. In addition, you learn how to write sentences that flow and are constructed in Standard English. Furthermore, when you read, you are exposed to figurative language, such as similes and metaphors, that help strengthen sensory details. Finally, through reading, you learn a variety of useful information that you can write about, such as where the first Olympics was held, tips on how to ace a job interview, or which is better: an Apple iPhone or a Samsung Galaxy.

HOW WILL WRITING IMPROVE YOUR READING SKILLS?

When you read, you must become fully engaged with the text. In other words, you must practice active reading to help your brain stay focused on the material so that you can better comprehend or understand what you are reading. **Active reading** means that you are utilizing reading strategies. When most students read, they read passively surrounded by distractions. **Passive reading** means you just read the material and hope some of it sticks in your memory banks. Never mind the fact that you are also listening to loud music blaring from your Beats headphones or actually watching the cussing and fighting taking place on the reality TV show instead of reading.

Writing is an active way to help you make sense of your reading material. Therefore, when you read an assignment for the first time—yes, this mean you will have to read it more than once—you should have a pencil in your hand so that you can write important information in the margins, put question marks by material you do not understand, and circle key words. The reason you should use a pencil instead of a highlighter for the first reading is that you have not yet ascertained or figured out what is most important. If you use a highlighter at this point, you may end up highlighting most of the text, which will not be helpful to you later when you review the material. On your second or subsequent reading of the material, you may then choose to use a highlighter because now you know what key information you want to stand out.

Some additional ways writing can help you read actively are to jot down possible quiz questions, predict what will happen next, and clarify and summarize key points. The key points can be jotted down in a scratch outline format, in a graphic organizer, or by using quickly drawn pictures. In addition, you can reflect on what you have read by writing down what you have learned about the topic, if your views have changed or been reinforced, or if the reading reminds you of something else you have read, learned, or experienced. Also, you can assess the reading passage itself by deciding what worked well, what could be improved, or how you would have written the passage. Making connections and writing helps you remember and understand what you are reading.

Read Write! Breaking down a Text and Building up an Essay is designed to help you understand the reading and writing connection so that you can strengthen **both** your reading and writing skills. Therefore, throughout this student-centered textbook, you will learn strategies and tools to help you stretch your reading and writing muscles. However, in order to maximize your workout, you must be willing to do the following:

- ◆ Read this textbook thoroughly and carefully.
- ◆ Find ways to connect with the material.
- ◆ Practice the strategies.
- ◆ Fully complete the activities in the textbook and on the website.
- ◆ Envision and work for your own success.
- ◆ Take advantage of campus resources.

Are you ready for the challenge that awaits you? The workout will be strenuous, but the reward—improving your reading and writing skills—will be worth it.

> ➤ **Read Write! Tip**
>
> When you are reading your textbook, writing an essay, or studying for a test, find a quiet place away from distractions like the TV and loud music. Also, turn off your cellphone and just check it when you take a break; then, turn it off again when your break is over.

SOME NOTES ABOUT THIS TEXT

Terminology

When you are reading this text, you will often come across the words "passage," "reading," or "text." Understand that these words are synonymous, meaning they mean the same thing. They will be used to refer to whatever you are reading—a short story, a novel, an essay, or a newspaper article. These terms mean a piece of writing that you are *reading*.

> ➤ **Read Write! Tip**

Additionally, throughout this text you will see Read Write! Tips like the one above. These tips are meant to help you better grasp a concept or to help improve your study skills. While there is no section specifically dedicated to study skills in this textbook, you will find that study skills are mentioned off and on throughout.

Color Coding

Lastly, this book has been color coded to make reading it and following ideas easier. Below is a legend for you to use as you go through this text.

- ◆ Chapter titles are **purple, bolded, and a larger font size**.
- ◆ Headings are **RED, ALL CAPS, AND BOLDED**.
- ◆ Subheadings are **orange and bolded**.
- ◆ Read Write! Tips are **golden and bolded**.
- ◆ Activities are **blue and bolded**.
- ◆ Key terms and examples are **bolded.**

Pages

This textbook is actually a workbook, which means it is designed so that you can annotate and highlight, jot down notes, and complete assignments directly on the pages. Moreover, the pages are perforated so that you can more easily tear them out and turn assignments in to your instructor.

The Reading and Writing Questionnaire

1. Do you have a positive or negative attitude towards reading? Why?

2. Do you have a positive or negative attitude towards writing? Why?

3. How do you think your attitude affects your ability to understand what you are reading?

4. How do you think your attitude affects your ability to complete writing assignments?

5. Were you read to as a child? If you have children, do you read to them?

6. Do you have a library card? Do you own a Kindle? Do you listen to books on tape or download books?

7. Do you read books, magazines, or online material? If so, what kinds? (Remember social networking sites count.)

8. What are some things you write for personal enjoyment, for school, or for work?

9. What is your strategy when you are assigned to read something difficult, like a chapter in a textbook?

10. What is your strategy when you are assigned to write a paper in a college course?

Author Bios

Selena Stewart-Alexander

Selena Stewart-Alexander has over 25 years' experience teaching in higher education. She is the 2015-2016 recipient of the Minnie Stevens Piper Full-Time Excellence in Teaching Award for Eastfield College in Mesquite, TX, where she teaches both English and integrated reading and writing. Stewart-Alexander has a master's degree in English from the University of Texas in Arlington and a BFA in communications from Southern Methodist University. Reading, traveling, participating in Delta Sigma Theta and church outreach activities, and spending time with her family and friends are how she spends her leisure time when she is not grading essays or writing.

Patrice K. Johnson

Patrice K. Johnson is an educator and textbook author. She is a full-time professor of developmental English at Eastfield College, which is a part of the Dallas County Community College District. She earned a bachelor's degree in English from the University of Central Missouri and a master's degree in Higher Education

From right to left: Stewart-Alexander, Johnson, and Stanford Kintner, presenting at the 2015 NADE Conference, in Greenville, SC.

from Texas A&M-Commerce. She is the co-chair for the English/Writing/ESL Special Interest Network for the National Association for Developmental Education. In her spare time, she enjoys spending time with her immediate and extended family, writing non-fiction, and traveling.

Caitlin S. Stanford Kintner

Caitlin S. Stanford Kintner is an educator and textbook author. She is a full-time faculty member at Eastfield College in Mesquite, TX, where she teaches developmental English and college English. She has a bachelor's degree in journalism and a Master's of Professional Writing, both from the University of Oklahoma, and has completed graduate hours in developmental education, reading, higher education curriculum and instruction, English, and sociolinguistics at Texas A&M-Commerce. She is a member of the National Association of Developmental Education, the Texas Association of Developmental Education, and the Texas Community College Teachers Association. She enjoys reading, writing, photography, and spending time with her husband, daughter, friends, family, and pets.

Stewart-Alexander, Johnson, and Stanford Kintner are also the authors of *Think Write! Essays, 1st ed., Read Write! An Introduction to Integrated Reading and Writing, 2nd ed.,* and *Think Write! Sentences and Paragraphs with Readings, 2nd ed.*

PART I

The Reading and Writing Processes

Chapter 1
The Reading Process

Key Terms

active reading, PAUSE, prereading, annotating, understanding, jargon, context clues, definition, synonyms, antonyms, examples, topic, main idea, supporting details, implied main idea, summarizing, evaluating

Reading college material is sometimes difficult, especially if it is about a topic that does not interest you or contains words you are unfamiliar with. Nevertheless, you must read and comprehend the material in order for you to be successful in your college courses. The purpose of this section of the textbook is to introduce the reading process so that you can develop or refine strategies to enhance your thinking and reading skills to help you be successful in all your college courses. Moreover, as you develop your reading skills, your writing skills will improve, as well. As you learned in the preface, reading and writing are intricately connected. The more you read, the better you write and vice versa.

"My strategy for a reading assignment is to read and then reread it until I understand the subject. I also make sure that I understand the instructions before getting started."

—Louis Cruz
Eastfield College
Mesquite, TX

What do you do when you sit down to read for a college class? Do you just read the assignment once and call it a day? Do you have a strategy or system you use to help yourself better understand the text? Do you read it over and over again and hope that makes it stick? It is important to have a strategy for reading comprehension, especially in college courses as they tend to be reading heavy, and the reading assignments themselves are often dense. Thus, it is important to read actively rather than passively.

Reading passively is what you do when you read something once and then put it down. **Active reading** means utilizing strategies to engage with the text, such as creating prereading questions and answering them, summarizing a passage, or annotating the text; it also means you read the text multiple times. Active reading is important to reading comprehension because it allows you to check your own understanding as well as helps you to tackle difficult readings, such as reading multiple chapters out of a history or biology textbook.

There are a variety of reading comprehension systems you can use to help yourself better understand a text. Perhaps you already know some, such as SQR3 (survey-read-recite-review) or KWL (what I already know-what I want to know-what I learned). For the most part, this book will utilize a reading comprehension system called PAUSE. **PAUSE** is a five step strategy to help you achieve better comprehension through the reading process.

PAUSE

PAUSE is an acronym and mnemonic device to help you remember the five steps of this reading comprehension system. It is also a reminder to *slow down* when you read as good reading is like good writing: they both take time. PAUSE stands for:

♦ Prereading
♦ Annotating
♦ Understanding
♦ Summarizing
♦ Evaluating

Image © Matthew Cole, 2014. Used under license from Shutterstock, Inc.

Prereading

Prereading is one of the most important steps in the reading process because it allows you to gauge material and mentally prepare yourself to read, especially if you are reading something difficult or particularly dense. The prefix "pre" means *before*, so this step is completed before you actually read the text.

Prereading Steps

Read any information that may appear about the author. This may appear before the text or at the end. While it is tempting to skip this information, knowing context about the author often helps you to better understand the text.

Skim the title and any headings or subheadings to get an idea of what the reading is about. Also, by scanning over these items quickly, they give you clues regarding how the passage is organized. If there are no headings or subheadings, you can look at the first and last sentences of each paragraph. These will help give you a general idea of what the passage is about and what each individual paragraph is about, as well.

Skim any pictures, charts, or other visuals that accompany the text. Authors sometimes use graphics to illustrate or to help explain a concept in more detail.

Notice if any difficult, key, or technical vocabulary words have been italicized or bolded within the passage or if they have been defined for you in the margin or at the bottom of the page.

Flip through the full reading to determine its length and difficulty. If the passage is long or appears difficult due to paragraph density and/or numerous unknown words, then you know you need to spend more time on it.

Answer any prereading questions provided with the text. Sometimes you will be given questions to answer before you read. These are to help you engage with the text and think about it before you begin reading.

If you are reading a chapter from a textbook, see if there are review questions and/or a chapter summary at the end of the chapter. If there are, then you should read these BEFORE you read the chapter to get an overview of what the chapter will cover. However, do not let these "fill in" for actually reading; you still need to read the chapter itself!

Now that you have completed the preliminary steps of the reading process, you are ready to actually read the passage for the first time. Remember that good reading takes time; you will read the text multiple times before you complete the reading process. When you read for the first time, you should not do anything but read. Take your time and get a feel for the passage, but save annotating or trying to answer questions for subsequent readings. The first reading of any text should just be to read.

Annotating

After you have read the text for the first time, it is time to read it again. Every time you read a text you will notice new things and also reinforce what you have already learned from the previous readings. As you complete subsequent readings, you should annotate. **Annotating** is when you write notes in the margins, circle unfamiliar words, underline, and make connections by jotting down what a particular section reminds you of that you have read before or have experienced. There is no right or wrong way to annotate a text; as you practice annotating, you will begin to find what

works best for you. However, it is suggested that you always annotate initially in pencil. Below are some suggested annotation symbols, though, as you practice PAUSE, you may begin to develop your own. You may also find that you want to use post-its or other page markers as you annotate.

Annotation Symbols	
Underline	Key information or details
⬭	Circle words that need to be defined
*	Important information
?	Don't understand
!	Interesting or surprising information

(continued)

Annotation Symbols	
↔ or ∞	Connection to previous knowledge, concepts, or other texts made
√	Something you already know
1, 2, 3	Number consecutive ideas
Notes	Notes can include definitions and connections. They can be jotted in the margins of the text. They may start with phrases like "I think . . ." "I notice . . ." "This is . . ." "This means . . ."

After your initial annotation, it is time to read again. During your subsequent (third or more) readings, it will be clearer what the reading selection is about and how it is organized. You will also be aware of which information is covered in depth and the importance of a section to the overall text based on how much time the author spends covering it. Furthermore, during subsequent readings, you should be able to erase some of your question marks. In addition, you may feel comfortable now using a highlighter to denote key information.

Example Annotation

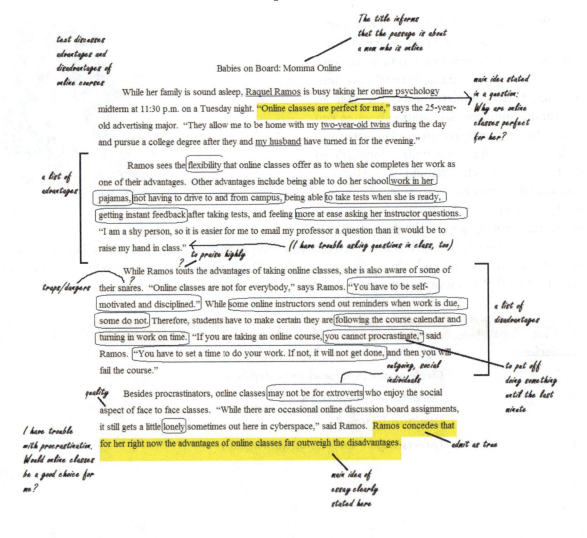

Understanding

By now you have read the material three or more times; you have also annotated it. Now it is time to check your **understanding**. Are you able to state aloud what the chapter, essay, or article is about and what you learned from reading it? Checking your comprehension is crucial. If you do not have a basic understanding of the reading material, then you are just looking at words on a page.

One way to check your reading comprehension is to create questions for yourself to answer based on the headings, subheadings, thesis statements of essays, topic sentences of paragraphs, or bolded words. Also, pay attention to information that is covered in great depth, the importance of a section to the overall text, or how much time the author spends covering it. For example, some questions you might ask yourself over this chapter so far are as follows:

1. What is the first step in the PAUSE reading strategy?
2. Why is this step important or what can be learned from completing this step?
3. What is the second step in the PAUSE reading strategy?
4. Why is it important to use a pencil instead of a highlighter during this step?

If you cannot readily answer these questions or anticipate other possible quiz questions your instructor may ask, then go back and read the section again; this time annotate as you read.

As you annotated, you may have circled unfamiliar words. If you are unfamiliar with any words in a reading, it will be difficult for you to make sense of the passage. Furthermore, it may cause you to misinterpret what the author is trying to say. Consequently, it is crucial that you familiarize yourself with the terms of a particular field of study, learn how to recognize the meaning of words using context clues, and be willing to look up the definition of unknown words during this stage of the reading process.

Are you aware that each college course has its own vocabulary words that you must learn in order to be successful in that class? For example, in reading and writing courses, some of the key terms that you must know are purpose, main idea, supporting ideas, thesis, topic sentences, and tone. What other courses are you taking? What are some of the key vocabulary words? Oftentimes, this specialized vocabulary is called **jargon.**

Besides familiarizing yourself with the terms, jargon, and vocabulary of a course, it is also important to know how to figure out the meaning of unknown words using **context clues**, especially when you do not have access to a dictionary, such as during a test. When you use context clues, you focus on the known words and phrases in a sentence to figure out the meaning of the unknown word. Four types of context clues are **definitions**, **synonyms**, **antonyms**, and **examples**.

Four Types of Context Clues

Type	Definition	Example Sentence	Answer
Definition	defining the actual word in the sentence	After WWII, Japanese Americans received **reparations**, a monetary settlement, for being placed in resettlement camps.	*Reparations* means financial settlement in this context.
Synonyms	using a word similar in meaning to the unknown word	The new mall is **ginormous**; it is so big that the last time I was there I got lost.	*Ginormous* means big.

(continued)

Type	Definition	Example Sentence	Answer
Antonyms	using a word that has the opposite meaning of the unknown word	The **gregarious** student invited his shy classmate to join his study group.	*Gregarious* is the opposite of shy. Therefore, you can infer *gregarious* means outgoing.
Examples	providing supporting details the reader can use to infer the word's meaning	Ebenezer Scrooge, a **miserly** old man, had few friends and refused to pay Bob Cratchit a decent wage.	From the example, you can infer that *miserly* means lonely and stingy.

If you are unsuccessful at determining the meaning of a word after using context clues, you should consult a dictionary.

> **Read Write! Tip**
>
> Today dictionaries are more than just dusty old volumes. You can look up the meaning of words using online dictionaries or smartphone apps, including ones you can download or ones that are preinstalled on your phone, like the iPhone's Siri or Microsoft's Cortana.

Read Write! Activity 1.1

Select the letter of the best meaning of the word in bold print.

1. _____ The **antagonist** in Westerns usually wears a black hat while the protagonist, or hero, often wears a white hat.
   a. sidekick   b. villain   c. mentor
2. _____ The parents were so proud of their **progeny** for winning the spelling bee that they took the whole family out to dinner.
   a. child   b. judge   c. teacher
3. _____ The **volatile** child threw a temper tantrum in the toy aisle at Target.
   a. volcanic   b. hungry   c. raging
4. _____ Gloria realized that her attempts to get her husband to wear matching outfits to the costume party were **futile** when he changed his mind about even going to the party.
   a. ineffective   b. possible   c. difficult
5. _____ Marcus was **ecstatic** when he became the starting quarterback; his shouts of joy could be heard throughout the locker room.
   a. pained   b. delighted   c. relieved

> **Read Write! Tip**
>
> Do not wait until the last minute to complete reading assignments as you may have to re-read them multiple times, define numerous words, or converse with a study buddy before you fully understand what you have read. Remember that good reading takes time! Give yourself adequate time to read well.

When you check your understanding, you can also begin breaking down the passage into its basic elements by identifying the topic, main idea, and supporting details. The **topic** is the general subject of the reading. It is not the point the author is trying to make but rather the overall subject matter the author has chosen to write about. You could be asked to find the topic of a paragraph, an essay, a passage, a short story, a book chapter, or perhaps even a larger piece of work.

Once you have established what the topic is, you can identify the main idea of what you are reading. The **main idea** is the point the author is trying to get across to his/her readers. It is the key concept the author is trying to convey through his/her writing. It can be directly stated or implied.

Tips for Determining the Main Idea

Ask yourself what the author is trying to convey about the topic. What is the author saying about the topic?

Examine the first and last sentences of the text. If it is a larger work, look at the first paragraph and the last paragraph. The main idea will often be present in the first sentence or paragraph and then reinforced in the last sentence or paragraph of the text. This may help you discern what the author is trying to get across to the reader.

Be careful about the smaller details. When finding a main idea, you do not need to include anything that appears to support a larger idea. Rather, focus on the big picture of the point the author is trying to convey.

The **supporting details** are the specifics an author uses to back up his/her main idea. The main idea always expresses some sort of point, and to strengthen and validate this point, the author must provide support. In essence, the supporting details expand on the main idea and help the reader better understand the author's point or, depending on the purpose of the writing, persuade the reader to even accept or agree with the author's point. When you are asked to identify supporting details, think about the main idea and then ask yourself what parts of the passage help to develop the main idea's point.

When you are determining an implied main idea, you must examine the supporting details to figure the author's point because an **implied main idea** is not stated. If you read through a passage and find no stated main idea, read through the passage again and ask yourself what the common theme is. What does each of the sentences have in common? As you ask yourself these questions, annotate your passage with a pencil. Make note of repeating ideas or concepts that seem connected. If you feel confident, highlight key ideas or phrases that help you answer your questions. Thinking about and annotating the passage this way can lead you to the implied main idea of the text because it allows you to make connections between the presented details. When in doubt, ask yourself what the controlling idea of the passage is. What is it that is holding all the smaller ideas together?

Tips for Determining Implied Main Idea

Check out the title. It will usually give you a clue as to what the author is trying to say.

Identify the topic of the passage. Remember that the topic will be included as a part of the main idea.

In a larger work, like an essay or a book chapter, you may have subtopics or headings. What is the larger idea that these subtopics are trying to explain?

Look at the supporting details. What are the smaller pieces of the text? Can you tell what they are trying to develop? That is your unstated main idea.

After prereading, annotate the passage. Use a pencil or highlighter to mark key ideas and supporting details. These will usually lead you to the implied main idea.

Ask yourself what the author is trying to tell you. What is the big picture of the author's point?

One excellent way to check your comprehension is to create a graphic organizer of the passage, such as a pyramid. A pyramid will allow you to create visual representation of the reading. It will also allow you to further break down the reading into major and minor supporting details. Graphic organizers are covered more in chapter 2.

Summarizing

Summarizing is the fourth step in PAUSE. When you **summarize**, you create a condensed version of a reading selection that captures the author's main idea and key points in the order that they were presented. A summary, therefore, is a shortened version of the original writing. Identifying topic, main idea, and supporting details will help you in this step.

Summarizing material aids in your reading comprehension and study skills because it requires you to sift through the material, locate key information, and state it mostly in your own words. While it is acceptable to quote the author in a summary, you want to do so sparingly, especially when the purpose of the summary is to help you learn new material to prepare for an upcoming exam.

When you summarize, you list the main idea and key points and leave out your opinions, your thoughts, and your reactions to the reading. The reporter's questions of who, what, when, where, why, and how (5WH) can be used to help you focus on the key information. However, you are not to answer all of the reporter's questions each time you summarize material; you will focus only on answering the questions that will help you extract the author's key information. Your instructor may require you to summarize something for a grade, or you may choose to do so because it is a good way to ascertain that you have a clear understanding of what you have read.

Summarizing can take various forms. One form is "Think-Pair-Share" or small group discussions. With partners or in small groups, you will be given a few minutes to jot down what the main idea is. Then, you share and compare your answers with others. If you cannot explain what you have read in your own words and/or verbally explain it to someone else, then you have not fully comprehended what you have read. Therefore, you must go back and reread the material again. Do not be discouraged if you have to read a chapter several times to understand it. Remember, you are not in a race with other individuals to see who can read the passage the fastest; you are working on improving your own reading and writing skills.

In the PAUSE strategy, summarizing serves as a way to actively ensure that you are processing what you are reading. In other words, if you can explain to a classmate or jot down the main idea and the key points of what you have read, then you have some understanding of the passage. How to create a more structured and formal summary as a mode of writing is discussed in chapter 14.

Evaluate

The fifth step in the PAUSE strategy is to **evaluate** what you have read. At this point you are ready to think critically about what you have read by analyzing, reflecting, and reacting to the text. You will synthesize information and make connections to what you already know. You will consider concepts like tone, mood, bias, and assumptions (both yours and the author's). You will also examine the reading at a deeper level, sifting through multiple layers of meaning.

The purpose of evaluating what you are reading is to reinforce what you are learning so that you are actively engaged with the text. For example, as you are reading about PAUSE, does it remind you about other reading strategies you might have learned, such as KWL or SQR3 and SQR4? If so, then will relating PAUSE to those reading strategies help you remember or understand this new strategy better?

Relating the information you are learning to what you already know helps you to make connections and reinforces learning. Furthermore, knowing about the author may help you to understand the reading better. Is the author known for being humorous or satirical? What happened in the author's past to make him/her feel so strongly about the topic he/she is writing about? If there is a mini biography about the author before the reading, some of these questions may be answered. Your instructor may assign you to research an author or a topic using multiple sources and then reevaluate what was presented to you in the text if no information about the author is listed or to ensure you gain a deeper understanding about what you are reading.

The three main purposes of writing are to entertain, to inform, and to persuade. Therefore, as you evaluate what you are reading, keep these purposes in mind. For example, after reading a text about a controversial topic, such as climate change, you may question what you can do to help. Did the reading inspire you to recycle and/or reuse your water bottle twice before tossing it into a recycle bin? If you are not inspired, what could the author have done better to show why recycling is important?

Image © Stuart Jenner, 2014. Used under license from Shutterstock, Inc.

The goal of good writing is to cause a reaction from readers, whether it is causing them to laugh at an embarrassing moment in the author's life, to incorporate new reading strategies into their learning arsenal, or to become involved in saving the planet. Evaluating what you are reading transforms you from being a mere sponge soaking up information into an empowered critical thinker. Evaluation and other critical reading concepts and strategies are covered more in depth in chapter 5.

Read Write! Activity 1.2

Using the first step of PAUSE, preread the passage below entitled "Campus Jewels." Skim over the title, subtitles, and gauge length and difficulty. Then, "Think-Pair-Share" with a partner. After you have discussed what you noticed as you skimmed, read the passage once just to take it in and get a feel for it. Do not annotate.

Campus Jewels

1   Campus resources are available to help students be successful in college. Unfortunately, not all students are aware that help is available. Three campus resources that savvy students know about are the tutoring center, the library, and the computer lab.

The Tutoring Center

2   One place that students need to know about is the tutoring center. At the tutoring center, students can receive free tutoring for their classes. For example, at most college tutoring centers, there are always math and English tutors available to help students whenever the center is open. For other subjects, like chemistry, accounting, or foreign languages, tutors are available at certain times.

The Library

3   Another campus resource that students should know about is the library, which offers much more than a quiet place to study. For instance, students can check out books, read popular magazines, ask librarians

for help with research papers, and borrow their current textbook to complete assignments if their instructor has put a copy on reserve in the library. In addition, at some colleges and universities, the library staff and faculty hold workshops on various topics from citing sources in research papers to acing job interviews in their libraries' meeting rooms.

The Computer Lab

4   The third well-kept secret that only some students know about is the computer lab. No longer can students use the excuse, "I don't have a computer, so I couldn't type my paper." Many college computer labs are open six days a week. Computers are available for students to use to do a plethora of activities, such as complete assignments, have access to the Internet, or check email. If students need help with creating a PowerPoint presentation, accessing Blackboard, or saving and opening files, the knowledgeable staff is available to assist them.

5   Once students unearth these hidden treasures, they will gain access to resources that can enhance their college experience. As they inform their peers of the services available, more students will use these valuable resources.

Read Write! Activity 1.3

Reread "Campus Jewels" and begin annotating with a pencil. Use the annotation symbols provided earlier in the chapter. When you feel confident about which sections are significant, such as main idea, supporting details, and key words or information, you may want to use a highlighter. Define any unfamiliar words you circled using context clues or a dictionary. You can write the definitions in the margin of the text or use the lines below.

_____

_____

_____

_____

_____

Read Write! Activity 1.4

Continuing PAUSE, you should check your understanding of the reading selection. One way to do this is to turn the title and subtitles into questions. Then, if you can answer them without referring back to the text, you know you have a good command of the basic information being presented. Answer the questions below based on the title and subtitles of "Campus Jewels."

1. What are the "campus jewels"?

_____

_____

_____

_____

2. How is the tutoring center a useful campus resource?

_____

_____

_____

_____

3. How is the library a useful campus resource?

_____

_____

_____

_____

4. How is the computer lab a useful campus resource?

_____

_____

_____

_____

Read Write! Activity 1.5

Now it is time for the fourth step of PAUSE: summarize. Circle the choice that provides the best summary of "Campus Jewels."

A. "Campus Jewels" informs students about three campus resources that they should take advantage of: the library, the Veterans Affairs Office, and the tutoring center. These services are there to help students be successful in college.

B. "Campus Jewels" highlights the services that the tutoring center, the library, and the computer lab offer. While students can benefit from using these resources, not all students know about the services these resources offer.

C. Students should definitely use campus jewels, especially these three resources because they are the best ones on campus, and they help students be successful in college. A marketing campaign is needed so that more students will know about these services.

> **Read Write! Tip**

When taking multiple choice quizzes, it is important to be able to eliminate answers in order to narrow down to the correct answer.

Read Write! Activity 1.6

Verbally or in the space below, explain why you eliminated two of the answers from Read Write Activity 1.5.

I was able to eliminate choice ___ because _____

_____

_____ .

I was also able to eliminate choice ___ because _____

_____

_____ .

I selected choice ___ because _____

_____

_____ .

Read Write! Activity 1.7

Look at the example writing that evaluates "Campus Jewels." Then use the lines below to create an extended list of resources available on your campus, including resources you may have used. This will help make connections with the reading and your own experiences.

> *The author does a pretty good job of informing about the importance of using these three resources, but if I were writing this essay, I would have mentioned a few more resources, like The Veterans Affairs Office for veterans or TRIO for first-generation students. Also, it seems the author puts the responsibility on students to inform other students about these campus resources. I wonder what the college is doing and how it can do more because if more students knew about these services, I think they would use them.*

_____

_____

_____

_____

_____

Ways to Improve Reading Attitude to Increase Altitude

Step 1: Admit that your reading skills need improvement. Did you voluntarily sign up for this class, or were you placed into it after taking an assessment test? If you signed up for it, what led you to do so? If you tested into the class, what areas do you need to improve in the most?

Image © michaeljung, 2014. Used under license from Shutterstock, Inc.

Step 2: Find a reason to want to improve your reading skills. Your motivation could be as simple as wanting to pass this class, being able to read aloud more confidently, or wanting to instill in your children a love of reading or at least a "like" of reading. It could also be more complex, like wanting to take college-level courses, earn a college degree, or have a certain career. Whatever your reason, remind yourself of it daily to stay focused and motivated.

Step 3: Read every day for at least 20 minutes. You can start by reading an online newspaper, a magazine, a novel, or an autobiography or a biography about one of your heroes. As you read, write down unknown words that you come across in your vocabulary journal. Use context clues to *decipher* what the words mean; if you cannot *figure it out*, then look the words up in a dictionary. Online dictionaries or dictionary apps may even pronounce the unknown words for you. Make certain that this reading is in addition to what you are assigned to read for your college classes or your job. Add any unknown words that you come across while reading for pleasure or self-improvement to your vocabulary journal, as well. Try to add at least a minimum of one word a day. Review and memorize these words. Eventually, they will become a part of your everyday vocabulary. Be on the lookout for newly learned words as you read various materials.

Step 4: Practice reading aloud. At first, you may sound choppy, meaning your words do not flow, you ignore punctuation marks, and skip over unknown words. After a while, you will find that you are reading aloud more easily and with more fluency. **Reading fluency** is the ability to accurately, smoothly, and expressively read a text, which are crucial to reading comprehension. Remember to pause at commas, stop at periods, and change the inflection of your voice when you read a question mark or an exclamation point.

If you are thinking, "I don't like to read" or "I don't have time to read," then you need to adjust your attitude and think of reading like eating your vegetables; it is good for you and essential to understanding what you are reading, so find the time to do it—silently and aloud—before you turn on the TV, talk on the phone, or go to sleep at night. Make reading and learning new words a priority.

As you utilize the strategies in the reading process, you will strengthen your reading comprehension skills, which is one half of the goal of this textbook. The other half, strengthening your writing skills, is addressed beginning in chapter 3.

Read Write! Review Questions: The Reading Process

1. Define prereading and what it entails.
2. Define annotating and what it entails.
3. Define understanding and what it entails.
4. Define summarizing and what it entails.
5. Define evaluating and what it entails.

Read Write! Connection: Chapter 1

Use PAUSE to go through Chapter 2: Success Strategies for College Students. Use the annotation symbols provided in this chapter.

Chapter 2
Success Strategies for College Students

Key Terms

paraphrasing, mnemonic devices, KWL, SQR3, prefix, suffix, root

College is a new experience. It is not like high school or other learning environments you may have been in. It is the academic arena, but it is also the professional arena. While the professors are there to facilitate your learning, there is also the expectation that you, too, must now take responsibility for your own learning, becoming your own advocate and getting yourself where you need to be. This chapter will cover some success strategies to help you take ownership of your collegiate educational experience.

© Monkey Business Images/Shutterstock.com

NOTE TAKING AND STUDY TIPS

A big part of college is taking notes over lectures, from textbooks, or from online course materials. Note taking does not mean writing down everything you hear or read verbatim. There is no time to do that, and it would be a waste of time because you cannot remember everything anyway. Therefore, you must devise systems for taking good notes.

Paraphrasing

Paraphrasing is a useful technique for condensing information that you read, listen to, or view. For example, in history class, your professor might use a PowerPoint presentation to show the causes and effects of World War II. You do not have time to write down every word on each slide, so you jot down notes in your own words to help you study and retain the information that was covered on the slides. When you paraphrase what you read, you are essentially doing the same thing—you are writing down the author's ideas in your own words because you will not have time to reread the entire chapter or chapters before the next test.

While paraphrasing, it is important to make sure you understand difficult vocabulary words or other important concepts so that you can put them in your own words. The most important reason you should master paraphrasing is so you can remember what you have heard or read and gain a meaningful understanding of the material. If you paraphrase the way you think, it will be easier to understand when you see the material again, such as on a test. For example, if you think in a linear fashion, you would want to make certain that all of your ideas are written in the order they appear in the text. However, if you think better by grouping similar concepts together or by using word association or mnemonic devices, then that is how you should paraphrase the information. For example, you might use a graphic organizer to arrange these concepts. Graphic organizers are covered more later in the chapter.

Mnemonic Devices

Studying is also a big part of college, and studying often requires memorization. By using or creating **mnemonic devices**, which are memory devices, you will be able to remember key information. The phrases, acronyms, rhymes, and songs help to trigger your memory and then enable you to recall information.

Some famous mnemonic devices are used to recall the year Columbus discovered America, the colors of the rainbow (ROY G. BIV), and the seven coordinating conjunctions (FANBOYS).

Below is an example of a student's paraphrase from "Campus Jewels" from chapter 1.

> In "Campus Jewels," the author discusses the *TLC services. At the T = the Tutoring Center, students can receive free tutoring. The L = the Library offers workshops and a place to study. The C = the Computer lab is the place to go to complete assignments that require a computer. Not all students know about these campus resources.

The student has created a mnemonic device to help remember the three campus resources discussed. The first letter of the first word of the three campus resources forms the well-known acronym TLC. However, instead of standing for tender loving care, in this case, TLC stands for **T**utoring center, **L**ibrary, and **C**omputer lab.

➢ **Read Write! Tip**

When you paraphrase or take notes, you do not have to use complete sentences; you can use single words and short phrases. In addition, you may want to use numbers and an outline format, leaving plenty of white space to add additional notes or to add more notes later. Outlines are covered later in this chapter.

Keys to Note Taking over Class Lectures

Tip #1   Make certain you have read the material that will be covered in advance. If your professor assigns an article, essay, or chapter and tells you to have it read before the next class meeting, then you need to have it read. That way you will be able to distinguish important information from less important information during the lecture. Also, it will mean that you have already completed PAUSE and have a good understanding of the material.

Tip #2   Listen and look for verbal clues from your instructor. If your professor says, "Write this down," then write it down. If your instructor goes to the smart board or white board and writes down information to clarify a point or spends a great deal of time on a PowerPoint slide, then you should add this information to your notes, as well.

Tip #3   Use outlining, indenting, and spacing to show where topics change. Leave plenty of white space so that if your instructor goes back and adds more information to a previously made point, then so can you.

Tip #4   Date and label your notes at the top of the page, such as Tuesday, April 8, 2018 "Notes on the Cause and Effect of World War II"—This way you will quickly know which notes to study before a quiz.

Tip #5   Avoid recording class lectures. This will lull you into passively listening during the lecture. Plus, you will miss visual clues from your instructor, such as him/her slowing down to emphasize key points, writing down information on the board, or going into more detail about what is on the PowerPoint slide. Your goal is always to be an active learner; therefore, note taking is essential. If you do record the lecture, you must get your professor's permission. Then, you must find the time to listen to the tape, stopping and starting it as you jot down your notes that could have been taken in class already.

Image © wavebreakmedia, 2014. Used under license from Shutterstock, Inc.

Keys to Note Taking over Readings and in General

Tip #1	Use the PAUSE strategy: Preread, Annotate, Understand, Summarize, Evaluate. After you have used PAUSE, then you can pull out key information and write it down on notebook paper in anticipation of quiz questions.
Tip #2	Do not take notes on tiny scraps of paper; use regular sized paper so that you can keep up with your notes and then place them in a three-ring binder. Then, you can easily add more information to them by inserting a sheet of paper that contains an outline of the material you just made or possible test questions. If your instructor gives you a handout over the information, punch holes in that and insert it where you want.
Tip #3	Take neat notes. Do not tell yourself, "I will rewrite my notes later, so they can be messy now." If you cannot read what you have written, then the notes are worthless. Plus, rewriting your notes is not a good use of time; instead, later you should be annotating and adding clarifications to them, not rewriting them.
Tip #4	Use a graphic organizer to take notes, especially if you are a visual learner. Graphic organizers allow you to create a visual representation of the material in a way that makes sense to you.

OTHER READING COMPREHENSION STRATEGIES

As mentioned in chapter 1, there are additional reading comprehension strategies besides PAUSE that you can use to actively read. It is possible that you have already learned some of these strategies and used them in the past. Two of the most recognized are KWL and SQR3.

KWL

The **KWL** strategy encourages you to recall what you already *Know* about a topic, jot down what you *Want* to learn about a topic, and then state what you *Learned* after reading. Below is an example of a KWL chart. There is a blank KWL chart located in the appendices.

Topic:		
Knowledge	**What**	**Learn**
*What I already **know** about the topic*	*What I **want** to know*	*What I **learned***

SQR3

The **SQR3** reading strategy consists of five key steps.

- **Survey** the material you are about to read; this allows your brain to prepare to learn. This is similar to the prereading step of PAUSE.
- Asking **Questions** helps you to anticipate possible quiz questions so that you are not passively reading. Jot down the questions in the margin or on notebook paper, leaving plenty of room to write your answers.

- **Read** to find the answers to your questions, to formulate additional questions, and to learn the information. Use highlighting, a pencil, circles, or your own short hand symbols to record your answers as you read.
- **Recite** after reading to verify what you can recall. Put the reading in your own words and pretend you are explaining it to a friend. You may have to reread a section again until you are able to easily restate what you have read.
- **Review** the material you have just read by looking at the headings, topic sentences, vocabulary words, highlighted words and phrases, and your margin notes to reinforce what you learned.

As you were reading this chapter, you probably noticed similarities among the various reading comprehension strategies discussed here and PAUSE from chapter 1. That is because everything is coming back to the same purpose: to get you reading actively and engaging with the text. Your instructor may ask you to try out a variety of reading comprehension strategies to see what works best for you. This textbook, however, primarily uses PAUSE.

© g-stockstudio/Shutterstock.com

GRAPHIC ORGANIZERS

Graphic organizers help you organize your thoughts and information in reading selections and lectures using visual representations. Sometimes you may gain a better understanding of the material if you see the information formatted using images instead of words. You do not need to be a Picasso or an art major to create your own graphic organizer because the work only has to make sense to you.

The purpose of graphic organizers is to help you condense large sections of information into small junks so that you can process, learn, and study the material. Graphic organizers help you understand the material because you must examine the whole and extract just the most important parts, ignoring or including minor details as you see fit.

If the term graphic organizer is not familiar to you, perhaps you can relate it to its writing counterparts used in the prewriting stage, such as clustering, building a pyramid, or outlining. In the writing process, graphic organizers help writers to organize their thoughts BEFORE creating their draft. However, in the reading process, graphic organizers are created AFTER reading to help you organize the main idea and supporting ideas about what you have read in a visual format.

Some of the most common graphic organizers include clustering, building a pyramid, outlining, VENN diagrams, pro and con lists, and drawing pictures.

Clustering

When you create a cluster graphic organizer, you actually draw a circle in the middle of a piece of paper and write the main idea or key phrase about the reading passage in it. Then, you branch out and put each of the supporting ideas in its own circle. If you choose, you can also add additional circles to include minor details for the supporting ideas.

Clustering Graphic Organizer Example

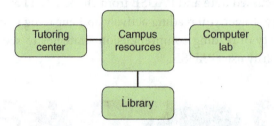

Building a Pyramid

A pyramid is another form of a graphic organizer. It is well suited for breaking down a five-paragraph essay; however, the parts of the pyramid can be expanded to include more than three main points. The pyramid consists of three sections. The top of the pyramid contains the main idea from the reading. It is a single box. The middle section has boxes that contain the major supporting details. The bottom section is for the minor supporting details.

Pyramid Graphic Organizer Example

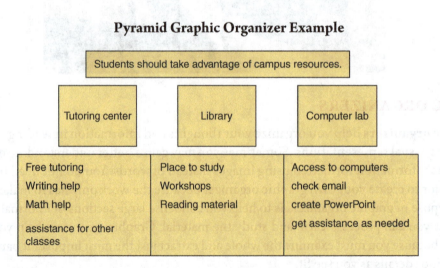

Outlining

Creating an outline graphic organizer is less formal than the one created for writing. Readers can use paraphrasing, short phrases, and words to illustrate the main idea and the supporting details. In addition, minor details may also be added. Outlines may either be typed or handwritten.

Outlining Graphic Organizer Example

Three Campus Resources (Main Idea)

1. *Tutoring Center   (Supporting Detail)*
   —free tutoring
   —different times for different tutors

2. *Library   (Supporting Detail)*
   —a place to study
   —workshops
   —check out books

3. *Computer Lab   (Supporting Detail)*
   —type papers
   —check email
   —access the Internet
   —get computer help

Based on the length of the reading, more supporting details can be added.

Venn Diagrams

A Venn diagram graphic organizer uses intersecting circles to show the similarities and the differences between two or more things. The similarities are placed in the intersecting sections of the circles, and the differences are placed in the non-intersecting sections of the circles. Venn diagrams are often used when writing a comparison-contrast essay or when wanting to highlight similarities or differences between two things.

Venn Diagram Example

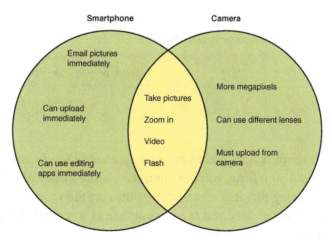

Pro and Con List

A pro and con list allows readers to sort information into one of two columns: either Pro (for) or Con (against). To create a pro and con list, draw a line down the center of the page. Then, label one side "Pro" and the other side "Con." Then, list the reasons the author is in favor of something on the pro side and the reasons against something on the con side. Below is a pro and con list for "Babies on Board: Momma Online."

Pro and Con List Example

Pros	Cons
(Reasons for	(Reasons against
taking online classes)	taking online classes)
Can take tests at any time	Must be self-motivated and
	disciplined
Do work in pajamas	
	Must follow calendar or will get
Do not have to drive to campus	behind
Take tests when ready	Cannot procrastinate
Get instant feedback on tests	
	Must set time to do work or will fail
Can email instructor questions	
	Lack of face to face interaction

Drawing Pictures

Drawing pictures can simplify note taking by creating a visual representation of a concept or key information. If drawing is not your forte, you can cut out a picture or download one from the Internet. Below is an example of drawing pictures when taking notes on the water cycle in biology class. This particular concept is more easily understood as a picture than as something written. Drawing it in your notes makes the information more accessible.

Drawing Pictures Example

Water cycle notes

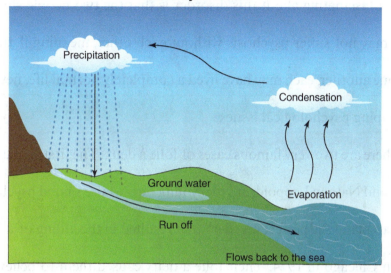

> ➢ **Read Write! Tip**

If you access the Internet and type in "graphic organizers" in a search engine, a plethora of options will appear, ranging from the ones above to charts for keeping track of characters in a novel. Then, you can copy and paste the one that fits your needs for a particular reading.

Read Write! Activity 2.1

Read the text below and then use the graphic organizer that follows to break down the text. You should be able to fill in all the boxes.

A Shared Madness

1   Folie à deux is a rare mental disorder involving two people. The phrase

"folie à deux" is French. Its literal translation is "the folly of two," but the

phrase itself has come to mean "madness shared by two" or the "madness

of two." It is a psychological term referring to a psychosis shared between

two people or a shared delusion imparted from one person to another. What is most fascinating about this disorder is that the two people sharing folie à deux may not suffer psychosis without each other, meaning if they had not met one another, each may have lived a completely normal life, never or rarely developing psychological issues.

2   There are two very famous cases of folie à deux. The first is that of Richard Loeb and Nathan Leopold, Jr., two young men whose shared psychosis caused them to plan "the perfect murder" that resulted in the killing of a 14-year-old boy in Chicago in 1924. Their folie à deux caused them to believe that they would be able to get away with the murder; however, they were caught by police and convicted, receiving life plus 99 years in prison. One of the conditions of their imprisonment was that they were to be kept separate. This was because of their folie à deux. It was believed that had they never met, the murder would not have happened because then the folie à deux would never have occurred. Thus, the judge who sentenced them believed keeping them separate was important for their own mental health and the safety of those around them.

3   A second example of folie à deux is that of Pauline Parker and Juliet Hulme, teenagers who murdered Parker's mother in Christchurch, New Zealand, in 1954. Their folie à deux developed out of their deep relationship based primarily on a fantasy world they had created together. The intensity of their friendship caused their parents to create a plan to separate them. In response to this, the girls planned and executed the murder of Parker's mother, irrationally believing that if she were dead, the two could remain together. They were arrested almost immediately and tried and found guilty. Like Leopold and Loeb, it is believed that if they had not met, the two would never have committed murder. They, too, were kept separate during their incarceration and were released separately.

4   It is important to note, however, that folie à deux is rare. Leopold and Loeb and Parker and Hulme are considered exceptional cases. Today folie à deux is often referred to as shared psychotic disorder or induced delusional disorder, and reported cases are few and far between.

Topic

[ ]

Main idea

[ ]

Supporting Details

[ ] [ ]

[ ] [ ]

VOCABULARY BUILDING

College is also about expanding your horizons, and that includes expanding the horizons of the vocabulary you come into the collegiate arena with. It is important that you continuously work to improve your vocabulary. The reasoning behind this is twofold. First, it will help you with your reading comprehension. If your vocabulary remains limited, you will continuously run into unfamiliar words when you read, and this will hamper your comprehension of the material. Secondly, increasing your vocabulary will help you as a writer. The more words you know the meaning of, the more choices you have when it comes to language and communicating concisely and effectively. Word choice is discussed more in chapters 5 and 6.

Recall that you must annotate as a part of reading actively. During prereading and annotation, it is important to mark words you do not know the meaning of, such as circling them or writing question marks over them. Then, during the understand step of PAUSE, you can come back to the unknown words and decipher their meanings either through context clues or by looking up their meanings using a dictionary. Afterward, it is important to record the new word somehow so that you can practice with it for the future. You can do this by keeping a vocabulary journal or by keeping vocabulary notecards.

Vocabulary Journals

Keeping a vocabulary journal is a great way to learn new words. A vocabulary journal is a place where you record the meaning of unknown words that you come across as you are reading. These lists of words can be kept in a spiral notebook or on sheets of notebook paper and placed in a binder.

To create a vocabulary journal, draw four lines down the page to create four columns. Label the first column "Vocabulary Word," the second column "Phonetics," the third column "Definition," and the fourth column "Synonyms." Each column has a more specific explanation below.

♦ Under "Vocabulary Word," list words you want to learn. The word may come from your textbook, a passage or novel you read, a list from your instructor, or anywhere else you encountered a word you are not familiar with.
♦ Under "Phonetics," write the word how it sounds. Phonetics means how it is pronounced out loud. You can find the phonetic spelling in the dictionary if necessary or look the word up online. Search engines and other online resources will pronounce the word for you.
♦ Under "Definition," put the denotation of the word, its dictionary meaning.
♦ Under "Synonyms," list other words that have the same meaning as the unknown word. Recall that synonyms are words that have the same meanings.

Review the example vocabulary journal page below to see how to lay yours out.

Vocabulary Journal			
Vocabulary Word	Phonetics	Definition	Synonyms
infamous	in-fuh-muhs	known for having a bad reputation	notorious, scandalous

Using Notecards

Using notecards is another way to expand your vocabulary. You can write the word on the front side of a card and its phonetic spelling below it. Then, on the back, put the definition, synonyms, antonyms, and a sentence that contains the word. Antonyms are words that have the opposite meaning.

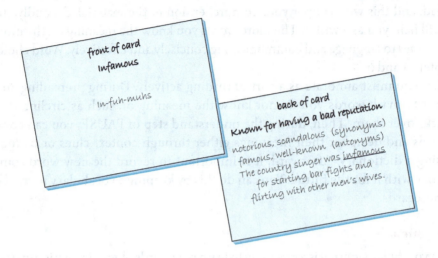

front of card

infamous

in-fuh-muhs

back of card

Known for having a bad reputation

notorious, scandalous (synonyms)
famous, well-known (antonyms)
The country singer was infamous
for starting bar fights and
flirting with other men's wives.

Carry your vocabulary cards with you and review them often to help expand your vocabulary. You can view them in between classes, while waiting at the doctor's office, or standing in the checkout lane at the grocery store.

Demystifying Words: Prefix, Root, and Suffix

Have you ever noticed that many words begin with a prefix, such as *in-, re-, pro-,* or *dis-* and end with a suffix, such as *-tion, -ment, -ing,* or *-less*? Familiarizing yourself with some of these common beginnings and endings and understanding how they change or modify the meaning of words will help you *demystify,* which means *rid of mystery or clarify,* the meaning of unknown words.

A prefix comes before a word while a **suffix** comes after a word; the **root** of the word is its base form before a prefix, a suffix, or both have been added. For example, take the word *preheated.* The prefix is *pre-,* which means *before;* the suffix is *-ed,* which signals the past tense of a verb; and the root word is *heat,* which means *to make warm.* A sentence using the word is the following: Guadalupe *preheated* the oven for five minutes prior to baking the chocolate chip cookies. Using the prefix, the suffix, the root word, and context clues, you can deduce or figure out that *preheated* means the stove was warmed up before it was used. In the appendix, you will find the common prefixes, roots, and suffixes quick reference.

Read Write! Activity 2.2

Circle the prefixes and underline the suffixes in the following words. Then, come up with at least two words that begin with the same prefix and at least one that has the same suffix.

Word	Words with matching prefixes	Words with matching suffixes
Biology		
Photosynthesis		
Prehistoric		

Expanding your vocabulary may be challenging because people tend to use the same words over and over. However, in order to become a better reader and writer, you not only need to learn new words, but you must also be honest about your reading abilities. Do you dread reading aloud in class because you cannot properly pronounce words? Do you skip over words that you do not know when you are reading instead of using context clues or looking them up in a dictionary? What is your attitude toward reading? Would you rather have a root canal than read a book? Are you aware that your attitude toward reading or anything else for that matter greatly determines your altitude, the extent to which you will be successful? In other words, attitude, which is derived from your thoughts and feelings about something, affects your altitude, the amount of improvement you make from where you started. Therefore, it is important that you assess your attitude about reading and your reading abilities so that you can take steps to improve them. This was discussed previously in chapter 1.

PRACTICES FOR SUCCESS

Lastly, keep the following practices of successful college students in mind as you work your way toward your certificate or degree. These practices, when used, will ensure your success.

The Ten Practices of Successful College Students

1. Become acquainted with an adviser who will assist you as you move through your college journey.
2. Read the class syllabus. It contains a wealth of information about course expectations, such as how to contact your professor and attendance and late work policies.
3. Attend class regularly. Do not miss the first day because important class policies will be reviewed.
4. Come to every class meeting with completed assignments, including keeping up with assigned readings.
5. Purchase textbooks and supplies. These are important learning tools for your success.
6. Communicate with your professors regularly. Ask questions if you do not understand a concept or what is expected on an assignment.
7. Take advantage of campus resources, such as the tutoring center, the library, and the computer lab.
8. Form a study group or find a study buddy early in the semester and meet often throughout the term.

9. Take notes and review them regularly. Use the PAUSE strategy outlined in chapter 1 to go through assigned readings.
10. Become involved on campus outside of class. Students who join clubs and participate in campus activities are more likely to stay in school and graduate.

Read Write! Review Questions: Success Strategies for College Students

1. True or False: When taking notes, you should write down everything you see and hear.
2. True or False: FANBOYS is an example of a mnemonic device.
3. True or False: Prefix and suffix are the same concept.
4. True or False: You should connect with an adviser who can help you throughout your college journey.
5. True or False: Missing class off and on is okay if you do the reading.

Read Write! Connection: Chapter 2

Read the passage "A Learning Secret: Don't Take Notes with a Laptop" by Cindi May. Then answer the questions that follow.

> Cindi May is a professor of psychology at the College of Charleston. This piece was originally published on the *Scientific America* website on June 3, 2014.

A Learning Secret: Don't Take Notes with a Laptop

by Cindi May

1   "More is better." From the number of gigs in a cellular data plan to the horsepower in a pickup truck, this mantra is ubiquitous in American culture. When it comes to college students, the belief that more is better may underlie their widely-held view that laptops in the classroom enhance their academic performance. Laptops do in fact allow students to do more, like engage in online activities and demonstrations, collaborate more easily on papers and projects,

access information from the internet, and take more notes. Indeed, because students can type significantly faster than they can write, those who use laptops in the classroom tend to take more notes than those who write out their notes by hand. Moreover, when students take notes using laptops they tend to take notes verbatim, writing down every last word uttered by their professor.

2   Obviously it is advantageous to draft more complete notes that precisely capture the course content and allow for a verbatim review of the material at a later date. Only it isn't. New research by Pam Mueller and Daniel Oppenheimer demonstrates that students who write out their notes on paper actually learn more. Across three experiments, Mueller and Oppenheimer had students take notes in a classroom setting and then tested students on their memory for factual detail, their conceptual understanding of the material, and their ability to synthesize and generalize the information. Half of the students were instructed to take notes with a laptop, and the other half were instructed to write the notes out by hand. As in other studies, students who used laptops took more notes. In each study, however, those who wrote out their notes by hand had a stronger conceptual understanding and were more successful in applying and integrating the material than those who used took notes with their laptops.

3   What drives this paradoxical finding? Mueller and Oppenheimer postulate that taking notes by hand requires different types of cognitive processing than taking notes on a laptop, and these different processes have consequences for learning. Writing by hand is slower and more cumbersome than typing, and students cannot possibly write down every word in a lecture. Instead, they listen, digest, and summarize so that they can succinctly capture the essence of the information. Thus, taking notes by hand forces the brain to engage in some heavy "mental lifting," and these efforts foster comprehension and retention. By contrast, when typing students can easily produce a written record of the lecture without processing its meaning, as faster typing speeds allow students to transcribe a lecture word for word without devoting much thought to the content.

4   To evaluate this theory, Mueller and Oppenheimer assessed the content of notes taken by hand versus laptop. Their studies included hundreds of students from Princeton and UCLA, and the lecture topics ranged from bats, bread, and algorithms to faith, respiration, and economics. Content analysis of the notes consistently showed that students who used laptops had more verbatim transcription of the lecture material than those who wrote notes by hand. Moreover, high verbatim note content was associated with *lower*

retention of the lecture material. It appears that students who use laptops can take notes in a fairly mindless, rote fashion, with little analysis or synthesis by the brain. This kind of shallow transcription fails to promote a meaningful understanding or application of the information.

5   If the source of the advantage for longhand notes derives from the conceptual processes they evoke, perhaps instructing laptop users to draft summative rather than verbatim notes will boost performance. Mueller and Oppenheimer explored this idea by warning laptop note takers against the tendency to transcribe information without thinking, and explicitly instructed them to think about the information and type notes in their own words. Despite these instructions, students using laptops showed the same level of verbatim content and were no better in synthesizing material than students who received no such warning. It is possible these direct instructions to improve the quality of laptop notes failed because it is so easy to rely on less demanding, mindless processes when typing.

6   It's important to note that most of the studies that have compared note taking by hand versus laptop have used immediate memory tests administered very shortly (typically less than an hour) after the learning session. In real classroom settings, however, students are often assessed days if not weeks after

learning new material. Thus, although laptop users may not encode as much during the lecture and thus may be disadvantaged on immediate assessments, it seems reasonable to expect that the additional information they record will give them an advantage when reviewing material after a long delay.

7   Wrong again. Mueller and Oppenheimer included a study in which participants were asked to take notes by hand or by laptop, and were told they would be tested on the material in a week. When participants were given an opportunity to study with their notes before the final assessment, once again those who took longhand notes outperformed laptop participants. Because longhand notes contain students' own words and handwriting, they may serve as more effective memory cues by recreating the context (e.g., thought processes, emotions, conclusions) as well as content (e.g., individual facts) from the original learning session.

8   These findings hold important implications for students who use their laptops to access lecture outlines and notes that have been posted by professors before class. Because students can use these posted materials to access lecture content with a mere click, there is no need to organize, synthesize or summarize in their own words. Indeed, students may take very minimal notes or not take notes at all, and may consequently forego the opportunity to engage in the mental work that supports learning.

9   Beyond altering students' cognitive processes and thereby reducing learning, laptops pose other threats in the classroom. In the Mueller and Oppenheimer studies, all laptops were disconnected from the internet, thus eliminating any disruption from email, instant messaging, surfing, or other online distractions. In most typical college settings, however, internet access is available, and evidence suggests that when college students use laptops, they spend 40% of class time using applications unrelated to coursework, are more likely to fall off task, and are less satisfied with their education. In one study with law school students, nearly 90% of laptop users engaged in online activities unrelated to coursework for at least five minutes, and roughly 60% were distracted for half the class.

10   Technology offers innovative tools that are shaping educational experiences for students, often in positive and dynamic ways. The research by Mueller and Oppenheimer serves as a reminder, however, that even when technology allows us to do more in less time, it does not always foster learning. Learning involves more than the receipt and the regurgitation of information. If we want students to synthesize material, draw inferences, see new connections, evaluate evidence, and apply concepts in novel situations, we need to encourage the deep, effortful cognitive processes that underlie these abilities. When it comes to taking notes, students need fewer gigs, more brain power.

1. In the context of paragraph 1, what does "ubiquitous" mean?

   _____

   _____

   _____

   _____

2. Students who take notes on laptops take more notes. Why, according to the text, is this not beneficial to learning?

   _____

   _____

   _____

   _____

   _____

   _____

3. What does the text say about professors posting lecture outlines or notes online? Is this beneficial to student learning? Why or why not?

   _____

   _____

   _____

   _____

   _____

4. If students have laptops in the classroom, what is the percentage of class time they are using applications unrelated to course work?

   _____

   _____

   _____

5. What is the main idea of the passage? Is it stated or implied?

   _____

   _____

   _____

   _____

6. Connect this study to your own note taking strategies. Do you use a laptop? Why or why not?

_____

_____

_____

_____

_____

_____

7. What can you take from this article to help with your own note taking and study skills? Explain your answer.

_____

_____

_____

_____

_____

_____

Chapter 3

The Writing Process

Key Terms

prewriting, metacognition, audience, purpose, topic, prewriting strategies, free writing, listing, clustering, asking questions, thesis statement, parallel structure, outlining, building a pyramid, revising, unity, support, coherence, transitional devices, editing, formatting, titles, publishing

Writing academic papers can be an arduous and intimidating task. It can be particularly hard if you have been assigned a topic you do not know much about or do not like. Additionally, it might be somewhat nerve-wracking if you have not had to write anything in several years, your job does not require you to communicate through writing, or if you do not feel like you are a "good" writer. However, writing, like reading, is a major part of many college courses; most classes require at least one paper, if not more. The purpose of this section of the textbook is to introduce the writing process so that you can develop or refine strategies to enhance your thinking and writing skills to help you be successful in all your college courses. As with the reading process, as you go through the writing process, it will in turn help to improve your reading skills. They are two sides of the same coin.

"If it's a prompt, I usually read it twice to make sure I understand what I'm supposed to be writing about, so I don't answer something it's not asking me. I write a thesis statement first because I want to make sure I have a good foundation for my essay. I do clustering to make sure I have three good, strong topics."

—Angela Miskell
Eastfield College
Mesquite, TX

Everything you read, whether it is an essay, a novel, an article, or some other form of writing, has been taken through the writing process by its author. The writing process is a series of steps any writer must take to create a polished piece of written work that communicates effectively with the reader.

PREWRITING

The first step in the writing process is actually a process in itself: the prewriting process. When you prewrite, you do everything you need to do *before* you write. A major part of the prewriting process has to do with the way you think about the writing task at hand, including the topic, audience, and purpose, as well as developing ideas.

A term that captures this ultimate thought process is called **metacognition**, or thinking about thinking. Essentially, metacognition is examining your thoughts for the purpose of analysis, including problem solving, connecting to prior knowledge, assessing your attitude toward the writing assignment, and evaluating your own thoughts. In other words, it is much like the last step of PAUSE, and those skills will help you to use metacognition for your writing tasks.

Audience and Purpose

Before you start generating ideas about the topic, you need to think about two important factors. One is your **audience.** Audience is who you are writing for, your reader. Audience is important because it determines how you will write—word choice and tone. If you are writing for a friend, you might use a conversational tone and slang words. However, if you are writing for your professor, a more formal, academic tone is needed in Standard American English. When you are reading, *you* are the audience, and the author is trying to communicate effectively with *you*. When you think about it this way, the concept of audience becomes even more important.

Purpose is your reason for writing. If you recall, there are three main purposes for writing: to inform, to persuade, or to entertain. It is possible for the purpose to overlap, but keeping your purpose in mind will help you stay on track. Oftentimes, purpose is determined by your mode of writing. If you are writing the descriptive-narrative essay, for example, your purpose is to entertain through descriptive storytelling. The argument essay, however, is meant to persuade the reader as you defend your position on an issue. Purpose is also important in terms of reading because it helps the reader better understand the author's point. Author's purpose is discussed more in chapters 5.

Topic

The **topic** is what you will be writing about. A topic may be assigned to you, or your professor may allow you to choose a topic. Oftentimes, you will need to narrow a topic down. When thinking about the topic, try to connect to prior knowledge if possible. Ask yourself what you already know about the topic and how you could use this information for your writing task. Prior knowledge may also help you narrow down a topic that is too broad. Your topic should fit the parameters of the assignment. For example, if you are asked to write a history paper about a topic from the American Revolutionary War, you would not write the paper over the entire war. You would choose a specific moment or significant battle to analyze, effectively narrowing down the topic to fit the assignment.

Prewriting Strategies

When you are ready to take your thinking process to the next step, you are ready to begin developing ideas about your topic and getting them on paper. There are several strategies you can use to generate ideas: free writing, listing, clustering, and asking questions.

When you use **free writing**, you write freely about whatever comes to mind about a topic. At this point, you are not worried about errors in grammar, spelling, mechanics, or formatting. At first glance, free writing may look like a paragraph or essay, but when you begin to revise and edit, you will find there is much correction needed to enhance the final draft. This strategy is popular because the writer is "free" and less apprehensive about writing.

Free Writing Example

Topic: entertainment

I think my favorite form of entertainment is the internet. Plaing on social networking sites like Facebook can be very amusing. I like to see whaty my friends are up to and see their pictures. That's whats fun about Instagram too. I can look at all the pictures. Some of the people I follow are good photographers. Filters too. TV is cool too. I watch a lot of different shows and keep track of them. DVR. Sometimes I record more shows then I have space for. Music is the best though. Music is just all over. I listen to the radio and iTunes and have so many albums. Seriously the best.

When you use **listing**, you write the topic at the top of the page and then write one word or a small phrase about the topic. This is usually done parallel down the margin. This list is similar to a grocery store list. You know that there are several reasons for writing a grocery list. First, you are writing items that you want or need (necessity). Secondly, you may write the list to keep you organized so you do not overspend on items that you do not need (irrelevance). Therefore, like grocery shopping, you create a list so that when you begin drafting, you use only the ideas you need and eliminate irrelevant ideas.

Listing Example

Topic: Gossip

- Talking
- Stories
- Backstabbing
- Exaggeration
- Snark
- Friends
- Enemies
- Workplace gossip
- School gossip
- Talking trash
- Is there good gossip?

Clustering is a graphic organizer. Graphic organizers, as you saw in chapter 2, can be used for both reading and writing tasks. To create a cluster for writing, you draw a circle in the middle of a piece of paper and write the topic in the circle. You then branch out from the "topic circle" and write whatever comes to mind about the topic. If necessary, you may even branch out from the "subtopics" for more ideas. The cluster provides you with a visual picture of organization. No matter how small or large the cluster may be, ideas are indeed being generated.

> ➢ **Read Write! Tip**
>
> Remember, during the prewriting process, there are no errors being generated, only ideas. You may find that what you thought was irrelevant may prove to be valuable when you begin to add supporting details to your essay. You are encouraged to jump right in and continue thinking!

Clustering Example

Swearing
Not cleaning up
Smoking
Bad hygiene
Not flossing
Always being on your cell phone
Nailbiting
Skipping class
Bad Habits
Drinking
Social media oversharing
Sleeping all day
Gossoping
Popping gum
Texting while driving
Letting dishes pile up
Speeding
Smacking
Running red lights
Letting laundry pile up

Asking Questions

Asking questions includes two steps. The first step is writing questions about a topic on a piece of paper or computer screen. After you have asked who, what, where, when, why, and how about a topic, then you go back and complete the second step, which is answering the questions as you can. The rationale behind asking questions is that you are actually generating ideas and support for your essay. Like free writing, listing, and clustering, asking questions will get you closer to the ideas you need to write an essay.

Asking Questions Example

Topic: Consumerism

What is consumerism?
Who participates in consumerism?
Why is consumerism around?
Where is consumerism common?
When did consumerism begin?
How did consumerism come about?

Read Write! Activity 3.1

Below are several topics. Use a different prewriting strategy to develop ideas for each topic. You can write your answers on notebook paper, type them on the computer, or use the outline and pyramid templates in the appendices.

1. Social media
2. Education
3. Politics
4. Relationships
5. Video games

DRAFTING

After developing and narrowing down ideas, all writers must draft their essay. As you know, there are many different types of readings: essays, novels, articles, short stories, research papers, and more. As a student, you will often be asked to write essays. One way to keep yourself organized and on topic is the traditional five-paragraph essay format. While not every essay in this textbook will use this construction style, many will. It is an excellent way to keep your ideas on track while also providing your reader with a clearly organized piece of writing.

Image © ronstik, 2014. Used under license from Shutterstock, Inc.

By now you most certainly have been assigned a topic or you have been directed to generate your own essay topic. You have the most valuable pieces of information: a topic and prewriting. Never throughout the prewriting or writing processes are you allowed to stop thinking. Thinking critically about ideas and about your topic must continue from start to finish. Then, when you have reviewed all of your ideas, it is time to start writing. The words **drafting** and writing will be used interchangeably throughout this book. At this point, you are beginning to pay attention to the rules of writing regarding formatting and length. Your instructor will specify all expectations regarding the essay.

The drafting stage of the writing process for a traditional five-paragraph essay can be encompassed in three steps: expressing a main idea, organizing ideas, and writing your rough draft.

Expressing a Main Idea

Everything you read has a main idea. When you write, you must express your main idea in the form of a **thesis statement.** A thesis statement is one sentence that will explain to the reader what the essay is about, meaning it presents the main idea of the essay to the reader. This statement will contain the topic of the essay as well as the controlling idea of the essay. In other words, it will state the point the writer is trying to make about the topic. Essentially, the writing term thesis statement is very similar to the reading term main idea. The only difference is that when you are writing, your professor may provide you with certain requirements for how you construct your thesis statement. It may only contain the topic and controlling idea. It may also contain a plan of development in which the writer lists three or more supporting details within the thesis. It can be stated or implied, and its placement can differ according to writing style. For the traditional five-paragraph essay, your thesis statement should always be the last sentence of the first paragraph, and it will often, but not always, take a three-part construction: topic, controlling idea, and three main points.

Topic: what you are writing about or the subject of your essay

Controlling idea: what you are saying about the topic; the controlling idea "controls" the rest of the essay. Everything will relate back to it. It is where you present your opinion or message to the reader.

Three main points: your three main reasons to support the topic and controlling idea; in a traditional five-paragraph essay, the three main points will be the topics of your three body paragraphs. This is the plan of development.

Below is an example of a thesis statement.

> Preschool should be a required part of public education because children can begin learning classroom behaviors early, they can begin devoloping social skills, and they can work on early literacy.

The topic is "preschool." The controlling idea is that it "should be a required part of public education." Therefore, the rest of the essay will be about why preschools should be required within the public education system because this idea "controls" the essay. Nothing regarding optional preschooling will be mentioned. The three main points, or plan of development, are *learning classroom behaviors (a), developing social skills (b), and early literacy (c).* These are the three main reasons why preschool should be a required part of public education; they are also the three body paragraph topics.

Every traditional five-paragraph essay must contain a sentence like this. As you begin to think about how to mold your ideas into a thesis statement, it is very important to write a thesis statement that possesses **parallel structure.** Parallel structure is a grammatical concept that refers to similarity in words and phrases. It means that all items in a list are "balanced" or "match" in regard to parts of speech. In other words, all items in a list contain –ing, to + a verb, verbs, nouns, adjectives, adjectives + nouns, or phrases.

If you reexamine the thesis statement below, you will see an example of correct parallel structure.

> Preschool should be a required part of public education because children need an early start learning classroom behaviors, social skills, and literacy.

Notice the words *classroom behaviors, social skills,* and *literacy.* They are all nouns—three reasons for requiring preschool. The words follow a pattern like a, b, c. If you choose, however, to change the words to phrases, you must do so with all of the words. Look at the thesis statement below about preschools. This time the writer decided to write phrases to describe the reasons why preschool should be required, which means the writer is using the aaa, bbb, ccc pattern.

> Preschool should be a required part of public education because children can begin learning classroom behaviors early, they can begin devoloping social skills, and they can work on early literacy.

The thesis statement you choose to incorporate into your essay should match one of these patterns. It is not correct to mix the two patterns into one thesis statement as doing so will yield a list pattern that is not parallel. Parallel structure is important to you as a reader because thesis statements that are not parallel are hard to read. Anything hard to read means you are not communicating effectively with your reader.

Read Write! Activity 3.2

Below are five thesis statements that are not parallel. Make corrections to the parallelism.

1. *Breaking Bad* is the best show on television because of the acting, the writing is clever, and the subject matter is fascinating.
2. My three favorite Friday night activities are eating out, dancing, and stayed up late.
3. The United States is a great country because of its political system, its diverse population, and there are so many national treasures.
4. Halloween is my favorite holiday because I get to wear a costume, spooky, and decorating is fun.
5. Three things that should scare everyone are natural disasters, there could be a zombie apocalypse, and someone's loved one could die.

Read Write! Activity 3.3

Choose three of the topics below and write three thesis statements that contain the topic, a controlling idea, and three main points. Try to use one the patterns discussed above (a, b, c OR aaa, bbb, ccc). Remember not to mix the two patterns.

Example:

Topic—Cats

a, b, c, structure: *Cats make good pets because they are easy, amusing, and cuddly.*

aaa, bbb, ccc structure: *Cats make good pets because they are easy to take care of, they are amusing to play with, and they are fun to cuddle.*

1. Community colleges
2. War
3. Advice
4. Terrorism
5. Movies

Remember, thesis statements are used to inform the reader of the direction of your essay. The thesis statement is sort of like a steering wheel in a car, and you, the writer, are driving.

Organizing Your Ideas

Once you have expressed your main idea, it is time to organize your thoughts in preparation for writing a rough draft. This can be done by analyzing your prewriting and creating an essay plan. The essay plan can take the form of an outline or a pyramid.

An **outline** is a written plan for your essay. However, it does not go into every small detail. It is a framework for your essay, almost like a map, that will help you logically organize your ideas and prepare to write. Numbers and letters are used to distinguish your main topics from subtopics. Remember, the outline can be used interchangeably to write paragraphs rather than a full essay. Simply change thesis statement to topic sentence, and fill in the supporting details. Remember also that an outline does not just apply to the writing process. You can also use it in the reading process to break down a passage. This was covered more in chapter 2.

Outlining Example for a Traditional Five-Paragraph Essay

Thesis Statement: Preschool should be a required part of public education because children can begin learning classroom behaviors early, they can begin devoloping social skills, and they can work on early literacy.

I. First, preschool should be a required part of public education because it is important for children to begin learning classroom behaviors early.
   a. Raising hands before speaking
   b. Staying seated
   c. These skills will prepare children for kindergarten and beyond
II. Additionally, young children can begin developing their social skills if they are required to attend preschool via public education.
   a. Some young children who stay at home do not socialize much outside of their families
   b. Social skills are very important to success
   c. Preschool forces all students to socialize in a safe and friendly environment
III. Lastly, if preschool were a required part of public education, children could work on their literacy skills at earlier ages.
   a. Some parents do not work with their children on reading skills prior to kindergarten
   b. Working with the alphabet and phonics
   c. This develops the foundations for successful literacy earlier in life, setting the child up for success in kindergarten and beyond

Conclusion: It is important that preschool become a required part of the public education. For one, it would allow students to begin learning classroom behaviors at an early age. It would also allow children to work on their social skills before kindergarten. Finally, it would cause children to learn foundational literacy skills earlier. Preschool programs should be implemented as a part of public education in all 50 states.

Building a pyramid is much like an outline, but it is more of a visual representation of the essay rather than a written framework. Like the outline, it, too, can be used to break down a text as well as build up an essay. When used as an essay plan, it offers a visual representation of the essay you will write. The pyramid works best with the traditional five-paragraph essay but can be adapted for essays of 6–7 paragraphs if necessary.

When building a pyramid, you must first draw the sections of the pyramid that you will use to organize your ideas. The top of the pyramid contains the topic and the controlling idea from the thesis statement. It is a single box. The upper middle section of the pyramid has three boxes that will contain the three points of the thesis statement. The lower middle of the pyramid is for the supporting ideas. It has three boxes that are divided up into three or more sections. Support for your three main reasons should be written in these boxes. Finally, the base of the pyramid will serve as the conclusion. The objective when filling in the pyramid is to gain as many supporting details as you can in order to complete the essay.

Pyramid Example for a Traditional Five-Paragraph Essay

Preschool should be a required part of public education because

children can begin learning classroom behaviors early	they can begin devoloping social skills	they can work on early literacy

Raising hands before speaking Staying seated These skills will prepare children for kindergarten and beyond	Some young children who stay at home do not socialize much outside of their families Social skills are very important to success Preschool forces all students to socialize in a safe and friendly environment	Some parents do not work with their children on reading skills prior to kindergarten Working with the alphabet and phonics This develops the foundations for successful literacy earlier in life, setting the child up for success in kindergarten and beyond

It is important that preschool become a required part of the public education system. For one, it would allow students to begin learning classroom behaviors at an early age. It would also allow children to work on their social skills before kindergarten. Finally, it would cause children to learn foundational literacy skills earlier. Preschool programs should be implemented as a part of public education in all 50 states.

Essay Construction

Once you have finished planning your essay, it is time to write the rough draft. Remember that at this point in the writing process, sentence skills such as grammar, punctuation, and spelling do not matter. This is the step to get the writing done, not polish it.

Recall that the thesis statement is a part of the introduction paragraph. The introduction is the first paragraph in the essay. It has three purposes: to introduce the topic, to catch the reader's interest, and to present the thesis statement, or main idea, of the essay. Introductions will be covered in depth in chapter 4.

The body paragraphs follow the introduction. The body can consist of as many paragraphs as necessary to express the writer's ideas, but in the traditional five-paragraph essay, there are three. Each body paragraph requires a strong, clear **topic sentence**. The topic sentence is the first sentence of each body paragraph; it tells the reader what the paragraph will be about, meaning it presents the main idea of the paragraph. The topics of the body paragraphs will come from the thesis statement; therefore, each body paragraph should reference one of the three main points in the thesis. For example, using the first example thesis statement about preschool, topic sentence number one will discuss how children can begin learning classroom behaviors early while in preschool, topic sentence number two will discuss how children can begin developing their social skills in preschool, and topic sentence number three will discuss how children can begin working on their early literacy in preschool. Once you have written the topic sentence, you must support it with details that relate to the thesis statement. Both body paragraphs and topic sentences will be covered further in chapter 4.

The last paragraph in the essay is the conclusion. The purpose of the conclusion is to sum up your main points by restating the thesis statement and to give the reader a sense of closure. Conclusions will be covered more in chapter 4.

The Traditional Five-Paragraph Essay Layout

Title (the first glimpse of what the essay will be about)

Introduction
- Background info about the topic
- An attention getter
- Thesis statement

Body Paragraph One
- Topic sentence: thesis point #1
- Support
- Concluding sentence

Body Paragraph Two
- Topic sentence: thesis point #2
- Support
- Concluding sentence

Body Paragraph Three
- Topic sentence: thesis point #3
- Support
- Concluding sentence

Conclusion Paragraph
- Summarize the essay
- Restate the thesis
- Bring the essay to an end

REVISING

When you have finished your rough draft, it may feel as if you are done with the paper. However, the writing process is not yet complete. The next step is to **revise**, which means to "relook." When you revise, you look at content and organization and make changes as necessary. As with the pre-writing process, metacognition plays a role. It is important to think about and understand the necessity for change and improvement in your writing. When revising, you consciously think about how to make what you are trying to convey clearer.

Image © Bacho, 2014. Used under license from Shutterstock, Inc.

When you revise, you should look over your essay for the bases or foundations of the writing process to ensure meaning is being conveyed clearly to the reader. These bases are unity, support, and coherence.

Unity

Unity refers to the essay having a clear topic and sticking to it throughout. Generally, the thesis statement will guide unity in that every sentence in the essay should relate back to it. It can sometimes be easy to venture off topic and allow new, unrelated ideas to infiltrate your essay; thus, it is particularly important to review your writing carefully to make sure that every sentence relates back to the main idea, effectively keeping the essay on topic. An essay that stays on topic is an essay that communicates effectively with the reader. If you find anything that does not relate to the topic in the essay, it should be removed.

Support

Support refers to providing the reader adequate and specific details. Adequate support means that you have provided the reader with enough details to make your point. Specific support means you include relevant details about the topic. For example, if you were asked to narrate or tell a story about an accident you witnessed, you would most likely include details about the color of the vehicle in question or the impact of the vehicle that caused the accident. As a witness, you would most likely leave out information about an airplane that was flying overhead when the accident occurred unless the airplane was involved in the accident. It may be true that the airplane flew overhead; however, it is not relevant to the accident and should be omitted.

You should think about this as a reader as well. Suppose you were reading a persuasive article that was attempting to convince you to vote for a certain political candidate. However, the writer did not have many supporting reasons for *why* you should vote for candidate. That is not very convincing, is it? Providing support for your reader helps you more effectively prove your point. If you find that you do not have enough support for your essay, you should develop the essay further by adding more. If you need more ideas, it may be necessary to return to the prewriting process to generate more.

Coherence

Coherence refers to organizing ideas in a logical, consistent, and parallel manner so that the reader understands what you are trying to convey. In other words, an essay that has coherence is easy to follow because the ideas flow effortlessly from one to another. There is no point in the text where the reader is confused or has to backtrack because the ideas are logically organized.

Traditional organizational patterns are very useful when working with coherence. Organizational patterns generally line up with rhetorical modes. For example, a narrative piece usually will use chronological (time) order because stories are most often told from beginning to end. It may be beneficial for you to choose an organizational pattern that fits your purpose and mode to help smooth out coherence. Organizational patterns are covered further in chapter 5.

Additionally, **transitional devices,** or transitions, will help you create coherency. Transitions are words and phrases that help a writer move from one idea to another, whether it is paragraph to paragraph or from idea to idea inside a paragraph. They are signal words that tell your reader when you are moving from one idea to another, allowing the ideas to flow easily. You will also encounter them when you read.

Below is a chart to help you remember and correctly use transitional devices. Which transitional device you use depends on how you plan to organize your ideas. You may notice that some transitional devices can be used in more than one way.

Space transitions **show direction or location.**	in front, in front of, behind, next to, beside, above, around, between, by, down, in, near, on, over, toward, under, to the right, to the left
Chronological transitions **show the order in which events occur(ed).**	first, next, before, after, then, as, during, immediately, later, meanwhile, now, often, previously, suddenly, when, while, second, third, last, finally
Addition transitions **show additional ideas.**	Also, next, furthermore, another, finally, first, in addition, as well
Cause and effect transitions **show the cause or effect of something.**	Therefore, as a result, as a consequence of, because, since, consequently, so, thus, ultimately, in conclusion
Contrast transitions **show contrasting or differing ideas.**	However, although, even though, nevertheless, on the other hand, but, in spite of, in contrast, instead, yet
Example transitions **help to show examples or illustrate your ideas better.**	For example, for instance, including, such as, like

If you find that your essay lacks coherence, you may need to add words or phrases in, such as transitions, or move ideas around to more effectively organize them. Do not be afraid to completely overhaul your writing. With coherence, as well as unity and support, understanding the function of each base will eventually yield your best writing.

Moreover, unity, support, and coherence are closely related. Biologically, brothers and sisters are more closely related than two cousins. Therefore, unity, support, and coherence are so closely related they are like brothers and sisters. You cannot omit one base and think the standards for the other bases will be met efficiently.

EDITING

Once you have thought about the topic, organized your ideas, written your first draft, and revised the essay, it is now time to make it shine. To do this, you must study and learn the process of **editing**. When you edit your work, you do so to ensure there are no errors in the essay. You must edit carefully because you want to submit an essay that exhibits mastery of the learning outcomes for that particular essay. When you edit, there are several factors to consider: grammar, punctuation, mechanics, spelling, and formatting. In the back of the book are editing symbols your instructor may use to mark your papers. Also in the back of the book are the Sweet 16 Rules of Writing, which is a handy list of common errors you want to watch out for. As a writer, you can use both the editing symbols and the Sweet 16 to revise and edit your essay before publishing.

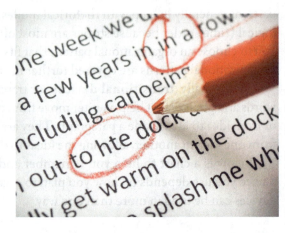

Image © B Calkins, 2014. Used under license from Shutterstock, Inc.

> ➤ **Read Write! Tip**

Editing is not just important in the academic arena. It is also important when you are writing online, whether it be posting your latest status to Facebook, captioning an Instagram photo, or sending an email. It is even important when you text. Everyone knows that autocorrect is notoriously wrong. Although sometimes this is funny, editing will help you avoid misunderstandings and enhance your credibility as a writer. In particular, emails play an important role socially, professionally, and academically in communication today.

Read Write! Activity 3.4

Below is an email sent from Ronald Carpenter, a student in Professor Ortega's MWF 9:30 a.m. U.S. history course entitled HIST 1301-43005. Revise and edit Ronald's email. Take into account the following concepts: audience, purpose, and mechanics, like spelling, punctuation, and grammar.

To: Professor Ortega
From: whatwhatron@worldnet.net
Subject: [no subject]

HEY I MISSED CLASS YESTERDAY CAN I MAKE UP THE WORK I WAS SICK. ALSO I KNOW U SAID I HAD TO HAVE A DOCTORS NOTE, HAVE ONE FOR U THO.

THANKS, SEE You Wendesday.

Ron C.

One concept in particular to edit for is formatting. **Formatting** refers to the presentation of the paper, such as double spacing and font face and size. Most professors will require you to write using a specific style, such as the Modern Language Association (MLA) or American Psychological Association (APA). These styles have specific formatting rules, like how to create a heading and how to number the pages. Most English and other communications courses use MLA style. In the Rules of Writing on the back inside cover of this textbook, MLA style formatting is covered in Sweet 16 numbers 1–5. When you edit your paper, is important to also edit for the format required by your professor. Check over it carefully to avoid these kinds of errors. Below is an example of MLA formatting.

Quintanillo 1

Aracely Quintanillo

Professor Fairbanks

DIRW 0310-67001

26 June 2018

Compulsory Preschool

Titles

Whether you add a title as you draft the essay or wait until you revise and edit, **titles** are an important part of the essay. They have two purposes: to let the reader know what your essay will be about and to capture the reader's attention.

Title Tips

Center your title.

Keep your title short; it should be a few words or a short phrase of four to six words at most.

Make certain your title is **NOT** a complete sentence.

Do not bold, enlarge, or put a period at the end of titles.

Do not italicize, underline, or use quotation marks in the title of your paper.

Do not use the prompt question as your title: What are three places you would like to visit?

Capitalize only certain letters of words in your title: the first letter of the first word, the first letter of major words in the middle, and the first letter of the last word.

Try to be creative with your title.

Here are some examples of titles. Pay close attention to what letters are capitalized and that none of the examples are complete sentences.

- *Compulsory Preschool*
- *Euthanasia: A Good Death*
- *Over the Hill*
- *A Day in the Life*

PUBLISHING

After you are finished prewriting, drafting, revising, and editing, it is now time to publish your work. **Publishing** means you are ready to turn in your essay to your professor because you are confident that all parts of the prewriting process and the writing process have been followed closely. When you publish essays consistently and correctly, it gives you a boost of confidence and encouragement regarding the writing process. Submitting well written essays gives you a positive feeling towards your work and signifies an end to another journey through the writing process.

Read Write! Review Questions: The Writing Process

1. Define free writing, listing, clustering, questioning, outlining, and building a pyramid.
2. What is the reading term for a thesis statement?
3. What are support, unity, and coherence? How do they apply to you as a reader? How do they apply to you as a writer?
4. What are transitional devices? Why are they important to both reading and writing?
5. Where else besides the academic arena is editing important?

Read Write! Connection: Chapter 3

Use a reputable news source, such as a newspaper, a magazine, or a news site like CNN, MSNBC, or Fox News, to find and read an article about a current event. Then, create a prewriting of your choice to generate ideas for a potential essay about the current event you read about.

Chapter 4
The Traditional Five-Paragraph Essay

Key Terms

introduction methods, thesis statement, topic sentence, supporting sentences, concluding sentence, thesis restatement, conclusion methods

In chapter 3, you learned the steps of the writing process, and one of those steps was drafting. When you write a draft, you must organize your ideas in the form of an academic essay, and the most basic way to do that is to use the traditional five-paragraph essay format.

The traditional five-paragraph essay has three parts: the introduction, the body paragraphs, and the conclusion.

Image © gresei, 2014. Used under license from Shutterstock, Inc.

INTRODUCTIONS

The purpose of the introduction is three-fold:

♦ To introduce the topic of the essay
♦ To catch the reader's interest/draw the reader in
♦ To present the thesis statement

The introduction can be broken down into two parts: the introduction method and the thesis statement. An **introduction method** is the way you choose to introduce the topic of the essay and draw the reader in. The **thesis statement** is the main idea of the essay that is expressed in one sentence and is usually the last sentence in the introduction. Notice that some reading terminology has appeared in this paragraph—main idea. Remember that the thesis statement and the main idea are the same thing. In a traditional five-paragraph essay, however, you will present your thesis statement using a specific construction. This is covered in more detail in chapter 3.

When writing, you should craft your thesis statement before writing your introduction because it is crucial that none of the specific information that will be covered in the thesis appears anywhere in the introduction. In other words, the first time the specific points that will be written about in the essay appear in the introduction are in the thesis statement.

Furthermore, when writing an introduction or a thesis statement, there are a few things to avoid. First, do not announce. This includes statements like "In this essay, readers will learn . . ." or "This essay will show. . . ." These kinds of statements are unnecessary because they are implied; let the essay speak for itself. Rarely do you see an author refer to the passage itself when you are reading. The same goes for you as a writer. Generally speaking, you should not mention the essay or any part of the essay when writing. Therefore, you should also avoid statements like "In this essay" or "in this paragraph."

There are many ways to write your introduction, and below are seven methods you can use when beginning your essay. Notice that in all of them the thesis statement is the same and is the last sentence in the introduction.

Background Information Method

This method gives your audience historical background information on the topic. The brief background information serves two purposes. One purpose is to draw the audience into the paper by including historical information about a current topic. Another purpose is to show that you are credible and knowledgeable about the topic being discussed. The same concept applies to authors when you are a reader. A passage that provides you with background information about the topic draws your attention and shows that the author is credible.

Example

In the mid-twentieth century, television replaced radio as America's main electronic device around which families would gather to spend time together. No longer did families have to just listen to their shows; now they could watch the news and other programs. Originally in black and white and primarily placed in living rooms, TVs now deliver shows in thousands of high definition colors, and today in some homes, there is a television in every room and a television for every person in the house. Families can watch all kinds of programs via local, cable, or satellite channels. Television has many benefits because it is educational, it is entertaining, and it is cheap.

Notice how this particular example includes both historical background information and general information on the topic of television. Then, the thesis statement is presented as the last sentence of the introduction paragraph.

General to Specific Method

The general to specific method is the most common type of introduction. In this introduction method, you begin with a general opening statement and then funnel or narrow the introduction to the thesis statement.

Example

In America, just about everyone watches television. Whether it is to escape from reality or to learn something new, people are pressing the on button on the remote control and tuning in. Individuals enjoy viewing a variety of TV programs, including fitness shows, sitcoms, and sporting events. Consequently, TV viewing has become a leisure activity for millions because it offers something for everyone. Television has many benefits because it is educational, it is entertaining, and it is cheap.

Anecdote Method

An anecdote is a brief story. Therefore, an anecdote introduction introduces the topic through a brief story that illustrates the topic. These can be written in first person, when you write about yourself and use I, me, my, or we, or third person, when you write about someone else and use they or he/she. Oftentimes, in academic writing, you will not use first person; however, the writing mode you are working on will determine whether you need to use first person or third person.

Example

Everyday Helen plops her three-year-old son, Jeremy, in front of the television set to watch *Sesame Street*. Jeremy sits enraptured while the Muppets dance on the screen, singing and talking in funny voices. Jeremy sings along with them, learning his alphabet and numbers as he does so. He watches the children on the show interact with the Muppets and the adults, and Jeremy learns about manners and behavior. Television has many benefits because it is educational, it is entertaining, and it is cheap.

Above is an example of a third person anecdote. It both introduces the topic of the essay, television, and illustrates the point the writer is trying to make: that television has many benefits. Then, the thesis statement is presented as the last sentence of the introduction paragraph. When using the anecdote method, it is important to note that some reference to the brief story must appear in the conclusion so that you come full circle with the story began in the introduction. This is important to your audience because it provides a sense of closure for your essay. Conversely, as a reader, such an introduction and conclusion would provide *you* with a sense of closure and finality by referring back to the original anecdote in the conclusion.

Contrast Method

When the contrast introduction is used, you summarize the opposite opinion of your own. You do not necessarily agree with the opposite opinion; you are only acknowledging it. After doing so, a key transition word that shows contrast is needed to let the audience know you are now moving to your own opinion. The contrast transition words *however*, *although*, or *but* are generally used for this purpose. This introduction style is particularly good for essays about a topic that has two sides, such as an argument essay.

Example

Some people believe television has many negative side effects. For example, people who watch it and do nothing else can become obese. Also, children can become desensitized to violence, and graphic images and foul language can negatively impact young adults. Additionally, television can waste too much time. However, television has many benefits because it is educational, it is entertaining, and it is cheap.

In the previous example, the writer begins by acknowledging the opinion opposite of his/her own. Then, a key contrast transition word is used to signal to the reader that the writer is changing to his/her own opinion, and the rest of the essay will stay on that side of the topic.

Quote Method

Another excellent way to begin an introduction is to start with a quote. This can be a direct quote, where quotation marks and attribution, stating where the quote is taken from or who said it, are needed, or an indirect quote, where you summarize the main idea of the quote. As a reader, quotes engage you very quickly, especially if you are familiar with them or recognize the name of the person or character being quoted.

Example

"Television! Teacher, mother, secret lover," Homer Simpson once said in loving reverence of his television set on an episode of *The Simpsons*. Truly television has as many uses as he claims. Since the 1950s, America has taken advantage of television's usefulness, and its worth has only expanded. Today television acts as not only "teacher, mother, secret lover" but also as a work out instructor, a relaxation technique, a radio, and more. Television has many benefits because it is educational, it is entertaining, and it is cheap.

Like the other examples, the thesis statement is the last sentence of the introduction. When using the quote method, it is important you correctly use quotation marks and punctuation. Note that commas and periods go inside of the closing quotation mark unless writing a research paper and citing sources within the sentence. Parenthetical citations are covered in chapter 7.

Question Method

When using the question method, you ask a question or several questions about the topic in the introduction. Readers will want to read the essay to find out the answer(s) to the question(s). It is crucial that any question asked in the introduction is answered after reading the essay. Otherwise, the reader will be left wondering and wanting more information. In addition, you should know that questions, besides those used in dialogue, should be limited to the introduction and not appear anywhere else in the essay. Using questions throughout the essay makes your essay appear too informal for academic writing.

Example

Why do people watch TV for hours? What do they get out of it? Do they watch it to learn new things, to laugh at comedians and sitcoms, or to spend an inexpensive evening at home? If every individual were asked these questions, he/she would give a different answer. However, TV viewers would agree that television has numerous positive attributes. Television has many benefits because it is educational, it is entertaining, and it is cheap.

When using the question method, you must also avoid the tendency to switch to second person and use the words *you* or *your*. Notice neither of these words is used in this introduction; it is written in third person. The only time the use of *you* or *your* is allowed occurs when you are writing dialogue, meaning quoting the exact words someone says, or composing a process or how to paper. However, even when writing a process paper, some instructors still prefer that you do not use second person.

Surprising Statement Method

One of the surest ways to catch your reader's attention is to begin your introduction with an unexpected or surprising fact or idea. This method piques your reader's curiosity, making him/her want to read the rest of your essay.

Example

Over 9 million people tuned in to watch some portion of the 2012 three-hour funeral of R&B superstar Whitney Houston, with CNN setting a record with 5.4 million viewers, ten-times its normal Saturday viewership, according to the Nielsen ratings. Millions sat transfixed in front of their TVs as a who's who list of entertainers paid tribute to Houston. From actor and *Bodyguard* costar Kevin Costner to singer Alicia Keys, the famous all shared their personal stories about the Grammy-award winning icon. Thanks to the power of TV, all who wanted to were able to be a part of the service and join the 1500 invited guests at the New Hope Baptist Church in Newark, New Jersey, to learn about Houston's roots, to cry, to laugh, and to remember a superstar. Television has many benefits because it is educational, it is entertaining, and it is cheap.

When using the surprising statement method, you must be careful to cite your source if you use specific data rather than common knowledge and to make certain that you do not fabricate or make up any information in an attempt to catch your readers' attention.

Think Write! Activity 4.1

Read the introduction below, and then answer the following questions.

Maintaining an excellent credit rating is essential today, not only for receiving good rates on mortgages or car loans but also for getting a job. Before companies hire someone, they check the potential employee's credit rating. If the rating is good, then the hiring process may continue. However, if the credit rating is poor, many employers will not hire a person regardless of their stellar educational background, their outstanding skills, or their impeccable references. Consequently, individuals must know their credit score, guard against identity theft, and live within their means.

a. The above introduction is an example of which introduction method:

____ historical background ____ general to specific or ____ surprising statement

Defend your answer. _____

_____

_____

b. According to the thesis statement, what three points will be developed in the essay? _____

_____

_____

THE BODY PARAGRAPHS

The body paragraphs follow the introduction. In a traditional five-paragraph essay, there are three. The body paragraphs are the meat of the essay; they are where you make your point and support your main idea. They are where all the explanation, elaboration, and support for the thesis statement occur. Each body paragraph is only about one topic and one topic only, and, in the traditional five-paragraph essay, these topics come from the thesis statement. They are the three main points listed in the thesis statement and the main ideas of each body paragraph. Developing one point only in each body paragraph helps your ideas stay organized and keeps your reader from becoming confused.

In reading terminology, the body paragraphs are where the supporting details can be found. Each main point from the thesis can be considered a subtopic because an essay is a longer piece of written work. Then, each subtopic is developed through the use of supporting details, a term that is used interchangeably between reading and writing.

The body paragraphs are made up of three parts: the **topic sentence**, the **supporting sentences**, and the **concluding sentence.** The topic sentence introduces the topic of the paragraph as well as serves as a link to the thesis by mentioning the topic and controlling idea of the essay. Topic sentences, which state the main idea of the paragraph, generally begin with a transitional device.

Below are the three topic sentences for the following thesis statement:

Television has many benefits because it is educational, it is entertaining, and it is cheap.

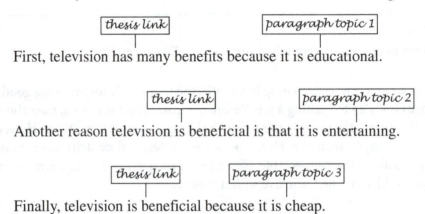

First, television has many benefits because it is educational.

Another reason television is beneficial is that it is entertaining.

Finally, television is beneficial because it is cheap.

Following the topic sentence are the supporting sentences. They give support to the topic sentence by providing details and examples that develop the point the topic sentence is trying to make, which in turn, refers back to the thesis statement. Supporting sentences are made of up examples, facts, and other details that help you make your point. Recall that in chapter 1 you learned how to identify supporting details in a text. The supporting sentences in your own writing are synonymous with supporting details in reading.

First Body Paragraph: First, television has many benefits because it is educational.

- Children often learn from watching different television shows.
  - They can watch documentaries and cartoons that are geared toward learning.
  - *For example,* the cartoon *Dora the Explorer* teaches kids to take pride in their heritage, to be adventurous, and to be kind to others.
  - With her friends, Diego and Boots, Dora goes on magical trips to find things or to help others.
- Adults can learn from television, *too.*
  - The Learning Channel, the History Channel, and other channels were specifically created to teach adults about different topics.
  - *For instance,* from these channels, adults can learn to bake, work out, or play a musical instrument.
- *Furthermore,* adults and children who do not speak English can learn the language from watching American television.
  - They can watch English speaking shows and learn vocabulary and sentence structure.
  - They can *also* learn pronunciation and dialect.

Notice how the supporting sentences contain transitional devices to help move from support to support. They keep the writing well organized and flowing. After the supporting sentences, the body paragraph wraps up with the concluding sentence. Generally, the concluding sentence restates the topic sentence in some manner and also gives the body paragraph's topic a sense of closure.

Concluding sentences for all three body paragraphs:

- There are many educational opportunities with television.
  - Restatement of "First, television has many benefits because it is educational."
- Television can be a great diversion from daily routine.
  - Restatement of "Another reason television is beneficial is that it is entertaining."
- Television is an inexpensive way to have a good time.
  - Restatement of "Finally, television is beneficial because it is cheap."

Full Body Paragraph Examples

| topic sentence | | support sentence 1 |

First, television has many benefits because it is educational. Children often learn from

| specific details for support 1 |

watching different television shows. They can watch documentaries and cartoons that

teach them to read, to count, and to learn about different cultures and new ideas. For

| specific details for support 1 |

example, the cartoon *Dora the Explorer*, teaches children to take pride in their heritage, to

| specific details for support 1 |

be adventurous, and to be kind to others. With her friends, Diego and Boots, Dora goes

| support sentence 2 |

on magical trips to find things or to help others. Adults can learn from television, too. The

| specific details for support 2 |

Learning Channel, the History Channel, and other channels were specifically created to

| specific details for support 2 |

teach adults about different topics. For instance, from these channels, adults can learn to

| support sentence 3 |

bake, work out, or play a musical instrument. Furthermore, adults and children who do

not speak English can learn the language from watching American television. They can

| specific details for support 3 |

watch English speaking shows and learn vocabulary, sentence structure, pronunciation,

| concluding sentence |

and dialect. There are many educational opportunities with television.

topic sentence

Another reason that television is beneficial is that it is entertaining. There are

support sentence 1 · specific details for support 1

countless dramas broadcast every night on television. For example, HBO's *True Blood*

is popular drama about vampires and other supernatural beings. HBO has other

specific details for support 1

entertaining drama series, as well, such as *Boardwalk Empire,* which takes place during

the Prohibition era, and *Game of Thrones,* which is a fantasy series about political

support sentence 2

intrigue in a feudal society. Viewers can also enjoy comedies and sitcoms, like *The Big*

Bang Theory, a show about four extremely intelligent "nerds" and their attractive female

specific details for support 2

neighbor. Other comedy examples include *The Office* and *Community.* Additionally,

support sentence 3 · specific details for support 3

reality television keeps the masses entertained. Reality shows cover a wide variety

of topics, from following celebrities in their daily lives to competitions. One such

specific details for support 3

competition is *The Voice,* a singing competition on which contestants train with celebrity

specific details for support 3

coaches like Christina Aguilera and Cee Lo Green. Then, they compete against one

specific details for support 3

another to win a recording contract. Shows like this one draw the audience in by making

them root for one of the competitors and keep viewers coming back week after week.

concluding sentence

Television can be a great diversion from the daily routine.

topic sentence · support sentence 1

Finally, television is beneficial because it is cheap. Local channels are free of charge

specific details for support 1

and can be received with an antenna or a basic receiver box. This includes stations like

specific details for support 1

NBC, ABC, PBS, Fox and the CW. These basic channels broadcast news shows, one-hour

support sentence 2

dramas, 30 minute sitcoms, and educational shows all for free. Cable and satellite, on the

other hand, do cost money, but they are cheaper than going to the movies, and there are various packages that can accommodate virtually everyone's price range. Viewers can

specific details for support 2

purchase access to specialized networks, like Nickelodeon, MTV, the Food Network,

support sentence 3

TNT, ESPN, and Showtime. Lastly, television can now be accessed online. Viewers can

specific details for support 3

watch their favorite shows on the networks' websites free of charge. Also, sites like Hulu

specific details for support 3

allow viewers to watch some shows for free or to pay a small charge for others. Other

specific details for support 3   concluding sentence

services, like Netflix, may be purchased for a nominal fee. Television is an inexpensive way

to have a good time.

All three body paragraphs are written in this manner. Transitional devices should be used to help move from idea to idea within the paragraphs as well as from body paragraph to body paragraph. Notice also that the way the body paragraphs are structured helps the reader easily follow the organization of the essay. The order, or organizational pattern, in which you arrange your main points and supporting details often depends on your rhetorical mode. For example, a narrative essay will use a chronological pattern. Can you tell which organizational pattern from chapter 5 has been used in the body paragraph examples about television?

Read Write! Activity 4.2

Below is a body paragraph excerpt taken from an essay about the habits of successful college students. Fill in the missing information to create a well-developed body paragraph.

Another habit successful college students practice is attending class regularly. One reason

this is an important habit is _____. For example,

_____. Another part of

attendance is being on time to class. Being punctual is important because

_____. For

instance, _____. Finally,

successful students contact their instructors when they must miss class. This is because

_____. Regular

class attendance is one of the most important habits of successful college students.

> **Read Write! Tip**

While the traditional five-paragraph essay is a useful tool to organize your ideas, you will certainly be asked to write longer essays as you progress through your academic career. One way to do this is to expand on the traditional five-paragraph essay by adding more body paragraphs. This also requires dropping the plan of development, or points listed, from the thesis statement, leaving it broad to focus on just the topic and controlling idea.

CONCLUSIONS

The conclusion is the last paragraph in the essay. It is used to summarize your point and bring the essay to a close. No new information should be included in the conclusion. In other words, this is not the place to include any information that you wanted to use in your essay but could not find a place for it.

Usually the conclusion begins with the **thesis restatement**. This means you summarize the main points from the thesis statement using new words. There are a couple of ways to do this.

Single Sentence Method

The original thesis statement should not appear in the conclusion word for word. However, the thesis statement can be reworded and placed in the conclusion to help you summarize the main points of the essay.

Example

Original thesis statement:	Television has many benefits because it is educational, it is entertaining, and it is cheap.
Thesis restatement:	Television is an instructive, enjoyable, and economical device.

Multi-sentence Method

It is also possible to break up the thesis into several sentences. Generally, the simplest way to do this is to put the topic and the controlling idea into one sentence and then put each of the main points into a sentence of its own.

Example:

Original thesis statement:	Television has many benefits because it is educational, it is entertaining, and it is cheap.
Thesis restatement:	Television is very beneficial. There are many ways to educate oneself with television. Additionally, television is a fun way to pass the time. Also, television is inexpensive.

> ## Read Write! Tip

When you are restating your thesis, you never just want to copy the thesis from the introduction and paste it into the conclusion. This should be avoided because you should never see the same sentence twice in one essay.

After the thesis statement has been summarized, the essay needs to close in a satisfactory manner. This can be done with one of the **conclusion methods**: summary, suggestion, prediction, or call-to-action.

Summary Method

The summary method is used to summarize your point one final time.

Example:

Television audiences can get so much out of their viewing experiences.

Suggestion Method

With this conclusion method, you suggest something to the reader about the topic.

Example:

Everyone should watch more television.

Prediction Method

The prediction method is used to predict something about the topic.

Example:

In the future, television will continue to teach and amuse Americans.

Call-to-action Method

This conclusion method calls the readers to get out of their seats and do something about the topic. This method is used mainly when writing an argument or persuasive essay.

Example:

Television audiences should write to television production companies about adding more shows and channels.

Two Full Conclusion Examples

Single Sentence Method Example

Television is an instructive, enjoyable, and economic device. Americans enjoy watching TV because of what it offers. Television is not only a way to learn new things, but it also allows viewers to have a good time in the comfort of their own home without spending a great deal of money. Television viewers can get so much out of their viewing experiences.

Multi-sentence Method Example

Television is very beneficial. There are many ways to educate oneself with television. Additionally, television is a fun way to pass the time. Also, television is inexpensive. In the future, television will continue to teach and amuse Americans.

Revisiting the Anecdote from the Introduction

Remember, in the introduction section, you were instructed that if you chose to use the anecdote method for an introduction that you needed to refer back to the anecdote in some way in your conclusion.

Anecdote Introduction:

Everyday Helen plops her three-year-old son, Jeremy, in front of the television set to watch *Sesame Street*. Jeremy sits enraptured while the Muppets dance on the screen, singing and talking in funny voices. Jeremy sings along with them, learning his alphabet and numbers as he does so. He watches the children on the show interact with the Muppets and the adults, and Jeremy learns about manners and behavior. Television has many benefits because it is educational, it is entertaining, and it is cheap.

Conclusion Example

Three-year-old Jeremy is too young to truly understand all of the benefits that television has to offer. Nonetheless, he, along with other Americans, enjoys watching TV. Television allows individuals to learn and to be entertained in an inexpensive manner. Television audiences can get so much out of their viewing experiences.

Read Write! Activity 4.3

Below is an example introduction using the general to specific method. Use the introduction to write a conclusion paragraph.

Every year students register for college classes, and they hope that they will be successful. However, many of them are not due to poor habits, such as skipping class, not reviewing their notes, and failing tests. In order for students to be successful, they must develop positive habits. Three habits successful college students practice are studying consistently, attending class regularly, and completing all assignments.

Conclusion: _____

_____

_____

_____

_____

_____

Traditional Five-Paragraph Essay Example

The Positive Attributes of Television

1   "Television! Teacher, mother, secret lover," Homer Simpson once said in

loving reverence of his television set on an episode of *The Simpsons*.

Truly television has as many uses as he claims. Since the

1950s, America has taken advantage of television's usefulness, and its worth has only expanded. Today television acts as not only "teacher, mother, secret lover" but also as a work out instructor, a relaxation technique, a radio, and more. Television has many benefits because it is educational, it is entertaining, and it is cheap.

2   First, television has many benefits because it is educational. Children often learn from watching different television shows. They can watch documentaries and cartoons that teach them to read, to count, and to learn about different cultures and new ideas. For example, the cartoon *Dora the Explorer* teaches children to take pride in their heritage, to be adventurous, and to be kind to others. With her friends, Diego and Boots, Dora goes on magical trips to find things or to help others. Adults can learn from television, too. The Learning Channel, the History Channel, and other channels were specifically created to teach adults about different topics. For instance, from these channels, adults can learn to bake, work out, or play a musical instrument. Furthermore, adults and children who do not speak English can learn the language from watching American television. They can watch English speaking shows and learn vocabulary, sentence structure, pronunciation, and dialect. There are many educational opportunities with television.

3   Another reason that television is beneficial is that it is entertaining. There are countless dramas broadcast every night on television. For example, HBO

has *Game of Thrones*, which is a fantasy series about political intrigue in a feudal society, and *West World*, a show about the ethics and dangers surrounding the use of artificial intelligence for human pleasure and vice. Viewers can also enjoy comedies and sitcoms, like *The Big Bang Theory*, a show about four extremely intelligent "nerds" and their attractive female neighbor. Other comedy examples include *The Office* and *Community*. Additionally, reality television keeps the masses entertained. Reality shows cover a wide variety of topics, from following celebrities in their daily lives to competitions. One such competition is *The Voice*, a singing competition on which contestants train with celebrity coaches like Blake Shelton and Adam Levine. Then, they compete against one another to win a recording contract. Shows like this one draw the audience in by making them root for one of the competitors and keep viewers coming back week after week. Television can be a great diversion from daily routine.

4   Finally, television is beneficial because it is cheap. Local channels are free of charge and can be received with an antenna or a basic receiver box. This includes stations like NBC, ABC, PBS, Fox, and the CW. These basic channels broadcast news shows, one-hour dramas, thirty-minute sitcoms, and educational shows all for free. Cable and satellite, on the other hand,

do cost money, but they are cheaper than going to the movies, and there are various packages that can accommodate virtually everyone's price range. Viewers can purchase access to specialized networks, like Nickelodeon, MTV, the Food Network, TNT, ESPN, and Showtime. Lastly, television can now be accessed online. Viewers can watch their favorite shows on the networks' websites free of charge. Also, sites like Hulu allow viewers to watch some shows for free or to pay a small charge for others. Other services, like Netflix, may be purchased for a nominal fee. Television is an inexpensive way to have a good time.

5   Television is very beneficial. There are many ways to educate oneself with television. Additionally, television is a fun way to pass the time. Also, television is inexpensive. In the future, television will continue to teach and amuse America.

Read Write! Review Questions: The Traditional Five-Paragraph Essay

1. How do you use introductions as a writer? How do introductions apply to readers?
2. What is the thesis statement synonymous with in reading terminology?
3. In reading, there are supporting details that develop a main idea. Where do the supporting details go in a traditional five-paragraph essay?
4. What usually determines your organizational pattern when you are writing?
5. What is the purpose of the conclusion? What does it do for the reader?

Read Write! Connection: Chapter 4

Refer back to the example introduction from Activity 4.3. This introduction is written using the general to specific method. Using the same thesis statement as in Activity 4.3, choose a different method to write a second introduction for the habits of successful college students topic. Then, search the internet for successful workplace habits. Find three success habits from the reading you chose and create an introduction similar to the one about student success using the information you gathered from the online reading.

PART II
Critical Reading and Writing

Chapter 5

Analyzing a Text

Key Terms

literal meaning, inference, inferential meaning, organizational patterns, thematic meaning, theme, purpose, audience, fact, opinion, word choice, denotative meaning, connotative meaning, tone, mood, bias

Think back to chapter 1 and remember the PAUSE strategy. You learned this process to make it easier to understand and break down a text. When you use PAUSE, you preread, annotate, understand, summarize, and evaluate. What this means is, thanks to the PAUSE strategy, you have already begun to read critically. Critical reading is what you do when you engage deeply with a text. It means taking your understanding into more complex levels of the reading.

Image © Dragon Images, 2014. Used under license from Shutterstock, Inc.

THE LEVELS OF READING

While some texts are fairly cut and dry, many also have multiple layers of meaning. These are called the levels of reading, and there are three: the literal level, the inferential level, and the thematic level. When you read for **literal meaning**, you are reading for what is directly stated on the page. There is nothing implied or hinted at. What you see is what you get. When you identify the topic, stated main idea, or supporting details, you are looking at the literal meaning of the text.

However, not everything is literally stated in a passage. Sometimes concepts are implied, which means you must make inferences about them. An **inference** is an educated guess based on what you already know and what you are reading. Anything implied has **inferential meaning**, which means it is not stated and must be inferred using context clues. When this happens, you are beginning to synthesize the information from the text with what you already know, allowing you to begin analyzing what you are reading at a deeper level.

Inference does not just apply to reading, however. Inferences can be made about images and graphics, as well. Look at the photo below. What do you see going on? What information is available?

You should recognize the environment: this looks like a classroom. Therefore, you can assume, or *infer*, that these are students working on an assignment or taking a test. The clues are there: a classroom and students bent over their work. However, what is that guy doing? From your own prior knowledge, you know that during an assignment or test, you are supposed to keep your eyes on your own paper. Thus, you can make another inference about this image: the guy is cheating off the girl's paper.

When you make inferences with a text, you follow the same process as with an image, but instead of asking yourself what you see, use what you have read "on the lines" to draw conclusions and make inferences. Fables are easy texts to practice inference with because all fables have morals to them, but the morals are rarely explicitly stated. Instead, you as the reader must *infer* what the moral of the story is. Look at the familiar fable of "The Tortoise and the Hare" below. What can you infer about this text?

"The Tortoise and the Hare"

from *Aesop's Fables*

1   Once upon a time there was a hare who, boasting how he could run faster than anyone else, was forever teasing tortoise for its slowness. Then one day, the irate tortoise answered back: "Who do you think you are? There's no denying you're swift, but even you can be beaten!"

2   The hare squealed with laughter. "Beaten in a race? By whom? Not you, surely! I bet there's nobody in the world that can win against me, I'm so speedy. Now, why don't you try?"

3   Annoyed by such bragging, the tortoise accepted the challenge. A course was planned, and the next day at dawn they stood at the starting line. The hare yawned sleepily as the meek tortoise trudged slowly off. When the hare saw how painfully slow his rival was, he decided, half asleep on his feet, to have a quick nap. "Take your time!" he said. "I'll have forty winks and catch up with you in a minute."

4   The hare woke with a start from a fitful sleep and gazed round, looking for the tortoise. But the creature was only a short distance away, having barely covered a third of the course. Breathing a sigh of relief, the hare decided he might as well have breakfast too, and off he went to munch some cabbages he had noticed in a nearby field. But the heavy meal and the hot sun made his eyelids droop. With a careless glance at the tortoise, now halfway along the course, he decided to have another snooze before flashing past the winning post. And smiling at the thought of the look on the tortoise's face when it saw the hare speed by, he fell fast asleep and was soon snoring happily.

5   The sun started to sink below the horizon, and the tortoise, who had been plodding towards the winning post since morning, was scarcely a yard from the finish. At that very point, the hare woke with a jolt. He could see the tortoise a speck in the distance and away he dashed. He leapt and bounded at a great rate, his tongue lolling, and gasping for breath. Just a

little more and he'd be first at the finish. But the hare's last leap was just too late, for the tortoise had beaten him to the winning post. Poor hare! Tired and in disgrace, he slumped down beside the tortoise who was silently smiling at him.

6   "Slowly does it every time!" tortoise said.

This fable is familiar to many people, so you may already know the moral. However, the moral is never actually openly stated; instead, it must be inferred. To make this inference, you would first have to look at what is happening "on the lines." The story is fairly straightforward when you take it literally, and you can easily summarize it as a way to pick out clues: A rabbit has boasted he can beat a tortoise in a race because the tortoise is so slow. The rabbit is cocky and decides to take a nap during the race. He naps too long, however, and loses the race at the last minute. The tortoise then lauds his own slowness.

After you have looked at the literal meaning of the text, you can ask yourself questions about your own experience with facts, examples, or situations presented in the text. In the case of the fable, maybe the story makes you think of a time you raced through a homework assignment and as a result earned a bad grade. Perhaps you are reminded of a time when you waited until the last minute to study for a midterm exam, and it did not work out well for your course average. Either of these experiences would easily connect to the fable, so they both work for making inferences about the moral of the story.

At this point, it is time to actually begin inferring something. Based on the literal meaning of the text and the connections you can make to what you already know or have experienced, you can infer that the moral of the story is that "slow and steady wins the race."

In both the image example and the text example, you went through some specific steps to make inferences. You want to follow these steps every time you are asked to make inferences about a picture, graphic, or reading. As you improve with practice, you will move through these steps more quickly.

Steps for Making Inferences

Text	Image/Graphic
Step 1: Break down the text for its literal meaning. Complete the first three steps of PAUSE to make sure you understand the text at the literal level.	*Step 1:* Ask yourself what you see in the picture. What is going on? Does anything stand out? Do you notice anything specific? Write anything down that you notice. In other words, create annotations for the image.
Step 2: Check your understanding by completing the fourth step of PAUSE. Summarize the text.	*Step 2:* Summarize what is going on in the image. Write your summary down.

Text	Image/Graphic
Step 3: Relate the text to what you already know or your own experiences. Does it make you think of a fact you already know? Does it remind you of something you have experienced?	*Step 3:* Relate the image to your prior knowledge. Are you familiar with anything in the image? Have you had an experience similar to what is going on?
Step 4: Make connections between what you read and what it reminded you of. Through your connections, begin to draw inferences from the text.	*Step 4:* Make connections between your knowledge and the image. Through your connections, begin to draw inferences from the image.
Step 5: Question your thinking. Does your inference make sense? Could you make other inferences? What other inferences could you make? Always remember to think about your thinking. Recall that this is called metacognition.	*Step 5:* Question your thinking. Does your inference make sense? Could you make other inferences? What other inferences could you make? Always remember to think about your thinking. Recall that this is called metacognition.

Read Write! Activity 5.1

Look at the photo below. What do you see? Connect what you see to your own experience or prior knowledge about what is going on in the image. Then, make two inferences about the image below.

Image © oliveromg, 2014. Used under license from Shutterstock, Inc.

What do you see?

_____

_____

What do you already know?

_____

_____

Inference #1

_____

_____

Inference #2

_____

_____

_____

_____

Read Write! Activity 5.2

Read the text below. Then answer the question that follows.

Maria's Dilemma

Maria was frantically looking around her house. She checked in the basket she kept by the front door. She checked on the hook by the garage door. She dug through her purse and even went back to look inside her locked car. Then, she came back in the house and checked under the couch cushions, in the pockets of her jacket, and under the stack of yesterday's mail. Finally, she sat on the couch, placed her head in her hands, and said, "I'm going to be late again."

After reading this paragraph, what can you infer?

_____

_____

_____

_____

> ### Read Write! Tip

In science classes, you will often be asked to make an inference about the outcome of a lab or experiment in the form of a "hypothesis." This means you will make an educated guess about what will occur during an experiment.

© Mino Surkala/Shutterstock.com

Read Write! Activity 5.3

Preread and annotate the passage below, using strategies from chapter 1 to infer what the implied main idea is. Use a pencil to circle related ideas or repeated phrases. Then, write the topic and implied main idea on the line below the passage.

VW Beetle: The Origin Story

When people think of the Volkswagen Beetle, they tend to think of hippies and the 1960s. They often think of a rainbow of colors and engines in the back. However, most people do not realize that the original Volkswagen concept was conceived by Adolf Hitler. In fact, "Volkswagen" means "people's car" in German. Hitler's idea, which was developed in 1934 prior to World War II, was that the "people's car" would be affordable, fast, and easy to repair. The designer of the original Volkswagen was Ferdinand Porsche. Porsche's last name should be familiar; it is now associated with high end sports cars like the Porsche 911. However, Porsche also designed the original Volkswagen, which was called the Type 1 but eventually became known as the Beetle or "Bug" in popular culture. Production on the Type 1 came to a halt in 2003, but the original Beetle design can still be seen on the road today around the world.

Topic: _____

Implied main idea: _____

Organizational Patterns

Something else that can be inferred is organizational pattern. Understanding organizational patterns will help you with both reading and writing. When you read, **organizational patterns** help you to understand how an author organized his/her ideas and also why he/she chose to organize the writing in such a way. As a writer, organizational patterns will help you structure your paragraphs and essays in a logical manner appropriate for the rhetorical mode you are writing in. Below is a chart of the common organizational patterns you will see in texts you read. You will also see which rhetorical modes tend to use which organizational patterns.

Organizational Pattern	Matching Rhetorical Mode(s)	Explanation
Chronological/time	Narrative	The passage is organized from beginning to end. This is time ordering.
Compare/contrast	Compare/contrast, argument	The passage is organized to discuss how two topics are similar or different or both.
Emphatic order	Exemplification, argument	The passage is organized in order of emphasis or importance. This can be from most important to least important or vice versa.
Sequence	Process	The passage is organized in a specific sequence or set of steps that must be done in a certain order.
Spatial/space	Description	The passage is organized by how the subjects relate to one another in a physical space, like a room.
Cause and effect	Cause and effect, argument	The passage is organized to show specific causes or effects or both.
Problem and solution	Argument	The passage is organized to first discuss the problem and secondly discuss a suggested solution.
Topical	Exemplification, argument	The passage is organized by topic. This organizational pattern is a catch-all for writings that do not fall into any of the other patterns.

In chapter 3, transitional expressions were discussed. Transitions play an important role in determining organizational patterns; in fact, they are signal words that well help you infer what the organizational pattern is. Remember that the chart on page 54 shows that certain transitional expressions are used for specific organizational needs. For example, the transitional device "as a result" might signal to you that the passage you are reading is organized in the cause and effect pattern because "as a result" shows effect. Thus, when you annotate a passage, circling transitions will often help you to determine the organizational pattern because they are signal words alerting you to how an author has organized the reading.

Read Write! Activity 5.4

Read the passage below and determine the organizational pattern by circling or highlighting the transitional expressions you see.

Campus Beauty

The University of Oklahoma's campus is one of the most striking in the Big XII conference. Its busiest area is the South Oval, which is lined with lecture halls. In the middle of the oval is a beautiful lawn dotted with billowing trees that provide shade for students studying, eating lunch, hanging out with friends, or even napping. Centered in the lush, green lawn is a marble fountain surrounded by rose bushes covered in creamy blooms in the spring and summer. South of the fountain are OU's seasonal flower beds which sit close to Lindsey Street. These take up about half the South Oval lawn, and the landscaping design changes from season to season, including choice of flower and how the flowers are patterned. Sometimes they are zigzagged, and the next time they might spell out "Oklahoma" in crimson and cream mums.

During the Oklahoma state centennial in 2007, the flowers were arranged into famous Oklahoma symbols, including a bison, an oil derrick, and a scissor-tail. On the opposite side of campus is the North Oval, which is a reflection of the South Oval and is lined with administration and office buildings that were once home to some of OU's original classrooms. In between the two ovals is the Bizzell Memorial Library, one of many buildings built in the campus' signature architectural style known as Cherokee Gothic. Bizzell's façade is cathedral-esque with two front facing turrets. It is composed of red brick and white granite details, including a number of small statuary that peer at students from on high as the students walk below. Included in the library complex is a great, freestanding clock tower that reaches to Oklahoma's sweeping blue skies. It sits in the middle of an open courtyard draped in weeping willows, and the soothing sounds of multiple fountainheads bubbling make it a quiet place to relax after a rigorous exam. To the northeast of the library is the student union, another Gothic inspired structure crowned with a thick, square clock tower that plays OU's school songs on the hour. South of the union is Oklahoma Memorial Stadium, the home of OU's football program. This massive structure reaches practically to the clouds and seats 88,000 people. The field below is a Neapolitan confection—white lines, green grass, and crimson end zones. South of the ovals and the stadium are the student dorms.

The ones that stand out the most are the towers, which are 12 stories tall and

shaped like giant Xs. Like most of the buildings on campus, the dorms are

built of stately red brick. Much of OU's campus is built in a similar style, all

of which is arrestingly remarkable.

Organizational pattern: _____

Beneath inferential meaning is the third and deepest level of reading: **thematic meaning**. When you look at a reading from a thematic standpoint, you make broader connections to the text, thinking outside of the reading and moving into more universal concepts. Ideas to consider during this step include why the text's meaning is universally important, what it means to you as a reader, and what it means to humanity as a whole. When you are reading thematically, you are critically evaluating the text. You want to try to connect the text to bigger ideas and think about how it appeals to a universal audience.

Theme

Theme is the author's message. It is the lesson you are supposed to get out of the story. If you think back to the fable of "The Tortoise and the Hare," you did more than infer something about the text. You discovered the moral of the story, which means you figured out the *theme*. While inference is not always about theme, discerning the theme of a text is *always* going to take skill in inference because an author will almost *never* blatantly state the theme. You must use clues within the text to decipher what the theme is.

Once you know what the theme is, you can take the theme beyond the reading and think about it in a broader scope. For example, in "The Tortoise and the Hare," recall that the theme, or moral, is "slow and steady wins the race." Can you give this moral universal meaning by connecting it to yourself or others? This could lead to the connection between "slow and steady wins the race" and procrastination. The hare waited until the last minute, and this led to poor results. Therefore, a universal interpretation might be that planning and taking the time to do something well will produce more satisfying results. This is not just an idea that applies to the hare—it can apply to anyone.

Read Write! Activity 5.5

Read the fable below. Then answer the question that follows.

"The Lion and the Bulls"

from *Aesop's Fables*

There was once a hungry lion who observed three bulls in a field in hopes of eating them. Every time he tried to attack the bulls, they herded together and drove him off so that no matter how quick or strong he was, the group was able to defeat him.

Then, one day the bulls had a fight. They were so angry with one another, they went to separate corners of the field and refused to speak to each other. When the lion saw this, he was pleased. It was now easy for him to pick them off one by one.

What is the theme of this passage?

_____

_____

_____

_____

CONSIDERING THE AUTHOR

Something important to take into account when you are reading critically is the author. While it is tempting to skip over this information, author bios, which are usually brief, will give you important information to consider about the author and will help you better evaluate the text. While there will not always be an author bio, if there is one, you *must* read it. You can usually find author bios before a text or directly after.

Author's Background

Oftentimes, the author bio will give you background information about the author. This may include his/her credentials and job title. It might also include the years of his/her birth and death. Why do you think these bits of information about the author might be important? For one, credentials tell you whether or not an author is credible. If you were asked to read an article about molecular biology, but it was written by a poet, that takes away from the credibility of the information in the article. Most poets are not molecular biology experts. A more credible author of such an article would be a molecular biologist. Thus, credentials and titles inform the reader of the author's expertise. Knowing whether or not the author is an expert in the field you are reading about plays a role in how you engage with a text.

The time period in which the author lives or lived is also important. Life is very different now from two centuries ago. In fact, life is very different now from just two decades ago! Thus, history plays a role in critical reading. This textbook contains writings from multiple periods in history, and reviewing the author bio can give you key historical context to use when evaluating a passage. It can also help you to think about vocabulary. You may find words in older pieces of writing that are unfamiliar to you because they have fallen out of use today. When you come across one of these words, use context clues to decipher its meanings or, as a last result, look up the definition in a dictionary and add it to your vocabulary journal.

Audience and Purpose

Remember that there are three main **purposes** for writing: to inform, to persuade, and to entertain. Some examples of informative texts include newspaper and magazine articles, exemplification and process essays, and even this textbook. Persuasive texts can include newspaper columns and editorials, blogs, argument essays and research papers, and speeches. Examples of entertainment include books, poetry, short stories, descriptive-narrative essays, and even TV shows and movies. Identifying an author's purpose helps you to understand *why* an author wrote the passage you are reading, which in turn helps you to better evaluate it.

Purpose goes hand in hand with an author's audience. **Audience** is who the author is writing for. A picture book author's primary audience, for example, is children, and this informs the way such an author writes. Think about a picture book. It is not full of multifarious types of sentences and extensive, obscure vocabulary words and jargon. It is written in simple sentences with simple vocabulary because it is meant to reach children. Alternately, a literary analysis of Shakespeare's *Macbeth* published in a scholarly journal has a different target audience. The author of such a work might be writing for his/her peers, meaning other experts in and students of Shakespearean tragedies. If this were the case, the language of literature would be used—words the author's peers would recognize, like allusion, allegory, and symbol. This textbook's target audience is reading and writing students. The fact that it was written for students like you informs the choices made when writing it. Therefore, knowing an author's audience helps to you evaluate the text further.

Fact vs. Opinion

As you are reading, sometimes you will have to determine the difference between a fact the author has presented you with and the author's opinion. **Facts** can be proven true while an **opinion** is something that the author believes. Facts are used in both informative and persuasive passages. For example, the author of a chemistry textbook will use facts to inform you about the subject of chemistry. A persuasive piece of writing would use facts to convince you of something. For instance, a political speech will provide you with facts, such as statistics, to convince you to vote for a certain candidate. That is where opinion comes in. Often, facts are used to support opinions.

Fact and opinion play a role in your own writing as well. For example, if you were to write an exemplification essay, some of the examples you use to explicate your topic might be facts. In an argument essay, you would use facts to support your thesis statement and convince your audience that your argument is valid. In an argument essay, your thesis statement is your opinion about a controversial topic. You will use the facts, which can be proven, to support whatever your opinion may be.

> ➤ **Read Write! Tip**
>
> Remember that facts are objective. This means they are impartial and neutral. Opinions, on the other hand, are subjective, which means they are personal and represent specific views or attitudes.

Author's Word Choice

As aforementioned, audience and purpose affect how an author writes his/her work. This means that these two important concepts drive **word choice**, also known as diction. Authors do not just conjure their words at leisure—they pick them carefully and with intention because they are writing for a specific purpose and for a certain audience.

All words have a denotative meaning. **Denotative meaning** is a word's literal meaning, its dictionary definition. Denotative meaning goes with reading for literal meaning because it is what it is—there is nothing to infer or think about too deeply. However, many words also have connotative meanings. **Connotative meaning** is a secondary meaning of a word drawn from associations with the word, usually emotional associations. Connotations can be positive or negative or neutral. For example, think about the word "intelligent." Intelligent has a positive connotation. People associate it with being well educated and clever. Then, there is the word "cunning." Cunning is a very similar word to intelligent, but it has a negative connotation. Why? Generally speaking, people tend to associate words like "cunning" or "shrewd" with being sneaky. Sneaking around has negative emotions associated with it. Even a word as simple as "red" has connotations to it. Many people might associate the word "red" with communism. Others might associate it with anger. Denotation and connotation, then, are two sides of the same coin. They both create meaning for a word.

Read Write! Activity 5.6

Read each word group below. Then, decide the connotation of each word: positive, negative, or neutral. In your own words, explain why you believe a word has a negative, positive, or neutral connotation.

1. Died   Passed Away   Deceased

   _____

   _____

2. Assertive   Bossy   Confident

   _____

   _____

3. House   Home   Dwelling

_____

_____

4. Horselaugh   Giggle   Snicker

_____

_____

5. Gaze   Gawk   Look

_____

_____

Thus, authors choose words for both their denotative and connotative meanings. If they are trying to create negative emotions in their readers, authors will choose words with negative connotations. This relates directly to tone. **Tone** is the author's attitude toward the topic. Word choice creates tone, and since word choice is informed by audience and purpose, that means tone is too. Tone is usually explained through the use of adjectives, like happy, sad, dark, sarcastic, inspiring, funny, or satirical. For example, earlier in this chapter you read a short passage called "Campus Beauty." The tone of this piece is appreciative or perhaps nostalgic. All of the author's word choices have positive connotations—beauty, blooms, confection, stately. All of these words inspire certain images in your mind as a reader. The author clearly associates this college campus with good things, and this informs the tone of the entire piece: it is one of appreciation.

Of course, tone is not something that is directly stated. Instead, you must infer it by looking at word choice. Authors deliberately use certain words to create a certain tone and make you as a reader think certain things or feel a certain way. Identifying tone requires you to read between the lines. Tone also helps create **mood**, which is how you feel when you read something. The mood of most of the writings of Edgar Allan Poe, whose work you will read later in this textbook, is creepy, melancholy, or chilling. It is meant to make you feel anxious or uncomfortable or scared or sad because of its **genre**, or type or mode of writing it is. In Poe's case, much of his writing falls into the horror genre, so it is supposed to frighten you.

> **Read Write! Tip**
> Be careful not to confuse tone and mood. Tone is the author's attitude toward the subject. Mood is how you as a reader feel when you are reading the author's words. Tone creates mood, but tone and mood are not the same thing.

You can also think of tone in terms of formal vs. informal. Most professional writings you read are formal as are most assignments you do for college. Informal pieces you might read are emails, Facebook statuses, text messages, bulletins, online announcements from your professor, and your own course notes. A formal tone tends to sound more serious—it uses richer vocabulary, more complex sentence structure, and avoids slang. It is also extremely polished, meaning there are no mechanical errors like spelling or grammar, and it usually follows a specific format, structure, or way of presentation. Informal writing, on the other hand, is more free form. It is how it is and can include slang and mistakes and does not follow any specific rules.

When you are asked to identify tone, ask yourself a few questions to help determine what the tone of a passage is:

- What is the word choice like? Do the words have negative or positive connotations or are they neutral?
- Are the words formal or informal sounding? Do you see slang?
- What is the mood of the writing? How do you feel while you are reading it? Did you laugh? Were you sad?
- What is the organizational pattern being used? In what order did you receive the information? Does this play a role in how it sounds?
- What inferences can you make? Is there anything implied that you can discern? What is it?
- Is there any information you know of that has been omitted or left out? When an author leaves something out, purposefully or otherwise, it can inform the tone.

Read Write! Activity 5.7

Use PAUSE to break down the poem below. During the evaluation step, focus on determining the tone and mood of the poem. Identify the tone and mood using an adjective and write on the line following the piece.

> Virginia Morris is a student at Eastfield College in Mesquite, TX. This poem was originally appeared in spring 2014 in *The Eclectic*, vol. VII, which is a literary and arts journal published by the Psi Beta chapter of Sigma Kappa Delta, the National English Honors Society for two-year colleges.

The Child Who Once Was Me

by Virginia Morris

Staring back into the memories blanketing my

past

Flipping through the snapshots makes the years

go by too fast

Each picture holds an instant—a single drop of

time

Yet photographs can't capture all the life that

has been mine

To someone else, perhaps a smiling child is all

they see

I see the joy and innocence of someone who was

me

Each picture is a window to the time when it

was made

And often gazing back through them, I wish I

could have stayed

Banishing my worries with a gleeful childish

grin

Rejoicing in simplicity and peace from deep

within

Wistfully, I carry on with the way that life must

be

Still envying the freedom of the child who once

was me

Tone/Mood:_____

Author's Bias

Tone can sometimes indicate that the author has a bias. A **bias** is a prejudice against or in favor of something. Bias is not always present in a writing, but if it is, you may be asked to identify it. Again, connotative meaning plays a role here. You want to look for "loaded" words—words that have powerful connotations. Think about the two primary political parties in the United States: the Democrats and the Republicans. Both of these words are very emotionally charged and depending on the author, can have either strong positive or negative connotations. Think again about the passage "Campus Beauty." The tone is appreciative and approving; it is definitely not neutral. Can you agree that the passage has a bias toward the University of Oklahoma, meaning a prejudice in favor of this university? Definitely.

It is particularly easy to identify bias when you are reading something persuasive. It becomes even more obvious when the argument is only one-sided. For example, if you are reading a text that is trying to persuade you to outlaw abortion and the pro-choice side of the argument is never addressed, it would be clear that the author is biased in favor of the pro-life agenda. You can also think about bias in terms of facts vs. opinions. Facts have no prejudice. They are what they are. If an author relies primarily on facts with neutral word choice, there is probably not a bias. Opinions, on the other hand, can be loaded with bias.

Keep in mind that bias is not necessarily a bad thing. Authors are allowed to have opinions and present them how they wish. Like everything else in this chapter, what is important about bias is that you as the reader are able to recognize it and take it into account when you evaluate a text.

Read Write! Review Questions: Analyzing a Text

1. What is inference?
2. Why might an author's background be important?
3. What is the difference between fact and opinion?
4. What is the difference between connotation and denotation?
5. True or False: Tone and mood are the same thing.

Read Write! Connection: Chapter 5

Go back to an essay or paragraph you have written from this class or a previous class, the older the better. Look at your writing through new eyes as though you are reading it for the first time. Use PAUSE to break down your text, focusing specifically on the "annotate" and "understand" steps. Underline the main idea of your essay and put a box around the topic, which should be included in the main idea. Use a highlighter to identify the subtopics and/or supporting details. Finally, circle the transitional devices you used within your writing. Use these to determine which organizational pattern you used in the essay.

Chapter 6
Analyzing Your Own Writing

Key Terms

credibility, general audience, purpose, facts, opinion, word choice, bias

Critical writing goes hand in hand with critical reading. Much of what was discussed in chapter 5 comes into play here in chapter 6. The only difference is now *you* are the writer instead of the reader. This means *you* are using the tools in your writing arsenal to communicate with and affect your audience.

Image © Diego Cervo, 2014. Used under license from Shutterstock, Inc.

CREDIBILITY

Recall that an author's credibility is important when you are breaking down a text. In turn, your own credibility is important when you write. As a student writer, your credibility depends upon the following things:

- ♦ Your ability to follow directions—Did your instructor ask you to present your writing in a certain way? Perhaps you were asked to use MLA style. When you do not follow your instructor's directions, you lose credibility.
- ♦ Your sentence skills—Did you edit your writing? Errors in mechanics, spelling, grammar, and punctuation hurt your credibility. Use the Sweet 16 Rules of Writing on the back inside cover of this textbook to help you with this.
- ♦ Proper acknowledgment of sources—Sometimes you will be asked to research a topic and use your research to write a paper. When you do this, you must cite the sources you used both in the text and on a Works Cited page. This is covered more in chapter 7.
- ♦ Avoidance of academic dishonesty—Academic dishonesty includes cheating, plagiarism, and collusion. When you are caught in the act of academic dishonesty, this destroys your credibility in the class you are taking. It is imperative that you avoid this ***at all costs***.

Credibility is also known as ethos. Credibility and ethos are discussed more in Chapter 13: Reading and Writing Arguments.

AUDIENCE AND PURPOSE

Audience and purpose have both been discussed at length several times in this textbook. Why do they keep coming up? It should be obvious by now that they are very important. Your purpose and audience inform *why* and *how* you write. When you are writing, your purpose is often defined by the rhetorical mode. If you are writing a descriptive-narrative, you are trying to entertain. An argument essay, on the other hand, is persuasive. The audience of a student writer is called **general audience**, or the broader public. However, you can also think about this more specifically. Who, really, is going to be reading your writing in this course? It is your professor and perhaps your peers. Remember, though, that your professor and peers *are* a part of the general audience.

Read Write! Activity 6.1

Below are several different audiences. On the lines below the audience type, explain how you would adjust your writing based on who your audience is.

1. Your best friend

   _____

   _____

2. Your professor

   _____

   _____

3. Your five-year-old niece

   _____

   _____

4. Your boss

   _____

   _____

FACTS VS. OPINION

When you are writing, you will use both fact and opinion. Facts will come in handy in most of your writing—exemplification, summary, argument, and even narrative. A **fact**, which is anything you can prove, is going to work well in support of a thesis statement. You can also use facts in informal writing, like journals and discussion boards.

Opinions, on the other hand, will play a larger role in certain rhetorical modes because **opinions** are what you as a writer believe. For example, if you are writing an argument essay, you present an opinion, or claim, in the form of a thesis statement and then defend it through the use of facts and other supports.

A cause and effect essay, on the other hand, might not include an opinion. Instead, it will neutrally explicate the cause(s) and/or effect(s) of something.

WORD CHOICE

Remember that authors do not just choose words at random when they write. You should not do that either. Instead, you want to be deliberate in your **word choice**, picking words to create a tone that goes with your purpose. For example, suppose you are writing a descriptive-narrative about your first date, which was a hilarious disaster. You would want to choose words with positive and humorous connotations. Perhaps you fell down as you tried to sit at the table, pulling the table cloth and dishes with you. If you were trying to make this humorous, you would not write it neutrally. Rather, you would write something that would inspire a humorous tone through specific word choice.

Neutral:	As I sat down, my chair rolled out from under me, and I lost my balance. In an attempt to steady myself, I grabbed the table but only ended up pulling down the tablecloth and dishes on top of me as I fell to the floor. Everything falling was very loud.
Humorous:	As I sat down, my chair took on a life of its own and rolled out from under me. Surprised, I lost my balance and began to teeter backward. In an attempt to steady myself, I grasped at the table top. Unfortunately, this was no help. I careened backward, ending up in a heap on the floor, followed shortly by the tablecloth and a shower of dishes and silverware. It made quite a hullabaloo.

In the second example, specific words are chosen to create the tone, which is humorous. It does not just say the narrator lost his balance—it says he "teetered." He does not just fall—he "careens." The dishes and silverware do not fall either—they "shower" him, and it is not just noisy, it is a "hullabaloo." Even the word "hullaballoo," which means to make a racket, is funny sounding. Everything in the second example has specific connotations that help create the humorous tone.

Read Write! Activity 6.2

Read the passage below. Currently, the tone is neutral. After you have read it, *rewrite* the passage to give it a funny tone.

The cat ran through the hallway. His eyes were very big, and he swished his tail back and forth. He was chasing the red dot from a laser pointer. He climbed over the couch and jumped on the dog trying to get it. The dog growled and barked at him, but the cat continued after the red dot. Eventually, the red dot disappeared when the cat's owner put the laser pointer away. The cat did not understand. He meowed loudly.

_____

_____

_____

_____

_____

_____

_____

_____

_____

_____

_____

_____

Recall that tone can also be formal or informal. Most assignments you do for school are going to be formal. Below are some tips on formal, academic writing:

+ Always follow your professor's instructions for presentation and format. That means if your professor asks that your writing look a certain way, such as following MLA format, you need check that you did it correctly.

+ Use varied sentence structure. If you write in all simple sentences, your writing sounds choppy and boring. Mix it up and use simple, compound, complex, and compound-complex sentences to spice up your writing. Sentence patterns are discussed later in chapter 18.

+ Be specific with your language. Do not say something is "good" or "bad." Use stronger adjectives like "fantastic" or "horrible." Do not say something is a "big" topic today. Write that it is "important" or "significant." Being specific helps you to get your point across more clearly.

+ Avoid being wordy. For example, the phrases "the reason for this" or "the reason being" are considered wordy—just use "because" instead. In this example, one word takes the place of three or four. Be concise with your language and avoid awkward sounding sentences in the process. This will help you communicate more effectively. Additionally, avoid the phrase "that being said." This is just filler.

+ Avoid clichés. A cliché is a phrase or saying that is overused. Examples of clichés include "in a nutshell," "he/she means the world to mean," and "at the end of the day." You have probably heard these phrases a million times—that is exactly why you do not want to use them in your writing. They make you sound unoriginal and boring.

+ Avoid conversational language, meaning do not let your tone become too familiar. Avoid words like "nowadays," "a lot," and contractions. While these are fine in conversation, they are too informal for academic writing. This includes avoiding slang words. An example of this is "cop." Use "police officer" instead. Never start a sentence with the word "well."

+ Think about your audience and purpose, and choose words that are appropriate to the task and reader at hand.

+ Be sure to follow all of your professor's directions. When in doubt, ask.

> ## ➢ Read Write! Tip

Do not fall into the trap of using "intellectual" sounding words in your writing, especially if you do not know what they mean. Formal writing does not mean you have to use an overabundance of winding, multi-syllable vocabulary words. While you are expected to use richer vocabulary in academic writing then in, say, a text message, avoid using words you do not really understand just because you think they make your paper sound "authoritative" or "smart." If you use the words incorrectly, it will take away from your credibility. Always be sure you understand the

meaning of a word before you use it in your writing. Additionally, keep your audience in mind as you choose your vocabulary. Use words appropriate for whom you are writing.

BIAS

Remember that chapter 5 explained that bias is not a bad thing. If you include **bias** in your writing, it just means you are prejudiced in favor of or against something. Whether or not bias is okay depends on your purpose. For example, imagine you are writing a descriptive-narrative essay about your wedding day. Many people consider their wedding day to be one of the best days of their lives. Therefore, of course you are going to have a bias in favor of your wedding day. That is perfectly fine.

It is different when it comes to persuasive writing. Bias is certainly required because you must be in favor of or against something to argue. However, you want to avoid presenting a strong bias because it will make you appear irrational and will leave your argument sounding one-sided. One way to lessen the effect of your bias, which could end up turning some readers off, is to acknowledge the opposition in some way and use tactful language. This is covered more in Chapter 13: Reading and Writing Arguments.

Read Write! Review Questions: Analyzing Your Own Writing

1. What are some ways you can ensure your credibility as a writer?
2. Explain how your word choice can affect your readers.
3. Name two things to avoid in formal writing.

Read Write! Connection: Chapter 6

Read the following paragraph and annotate the passage for anything that should be avoided in formal writing. Then, revise and edit the paragraph for word choice, such as slang, clichés, contractions, wordiness, and vague language. Utilize the Sweet 16 on the back inside cover of the textbook to help you do this.

The Game of Football

Football is an extremely krunk and entertaining sport to play because it involves a high amount of teamwork, a high reliance on yo skillz, and also the mental aspect of outsmarting your haters. Teamwork in football requires all teammates to bear the load. When playing on offense, the offensive line is required to play good at the start of any play. Without the offensive line, the running back cannot get into open space. The quarterback better be dope. The quarterback must have time to throw the ball. The wide receivers need time to get open. However, an open wide receiver and a good offensive line ain't nothin if the quarterback can't throw the ball. All teammates must play together as a single unit to be successful in moving the ball. A player cannot pick up the slack just cause someone fell off. Due to each player being a cog in the machine, all players must do their thing while on the field. Each player has a high accountability because at the end of the day, if you personally do not have mad skillz, the team won't be about nothing. Every player is important. This also gives a huge feeling of satisfaction when you beat the haters who were trying to beat you. However, it is not all about beating your opponent physically. Smaller and more wack teams have found success faking directions with where they are running. Faking a handoff to the running back only to throw the ball downfield or faking as if the quarterback will throw the ball only to hand it off to the running back at the last second will make y'all look like a beast if it is done correctly. This can cause an opponent to be out of position so that you have a greater chance of completing your own personal assignment. Knowing when to fake out the opponent is an incredible part of the mental game. Another high mental aspect is mental conditioning. Can you hold your concentration longer than your opponent? Can you go longer than your opponent without making a mistake and show that you are ride or die when you are exhausted and sore? This is an incredibly important part of football. It is what is. Football is a team game that requires each player to contribute individually for the team to be all that and a bag of chips. There are a lot of strategies that can allow players from different necks of the woods to be successful, but each player must be down with the squad to be successful as a group.

Chapter 7
Writing with Sources

Key Terms

sources, parenthetical citations, the sandwich method, Works Cited

Sometimes your professor will ask you to research a topic and use your research to write your paper, meaning your professor will want you to integrate the writing of others into your own writing. This is tricky business because it is important to both make the writing of others sound smooth and cohesive with your own writing as well as to acknowledge the source of the ideas that are not your own. The **source** is where the ideas that do not belong to you come from.

© Monkey Business Images/Shutterstock.com

EVALUATING SOURCES

While this textbook is not necessarily a research text, below are some quick tips for evaluating sources when trying to determine whether or not they are credible to use for an academic paper. Ask yourself the following questions:

Who is the author? Can you find information on the author to determine his/her credibility?

Who is the sponsor of the information? For example, Mayo Clinic publishes many studies.

How old is the information? Try not to use anything older than 10 years.

What is the purpose and who is the intended audience of the piece?

Can you detect bias in the piece? How does it affect the writing?

You can also think about types of credible sources, such as newspapers, magazines, books, scholarly journals, peer reviewed journals, television shows, documentaries, and films. Generally speaking, you should avoid using personal webpages and blogs, forums, and wikis as sources for academic writing.

INTEGRATING SOURCES

Once you have completed your research or reviewed pieces provided by your professor, you must figure out how to use the source in your writing without it feeling out of place to the reader. There are a few things to keep in mind as you do this.

The Quarter Rule

How much of your paper should be from sources? A good rule of thumb for an undergraduate research paper is no more than a quarter, or 25%. In other words, most of the paper should be your writing and your words. This also means that quotes should be brief. Do not pull a whole paragraph from another writer and stuff it into your paper. Try for one to three sentences maximum.

Direct Quotations

When you use a direct quotation from a source, you are using the source word for word. When this is done, you *must* put the information inside quotation marks followed by a parenthetical citation immediately acknowledging the source of the writing.

Direct Quotation Example

"Putting on a mask of black silk, and drawing a roquelaire closely about my person, I suffered him to hurry me to my palazzo" (Poe 67).

How do you know when to use direct quotes? Generally speaking, you should use them when numerical data is provided, as well as when you are presenting an opinion that is not your own.

Paraphrasing

Recall that paraphrasing was discussed in the context of note taking during chapter 2. When you paraphrase, you take the source's writing and put it in your own words. This does not, however, absolve you of the need for a parenthetical citation. Any time you use ideas that are not your own within your writing, you must acknowledge the source of that information. On the other hand, when you paraphrase, you do not need to put the information inside quotation marks. You do, however, still need to cite the source using a parenthetical citation.

Paraphrasing Example

Poe writes that Montresor dons a black mask and conceals his body in a cloak (67).

The Sandwich Method

Integrating someone else's writing into your own writing is the hardest part of using sources. However, there is a simple method to make this easier: **the sandwich method**. Every piece of researched information you use in your paper must be both introduced and explained. Thus, you sandwich your directly quoted or paraphrased information between the introduction and the explanation. The introduction allows the researched information to integrate smoothly into your own writing and keeps it from seemingly popping out of nowhere. The explanation connects the research to your main idea, effectively explaining how it supports your point. This draws threads between your research and your thesis. Directly following this paragraph is a sandwich method example.

Sandwich Method Example 1

In *The Cask of Amontillado*, Poe writes that Montresor hides himself in dark, concealing clothing. "Putting on a mask of black silk, and drawing a roquelaire closely about my person, I suffered him to hurry me to my palazzo" (67). This clearly shows that Montresor has malevolent intentions toward Fortunato, even going so far as to foreshadow his death. Montresor wears black, the traditional color of death in Western culture, and he brings death to Fortunato by burying him alive.

© Pressmaster/Shutterstock.com

Read Write! Activity 7.1

Using the previous sandwich method example, identify the introduction for the research, the research itself, and the explanation of the research. Put a box around the introduction, put brackets around the research, and underline the explanation.

Sandwich Method Example 2

In *The Cask of Amontillado*, Poe writes that Montresor dons a black mask and conceals his body in a cloak (67). This clearly shows that Montresor has malevolent intentions toward Fortunato, even going so far as to foreshadow his death. Montresor wears black, the traditional color of death in Western culture, and he brings death to Fortunato by burying him alive.

Common Signal Phrases for Introduction of Research

Acknowledges	Asserts	Believes	Claims
Comments	Contends	Disputes	Emphasizes
Illustrates	Implies	Notes	Observes
Points out	Refutes	Suggests	Writes

Common Signal Phrases for Explanation of Research

This demonstrates…	This explains …	This explicates…	This expresses…
This indicates …	This illustrates…	This proves …	This verifies …

MLA STYLE PARENTHETICAL CITATIONS

MLA style is used in most humanities courses, including your English, reading, writing, and other communications courses. MLA stands for Modern Language Association, and this group provides the guidelines for citing sources in your writing.

> ➤ **Read Write! Tip**
>
> MLA is not the only formatting style you will be asked to use in college. The social sciences often use the American Psychological Association (APA) style, and some other courses may call for the Chicago Manual of Style (CMS). Be sure to check with your professor to be certain which style is required before beginning an assignment. Again, most English classes will use MLA.

In the two previous examples, you saw the use of MLA style parenthetical citations. The **parenthetical citation** is the immediate acknowledgement of the source inside your own writing. This acknowledgement is inside parentheses at the end of the direct quotation or paraphrased idea and is considered a part of the sentence. Another example follows.

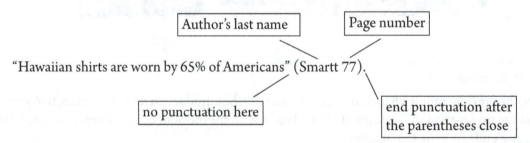

Notice that there is no end punctuation inside the quotation marks. That is because the parenthetical citation is considered a part of the sentence. Once the quotation marks close, the parentheses open, and the standard MLA parenthetical citation will include the author's last name and the page number the quoted information comes from. Then, the parentheses close, and the end punctuation is provided. Notice also that there is no punctuation inside the parentheses: just the author's last name and page number.

It is also possible to use the author's name as a part of the sentence, like the following example that paraphrases.

Smartt believes that Hawaiian shirts became popular when tourism to Hawaii increased during the late 20th century (88).

In this case, because the author's name has already been mentioned, it would be redundant to write it again inside the parentheses. Thus, only the page number is required. Otherwise, the citation style is the same.

No Author

Sometimes you will find a credible source that has no author. When this is the case, you can use the title in place of the author's name. Abbreviate the title to the first significant word, excluding articles, such as "the," "an," or "a."

"Bluebonnets arrive in early spring and, for a brief, startling moment, blanket Texas hillsides in splashes of indigo, violet, and azure" ("Texas" 22).

In the previous example, the title is a magazine article, so it is put in quotation marks to signify this. Larger works, such as books, are italicized (see The Rules of Writing: The Sweet 16 #10 for more information on this). The full title of the article is "Texas Wildflower Explosion," but for the purposes of not slowing down the reader with a lengthy parenthetical citation, it is abbreviated within the parentheses as "Texas." Later, on the Works Cited, the reader will find the full title of the source.

No Page Number

If there is no page number, such as with an online source, you should list the author's name alone.

"Feral cats kill large portions of native bird populations every year" (Alcarez).

Two Authors

If the source has two authors, name them both in the parentheses or within the signal phrase introducing the research.

"Most plastic bags with end up moldering in landfills for centuries, if not longer" (Danes and Qualley 249).

More than Two Authors

If there are more than two authors, list the first author, followed by "et. al."

"Most hand sanitizers are able to kill up to 99% of bacteria" (Jones et. al. 610).

> ➢ **Read Write! Tip**
> While these are the basics of MLA style parenthetical citations, there are myriad sources you can use in your writing, and specialized sources often require specialized parenthetical citations. Not all types of sources can be covered here. See your instructor for help with specialized citations, such as for songs, poems, bible quotes, or YouTube videos.

MLA STYLE WORKS CITED PAGES

Parenthetical citations require a Work(s) Cited page. A **Works Cited** page is a bibliography of all the sources used in the writing. The parenthetical citations within the essay give immediate recognition to sources, but the Works Cited gives the full citation for the source so that the readers can follow up with the information and, if desired, continue researching on their own by checking out the presented sources.

Here are some tips for your Work(s) Cited page:

♦ It should be on its own page. If the conclusion ends on page 4, your Work(s) Cited should begin at the top of page 5. This still applies even if there is a large amount of open space on the last page of the essay. You must begin a new page for the Works Cited.

♦ It is double spaced.

♦ It is titled Works Cited if there is more than one citation or Work Cited if there is only one.

♦ The sources should be alphabetized by author's last name. If there is no author, alphabetize using the first significant word of the title, excluding "the," "an," or "a."

♦ The first line of each source listed should be flush with the left margin. Any subsequent lines of each source should be indented. This is called a hanging indention.

♦ Book, movie, or play titles are italicized. Article titles are put in quotation marks. See the Rules of Writing: The Sweet 16 #10 for more information on this.

Like parenthetical citations, Works Cited citations have a specific format to follow. The basic formats for some common source types are below.

One Author

Author's last name, First name. *Title.* Publisher, Date.

Jefferson, Olaf. *The Stars in Her Eyes*. Simon Pulse, 2015.

Two Authors

1st Author's Last Name, First Name, and 2nd Author's First and Last Names. *Title.* Publisher, Date.

Alexander, Quentin T. and Riley Hershey. *Marching Bands in Action*. Hyperion, 2009.

Three or More Authors

1st Author's Last Name, First Name, et. al. *Title.* Publisher, Date.

De la Cruz, Alberto, et. al. *When They Were Gone*. University Press, 2011.

No Author or Editor

Title. Publisher, Date.

All the Flowers in the World. Blue Sea Press, 2012.

Article in an Online Journal

Author's Last Name, First Name. "Title of Article." *Name of Journal,* Volume, Issue, Date, Pages (if any),

URL. Accessed Day Month Year.

Phillips, Leon. "Gardenia in Bloom." *Gardens and Yards,* vol. 8, no. 6, Feb. 2010, www .gardensandyards.com/feb2010/8-6/gardenia.htm. Accessed 22 March 2017.

Article in an Online Newspaper

Author's Last Name, First Name. "Title of Article." *Name of Newspaper*, Date on web, URL. Accessed

Day Month Year.

Summers, Carley. "Archeology in the Amazon: Lost Culture Begins to Emerge." *The Sun Valley*

***Sun*, 8 August 2009, www.sunvalleysun.com/august2009/archeology-culture-emerge.htm.**

Accessed 15 April 2017.

> ➢ **Read Write! Tip**
> Be sure you punctuate each citation correctly, both in the essay and on the Work(s) Cited page. Because it is a specific format, it must be followed exactly. Otherwise, it will be considered out of format, and your instructor will likely penalize you for formatting mistakes.

> ➢ **Read Write! Tip**
> Again, while these are the basics of MLA style Works Cited pages, there are myriad sources you can use in your writing, and specialized sources often require specialized Works Cited page citations. Not all types of sources can be covered here. See your instructor for help with specialized citations, such as for songs, poems, bible quotes, or YouTube videos.

Following is an example Works Cited page with alphabetized entries.

Molina 5

Works Cited

Alexander, Quentin T. and Riley Hershey. *Marching Bands in Action.* Hyperion, 2009.

All the Flowers in the World. Blue Sea Press, 2012.

De la Cruz, Alberto, et. al. *When They Were Gone.* University Press, 2011.

Jefferson, Olaf. *The Stars in Her Eyes.* Simon Pulse, 2015.

Phillips, Leon. "Gardenia in Bloom." *Gardens and Yards,* vol. 8, no. 6, Feb. 2010, www
.gardensandyards.com/feb2010/8-6/gardenia.htm. Accessed 22 March 2017.

Summers, Carley. "Archeology in the Amazon: Lost Culture Begins to Emerge." *The Sun
Valley Sun*, 8 August 2009, www.sunvalleysun.com/august2009/archeology-culture-emerge.htm.
Accessed 15 April 2017.

➢ **Read Write! Tip**

Creating citations is not easy. There are resources online that can help you to generate your citations in MLA style. Sometimes the citation is even provided for you at the end of the article. Additionally, library databases have citation tools that can generate the citation for you. Always check that the citation you are using is in the style required by your professor.

© Rawpixel.com/Shutterstock.com

Read Write! Review Questions: Writing with Sources

1. What does MLA stand for?
2. What is a source?
3. Generally speaking, how much of your paper should be from sources?
4. What is the sandwich method?
5. What is a Works Cited page for?

Read Write! Connection: Chapter 7

Search an online newspaper and find an article you are interested in. After reading it, create an MLA style Works Cited page citation for it using the format for an article from an online newspaper included in this chapter.

PART III

Reading and Writing the Rhetorical Modes

Chapter 8
Reading and Writing Exemplification

Key Terms

Exemplification writing, first person, third person, example transitions, emphatic, topical, addition transitions, series of examples, extended example

When you are asked to clarify or explain a general idea with one or more specific examples, the **exemplification** mode of writing is extremely useful. For instance, if you are asked to explain why you should be promoted to a supervisory role at your place of employment, you would give examples of skills that prove you are the best candidate for the job. Exemplification essays about aspects of your life, such as experiences, skills, or preferences, are written in **first person**, meaning the pronouns *I, me, my,* and *mine* are used.

Image © bikeriderlondon, 2014. Used under license from Shutterstock, Inc.

If you are a student in a nutrition class and you are assigned to write a paper on healthy meals that aid in metabolism, you could peruse through a cook book and provide several examples of nutritious dishes. Depending on whether or not you are allowed to incorporate yourself into the essay will determine if your exemplification essay is written in first person or third person. **Third person** uses the plural pronouns *they, their,* and *them* and the singular pronouns *he/she, his/her,* and *him/her.*

> ➤ **Read Write! Tip**
>
> Most academic essays are written in third person, so it is imperative that you check with your instructor for clarification regarding whether you should use first person or third person.

This chapter will teach you to utilize examples when you read and write exemplification essays. As a *reader*, you will learn to identify the examples to help you to understand, analyze, and evaluate the essay. As a *writer*, you will include this key element in several formats in your body paragraphs to illustrate your point and to clarify meaning for your reader.

When you write an exemplification essay, you express your point to the reader in the format of the traditional five-paragraph essay. Therefore, your thesis statement, which is usually the last sentence in your introduction, will state your main idea, your body paragraphs will develop the three concepts in your thesis using examples, and the concluding paragraph will bring the essay to an end.

EXEMPLIFICATION ELEMENTS

When you write any essay, you want to make certain that you provide numerous supporting details in your body paragraphs so that you are creating vivid pictures for your reader. In exemplification writing, the supporting details are the examples used to illustrate or clarify your point.

There are two organizational patterns that can be used in exemplification writing: **emphatic** order, which means order of importance, and **topical** organization, which means your body paragraphs are organized by the three main points or the plan of development presented in the thesis statement.

As you read exemplification passages, look for **example transitions** and **addition transitions** to set up or introduce examples. Below is a small chart of the example and addition transitions. These words also signal which organizational patterns the author has used.

Example transitions **help to show examples or illustrate ideas more clearly**	For example, for instance, including, such as, like
Addition transitions **show additional ideas**.	Also, next, furthermore, another, finally, first, in addition, as well

Examples must be specific in order to avoid providing vague information. Paragraphs that are generic, meaning they lack specific examples so that anyone could have been the author or the topic could be about anything, do not illustrate a clear point. In fact, they are usually boring, repetitive, and say nothing.

Example of a vague or say-nothing paragraph:

Momma's Day

Every year I look forward to Mother's Day. It is a great day. My family is wonderful to me. I do not have to do anything. My family takes care of everything. It is a really wonderful holiday. I wish every day could be Mother's Day. I love this day.

This paragraph lacks specific examples that show why the author looks forward to Mother's Day; in fact, instead of discussing Mother's Day, the author could easily swap out that holiday and put in her birthday. Not only could the holiday be switched to another one but so could the author. Anyone could have written this paragraph; there are no specific examples that make it unique to the author. Not only is the paragraph vague, but it also raises more questions than it answers, causing readers to be bored, annoyed, and confused. For example, readers may wonder about any of the following questions:

1. What makes this day so great for the author?
2. Who does the author mean by family— spouse, kids (how many), siblings, nieces, cousins?
3. What does "everything" really mean?

When you read this paragraph, what other questions come to your mind? Poorly written texts sometimes contain "say-nothing" paragraphs. This happens because what the authors are writing is clear to them. In other words, they are "seeing" in their minds all the missing information. However, unless they are able to get the missing information out of their minds and into their work, the authors will fail to communicate clearly to their readers who are not mind readers. This concept will be discussed in depth in chapter 9 when the elements of showing and not telling are introduced. Mastering this skill is important because communicating your message visually is crucial.

When you are writing your exemplification essay, you can help your readers "see" by providing a series of examples, an extended example, or a mixture of both.

A Series of Examples

When you use **a series of examples**, you develop an idea using several related examples that are expressed in a singular sentence or over several sentences.

Below is a revision of the "say-nothing" paragraph "Momma's Day." Notice how a series of examples are used to convey how the author is treated like a queen on this holiday.

Example of a paragraph with a series of examples:

Momma's Day

Every year I look forward to Mother's Day because on this day I am treated

like a queen. My husband, Brian, and our son, Malik, have to wait on me all

day long. Whenever I need something, I just ask one of them, and they have to

do it on this day. For example, if I am feeling cold, one of them must get me a blanket and spread it out over me. If I cannot reach the remote control, one of them must turn the channel for me. After church, they make breakfast, do the dishes, and make plans for dinner. They either take me out to eat or cook. They usually choose to cook because the lines are so long at restaurants on Mother's Day. For example, one year we had to wait two and a half hours until our beeper lit up, informing us that our table was ready. We were so hungry that we devoured the rolls and crackers and asked for more three times until our entrées arrived. To avoid that nightmare, I prefer to dine at *mi casa*. My favorite meal that I have my family prepare consists of a fish entrée, such as salmon, a baked potato, and broccoli. After a satisfying meal, I spend the rest of the day lounging and having my personal servants wait on me. I love this day because I do not have to do any work—everything is done for me.

Read Write! Activity 8.1

See if you can now provide answers to the previously asked questions and to the ones you had.

1. What makes this day so great for the author?_____
   _____
   _____

2. Who does the author mean by family—spouse, kids (how many), siblings, nieces, cousins?
   _____
   _____

3. What does "everything" really mean?

_____

_____

The Extended Example

In addition to using several examples, you may want to use an **extended example**. An extended example is a long example that either provides the sole support or the bulk of the support for a body paragraph.

Example of a paragraph with an extended example

Filling the Bin, not the Landfill

There are numerous ways that people can go green. One of the easiest ways is to actually use the recycling bin for its intended purpose instead of as a storage container for motor oil and other car maintenance items kept in the garage. In a week's time, individuals who take the recycling challenge will be surprised how many plastic bottles, cans, and cardboard boxes they throw away. Are there any juice, milk, or water drinkers out there? In houses across the country, millions of plastic bottles of Minute Maid, Sunny D, apple juice, cranberry juice, milk, and Evian and Ozarka water bottles are

Image © GraphEGO, 2014. Used under license from Shutterstock, Inc.

being tossed daily into trash cans and hauled away to overflowing landfills.

Instead, these items could be placed in that lovely green bin, along with rinsed

out Bush's baked beans and Campbell soup cans, empty Captain Crunch,

Sugar Pops, and other cereal boxes, and Nike, Adidas, and DSW shoe boxes.

To think, people were concerned that they would not make a dent in that green

bin; now they are contacting their city officials to see if their city can pick up

recycled items twice a week instead of just once.

Read Write! Activity 8.2

Answer the following questions about "Filling the Bin, not the Landfill."

1. Circle your answer: The extended example illustrates how *hard* or *easy* it is to recycle.
2. What are the three broad categories of items that are discussed?
3. Why do you think the author lists some specific items that readers might throw away?

Sometimes the writer may use a combination of a series of examples and an extended example to illustrate or clarify an idea within a body paragraph. In "Going Green," the writer uses a mixture of types of examples to clarify additional ways people can go green.

Example of a mixture of a series of examples and an extended example: Note that the sequences of various series of examples are highlighted in blue, and the extended example is highlighted in orange.

Going Green

Besides recycling, there are some various things individuals can do to go green. One example is to conserve energy. **This can be done by turning off lights** when people leave a room. Not only will this eco-friendly endeavor save energy, but it will also save consumers money on their electric bill. **Utilizing natural light** will help, too. For example, during the day, people can open up their curtains and blinds and let the sun shine in, allowing its rays to provide natural light. Also, **switching out regular light bulbs when they burn out to compact fluorescent light bulbs** is another energy saver. In addition, **riding a bike to run errands** close to one's house is a great green idea. Not only will it save on gas, but the rider will get some exercise, too. If pedaling does not appeal to people, they can still use their car, but they can try to **combine errands and consider carpooling** to work, church, or other places. **If drivers stop speeding and drive the posted speed limit, they will also help the environment and save money. They will find that they use less gasoline and save money on speeding tickets. For example, when Marvin Carter decided to slow down, he could not believe how much money he saved. "I only had to fill up my Honda Civic once a week instead of twice a week," he said. "Also, I am feeling less stressed and have more money in my pocket**

because I am not spending money on court costs for speeding offensives," he continued. Like Marvin, individuals who join the green wave will be glad they did.

Read Write! Activity 8.3

1. Besides the ones listed in the paragraph above, list some other examples of ways people can go green.

   _____

   _____

2. Which of the examples in "Going Green" or that you listed in question number 1 do you practice?

   _____

   _____

READING EXEMPLIFICATION

As you read an exemplification essay, you should focus on the examples that the author provides. The depth and/or number of the series of examples and/or the extended examples will help you determine if the essay has accomplished its goal: to illustrate through the key elements the point the author is trying to make. Below are some additional tips for reading exemplification passages.

♦ What does the title tell you about what the passage will be about?
♦ Does the text use first person or third person?
♦ What is the main idea of the passage? Where is it located?
♦ Is the passage written in the standard five-paragraph essay format? If so, does it contain a plan of development (the three main points listed)?
♦ What is the organizational pattern of the text?
♦ What additional examples could have been provided?
♦ Is the author credible? Do you believe what he/she has to say?
♦ Does the author make any comments that make the passage or any aspect of it memorable?

Read Write! Activity 8.4

Read the exemplification essay "My Influential People" by student Rhonda Lee. As you do so, utilize PAUSE to work through the reading. Then, answer the questions that follow.

My Influential People

by Rhonda Lee

Looking back over the last few years of my life, I can see how much I have grown. Even though my childhood was not the best, I feel it played a significant role in the things that I admire and value today, such as my religious beliefs, my family goals, and most importantly, my educational aspirations. None of these things would be important if I did not experience many traumatic events throughout my teenage years. With the help of three memorable people, I was able to become the person I am today. The three people who have influenced me are Ms. Emily Irby, Ms. Nicole Holloman, and Professor L. Rodgers.

One person who has influenced me is Ms. Emily Irby. I met Ms. Emily Irby when she was a staff worker at a youth group home where I lived for two years. Looking back, I cannot recall a person who stayed on me as hard as Ms. Emily. She had her own way of getting her point across without ever having to actually say it. Shortly after I turned fifteen, she came into my life when I needed a fresh face around, but the first meeting with her was almost like a test of who was going to be in control. After weeks of finally realizing that I was not going to get anything by her, I slowly gave in and let her get her point across to me. Not only did Ms. Emily teach me things about myself I never knew, but she also helped me realize that I could learn something from everyone I encountered. Finally, she taught me to feel better about myself and how to build my self-esteem. Meeting Ms. Emily was the wakeup call I needed, and I will forever be grateful I had the pleasure of meeting her.

Another person who has influenced me is Ms. Nicole Holloman. Ms. Nicole was my childhood social worker for four years. After being placed in foster care and moving from place to place, I greatly appreciated being able to meet a person who took her time to understand me yet at the same time gave me structure and balance. Ms. Nicole was by far the most memorable person I have ever met; because of her, I realized I wanted to attend college and obtain my bachelor's degree. She motivated me by showing me that just because I did not come from a productive family did not mean I could not succeed in life. To this day, I push myself harder just because I want to prove to her I can overcome what I went through. Ms. Nicole never gave up on me, and every time I see her, she still pushes me to stay focused and finish what

I start. By meeting Ms. Nicole, I have been able to change my mindset and set out to obtain a college education.

The third person who has influenced me is Professor L. Rodgers. I truly believe God placed her in my life when He knew I needed the extra encouragement to return to college. Professor Rodgers saw potential in me and made sure she acknowledged it. Days when I wanted to sit in the back of her class, she would make sure to call on me to read or answer questions. I recall wanting to give up and discussing it with her, and she assured me that I was not alone. At a time when I was ready to quit, Professor Rodgers really inspired me to keep going.

While most people are more than just the sum of their influences, I think there is no debating the positive qualities I have obtained from Ms. Irby, Ms. Holloman, and Professor Rodgers. Some of those qualities are integrity, dedication, and assertiveness. When I was a teen, I might not have appreciated all that Ms. Emily had to offer, but her determination to get through to me allowed me to be more open to accepting what Ms. Holloman and Professor Rodgers had to teach me. I hope my children are able to meet individuals who can influence them as much as these women have influenced me.

1. What does the title tell you the essay will be about?

   _____

   _____

   _____

2. Is the essay written in *first person* or *third person*? Circle your answer.
3. Is the main idea (the thesis statement) *implied* or *stated*? Circle your answer.
4. Underline or highlight the thesis statement. Then, circle the three concepts that the author discusses.
5. Underline or highlight the three topic sentences.
6. Based on the reading, circle the statement that is a fact about the author's teen years.
   a. She grew up in an unstable two-parent home.
   b. She was an orphan.
   c. She lived in foster care.

7. What is the author's educational goal? _____

   What is your education goal?

   _____

   _____

8. According to the author, these three individuals influenced her. Did you find the essay convincing? Why or why not?

   _____

   _____

   _____

   _____

   _____

   _____

9. What organizational pattern is used? _____

10. In body paragraph 1, the writer uses the phrase "fresh face." What do you think this means? Does this phrase have a specific connotation?

    _____

    _____

    _____

Read Write! Activity 8.5

Google the Department of Family and Protective Services. Write down three different things learned from the website about foster care. Be prepared to share what you learned with your classmates.

_____

_____

_____

WRITING EXEMPLIFICATION

When you are asked to write an exemplification essay, you want to follow the writing process. As you complete the steps, focus on the clarity and depth of the examples, the key elements of exemplification writing.

Exemplification Essay Prewriting

When creating an exemplification essay, you should complete several prewriting strategies, such as free writing, listing, clustering, asking questions, outlining, and building a pyramid, to help you generate ideas. If you get stuck while writing, you can return to any of the prewriting strategies discussed in chapter 3 to generate additional ideas.

Exemplification Thesis Statement

The thesis statement states the main idea of the essay and the three topics that you plan to develop with specific examples in the rest of the essay.

Exemplification Body Paragraphs

Each body paragraph begins with a topic sentence that states one of the three topics listed in the thesis statement. Then, numerous supporting sentences follow. These supporting sentences are examples that can be a series of examples, extended examples, or a mixture of both. These examples help to clarify the point of the essay. A concluding sentence ends each body paragraph.

Exemplification Conclusion

The conclusion paragraph lets the reader know that the exemplification essay is coming to an end. Various techniques can be used to end the essay.

Exemplification Outline

The format of an exemplification essay is the same as a standard five-paragraph essay. Below is a basic outline.

    I. Introduction
       a. Introduction method
       b. Thesis statement containing the three topics that will be developed

II. Body 1
   a. Topic sentence for main point 1
   b. Series of Examples and/or Extended Example
   c. Supporting details
   d. A concluding sentence
III. Body 2
   a. Topic sentence for main point 2
   b. Series of Examples and/or Extended Example
   c. Supporting details
   d. A concluding sentence
IV. Body 3
   a. Topic sentence for main point 3
   b. Series of Examples and/or Extended Examples
   c. Supporting details
   d. A concluding sentence
V. Conclusion
   a. Thesis restatement
   b. Conclusion method

Read Write! Activity 8.6

Read the exemplification essay "College Student of the Year" from the standpoint of a writer, looking at structure. Then, answer the questions that follow.

College Student of the Year

"And the award goes to . . ." is the phrase that precedes someone's happiest moment and several other people's disappointing moment. However, before individuals can anticipate having their name called, they must be nominated. Each year peers, colleagues, supervisors, or fans seek out individuals worthy of being honored. At college campuses, administrators, professors, staff members, and fellow students nominate an outstanding student. Although the criteria for being nominated Student of the Year differ from college to college, the end result is the same: recognizing students whose achievements exceed those of their peers. Jasmine Morales is the perfect candidate for the Student of the Year award because she is intelligent, helpful, and involved.

One reason Jasmine should win the award is that she is very smart. For example, during her two years at the University of Michigan, Jasmine has maintained a 4.0 G.P.A. This is an outstanding feat in itself; however, it is even more worthy of recognition because Jasmine is a double major: nursing and international business. Last semester Jasmine was not certain that she would receive all A's because she was struggling in Chemistry 1402. Instead of bemoaning her predicament, she took action. She met weekly with her chemistry professor, Dr. Nguyen, during her office hours and spent two hours in the tutoring center every day. Focused and determined to not only learn the material but master it, Jasmine went from a C+ average to an A in the course. Jasmine's pristine academic record is definitely an achievement worthy of recognition.

Her willingness to help her fellow students at the university is another reason Jasmine deserves to win the Student of the Year award. For instance, when her English professor asked for someone to volunteer to be the scribe for a student with limited mobility with his hands, Jasmine immediately agreed to assist the student. Not only does she take notes for the student, but she also meets him on Saturdays at the computer center and assists him in typing up his essays. Another example of her helpfulness is her willingness to give one of her History 1302 classmates a ride to the campus two days a week. After she overheard her fellow classmate explaining to their professor that she was late on Tuesdays and Thursdays because she had to wait for her son's school bus to pick him up before she could catch her own bus to the college, Jasmine offered to give her classmate a ride to campus. Jasmine's willingness to assist her peers is remarkable.

The third reason that Jasmine is the perfect choice for the award is that she is involved in numerous campus organizations. For example, she is the student government treasurer, co-captain of the girls' intramural soccer club, and historian of the international business organization. As vice-president of the nursing club, Jasmine spearheaded a health fair that provided free pregnancy and HIV/AIDS testing for students. One of her favorite extracurricular activities, however, is serving as the program chair of the salsa club. In this capacity, Jasmine is responsible for not only finding opportunities for the club to dance but also for securing volunteer opportunities for the members on and off campus. For instance, last week Jasmine arranged for the club to dance in a Cinco de Mayo celebration at the college's satellite campus and to assist in the letter writing campaign "Thank the Troops" for their service to the country, sponsored by the college's Veterans' club. An off campus volunteer opportunity for the salsa club that Jasmine is spearheading will begin this fall. Two Friday afternoons a month the club will read to students at Cesar Chavez Elementary.

Jasmine Morales deserves to win the Student of the Year award. Her academic work is impeccable. In addition, her altruism she displays in her willingness to help her fellow classmates is commendable. Also, her commitment to being involved in campus organizations at such a high level is exceptional. Not only should Jasmine win this award, but in the future, she will probably win the Outstanding Alumna award, too.

Answer the following questions about "College Student of the Year."

1. What introductory method is used?
   a. anecdote   b. contrast   c. quote   d. question

2. Underline the thesis statement.

3. Which topic sentence has the transitional device towards the end of the sentence instead of the beginning?

   _____

4. How is the first body paragraph developed?
   a. a series of examples   b. an extended example

5. How is the second body paragraph developed?
   a. a series of examples   b. an extended example

6. How is the third body paragraph developed?
   a. a series of examples   b. several examples and an extended example

7. Which body paragraph is missing a concluding sentence? ___1st, ___2nd, ___3rd

8. Write a concluding sentence for the missing body paragraph:

   _____

   _____

   _____

9. Define the words based on their context in the essay. Use a dictionary as needed.

   altruism _____

   alumna _____

   bemoaning _____

   impeccable _____

   pristine _____

10. What method of conclusion is used?
    a. summary   b. suggestion   c. prediction   d. call-to-action

Read Write! Review Chapter 8: Exemplification

1. What does exemplification writing use to provide specific details in the body paragraphs?
2. Define a series of examples.
3. Define extended example.
4. What is the difference between first person and third person?
5. List two example transitions and two addition transitions.

Suggested Exemplification Essay Topics

1. What are your three favorite holidays?
2. What are the qualities of good parents or of good teachers?
3. Why should you or someone else win Employee of the Month, Spouse of the Year, or Parent of the Year?
4. Who are three people who have influenced you?
5. Who are your most memorable teachers?
6. What are some challenges college students face?

Read Write! Connection: Chapter 8

Use one of your other textbooks and look at one of the chapters to analyze how the author uses a series of examples, an extended example, and/or a mixture of both to explain a concept. Use the PAUSE strategy as you do so.

Chapter 9

Reading and Writing
Descriptive-Narrative

Key Terms

Narrative, descriptive, descriptive-narrative, foreshadowing, time order, 5WH, conflict, exposition, scene, pacing, showing and not telling, literary devices, mood, simile, metaphor, figurative language, personification, onomatopoeia, sensory imagery, plot, rising action, climax, falling action, resolution

Narrative is a part of life. You experience narrative every day when you watch television, read books, view movies, play video games, or even just talk with friends and family. This is because narratives are stories, and narrative writing is storytelling. The term **descriptive**, on the other hand, means to describe. Taking that one step further, descriptive writing should create a vivid image in the reader's mind using only words. Thus, a **descriptive-narrative** will be a story that includes vivid descriptive details.

Whether you are writing a narrative or reading one, there are specific elements that should be included in the art of storytelling. As a reader, this chapter will teach you to identify and break down these elements to understand meaning. As a writer, you will use these elements to create meaning for your reader.

A narrative essay, then, is a story *that has a point*. This means the writer learned something from the experience being written about. It does not always have to be profound or deeply meaningful, but the writer must have a reason for telling the story. For example, if you chose to tell the story of how you climbed a mountain despite a fear of heights, the point would be that you overcame the fear and accomplished something. Narratives without points are extremely boring and have a tendency to ramble on without actually going anywhere; the point keeps the narrative focused and drives the story forward.

When you *write* a narrative essay, you must explicitly express your point to the reader just as you would for the traditional five-paragraph essay. However, it will not be in the form of standard thesis statement.

This is because the narrative's format is not that of the traditional five-paragraph essay. Instead, it is more free form, and the point will not be revealed until the *end* of the narrative.

When you are *reading* a narrative, the point is the main idea of the essay; it is what the author is trying to communicate to the audience, and it can either be explicit or implied. Generally speaking, the point of a narrative does not just apply to the author but to the audience as well. This means that you can look at the point thematically by reading beyond the lines. In the example above, the point of overcoming a fear can be applied universally—it is not just about you as the author of the narrative. Overcoming fears to accomplish something is a part of the human condition. Therefore, even though the point itself is not necessarily profound, when you think about it thematically, you can apply it across a broader scope, and, in this way, you find deeper meaning.

As a student writer, when you compose a descriptive-narrative essay, you will often begin with an introduction similar to that of a traditional five-paragraph essay. However, narrative essays do not use the traditional thesis statement. Instead, after you have introduced the story, a foreshadowing sentence is placed as the last sentence of the introduction. **Foreshadowing** is a literary device used to hint to your reader that something is about to happen. It will draw the readers in and keep them reading. Foreshadowing in a narrative essay hints at what you will learn from the experience. On the other hand, just as you will draw the reader in with *your* foreshadowing sentence, an author will use foreshadowing to draw *you* in as a reader. It is important to note, however, that in a professional writing, the foreshadowing is not always a single sentence, nor is it always the last sentence of the introduction. However, foreshadowing will always occur early in the narrative.

> ➢ **Read Write! Tip**
>
> Much of the formal, academic writing students do in college avoids the use of first person (I, me, my, mine). Narratives, however, can be written in first or third person. Many times instructors ask their students to write personal narratives, which means that the use of first person is acceptable and oftentimes expected in narrative writing.

Example of background information and foreshadowing:

The Camping Nightmare

I had always enjoyed camping. My family and I camped all throughout my childhood at different sites around the state. It was always so fun to spend time enjoying the outdoors, cooking over the fire, fishing, and swimming. When I got to college, I thought camping over spring break with friends was an excellent idea. *Unfortunately, this turned out to be one of the worst experiences of my life.*

In this example, some background information is given on the writer. Consequently, you know the writer considers himself/herself an experienced camper, and, thus, the foreshadowing statement is intriguing, pulling you in. How could it have been such a bad experience if the writer is an avid camper? You must now continue reading to find out.

After the introduction, a descriptive-narrative is told from beginning to end, which is the chronological organizational pattern. This is called **time ordering**. Time order requires time transitions to help move from idea to idea in the story. Below is a chart of time transitional devices.

Time (chronological) transitions **show the order in which events occur(ed).**	first, next, before, after, then, as, during, immediately, later, meanwhile, now, often, previously, suddenly, when, while, second, third, last, finally

As you read narratives and begin to write your own, you will notice that, as aforementioned, this essay mode does not fall into the traditional five-paragraph format like some of the other rhetorical modes in this textbook. In fact, with the descriptive-narrative, an author may take as many paragraphs as needed to tell the story. Therefore, there will not just be three body paragraphs. There can be five, six, seven, or even eight. The narrative essay is as long as it needs to be to get the story told. Additionally, paragraphs do not have to be a certain number of sentences. Paragraphs that include dialogue, for example, may be only one or two sentences while paragraphs that give descriptive detail might be five, six, or more.

DESCRIPTIVE-NARRATIVE ELEMENTS

As you are reading descriptive-narrative, you will need to be aware of the specific elements that this rhetorical mode requires. Then, when you begin to write your own descriptive-narrative essay, you will use these elements to tell your story effectively.

The 5WH

5WH stands for who, what, where, when, why, and how. "Who" refers to the story characters, including the narrator. When you write your own personal descriptive-narrative, that means you, as the writer and narrator, are in the story. "What" refers to what is happening; it is the action of the story. "When" and "where" comprise the setting. "Why" and "how" encompass the reason the action is occurring. As a reader, you need to be able to identify these important elements because they help you understand the story's meaning, and, as a writer, it is imperative you include them to create meaning for your audience. If one of these key elements is missing, the reader has lost significant information.

Conflict

Narratives also need to have **conflict.** Conflict is a problem or issue occurring in the story. There are four different kinds of conflict: human vs. human, human vs. society, human vs. nature, and human vs. self. Conflict is necessary because it drives the action of the story. Without it, a narrative can become extremely boring. Think about a time when you went to see a movie and nothing happened during the film. How did you feel? You were probably bored during the movie and afterward felt like you wasted time and money. When you read a descriptive-narrative, conflict will keep you interested because you will want to know how the conflict will be resolved. As a writer, you will need to include conflict to keep your audience drawn in.

The Scene

At the beginning of a narrative, the writer introduces the topic with a foreshadowing sentence and then sets the scene with any background information necessary for the reader to understand what is happening. This is called **exposition.** All of this is written in summary, meaning there is not much descriptive detail. Then, it is time for the **scene**. The scene is the place where the action of the story occurs. It is the middle of the story, and it is also where the conflict of the narrative happens. Scenes are written to include lots of descriptive detail, and also dialogue can be used. Additionally, scenes are not meant to cover days at a time from your life; they are usually 15 minutes or less. Even though it is such a short period of time, much of the narrative is spent describing and explaining what happened during this moment. This is called **pacing** because the beginning and end of the story are summarized at a quick pace while the scene is taken at a slow pace, including as much detail as possible. The majority of the paragraphs in a narrative are written about the scene.

Showing, Not Telling

During the scene, it is important for a writer to "show and not tell," and this is where the descriptive part of the descriptive-narrative comes in. **Showing and not telling** is giving readers descriptive detail to help them imagine the scene taking place. "Telling" is boring and too quick of a pace for a scene. When you are reading, good description allows you to better imagine the story the author is telling. When you are writing your own descriptive-narrative essay, "showing" rather than "telling" will allow your audience to better visualize the action of your story.

Look at the example below to see the difference between telling and showing.

Telling: Bob was angry, so he left.
Showing: Bob's eyes narrowed, and a deep frown creased his face. For a moment, he stared at me, his expression as cold as ice, but then he stormed out of the room, slamming the door behind him with a loud bang.

The difference is immediately apparent. As a reader, you know what happened in the "telling" example, but you cannot imagine it very well, can you? However, the "showing" example is far more vivid. When you are writing, "showing" will allow you to present a stronger image to your audience. It also helps you with pacing because it takes more writing and thus more sentences, effectively slowing the pace of the scene down.

Literary Devices and Figurative Language

The best way to provide descriptive detail for a scene is to use literary devices. **Literary devices** are used to convey meaning to readers, and they can also help to set the **mood**, or how the story feels. While there are many forms of literary devices, this section will talk specifically about five that you are likely to see in descriptive-narrative and that your instructor will ask you to use when writing your own. For more literary devices, check out the literary devices quick reference on page 403 in the appendix.

> ### Read Write! Tip
> Literary devices are not just used in descriptive-narrative essays. They can be found across the rhetorical modes, in other forms of writing, and elsewhere. Perhaps you have seen a Shakespearean play. Literary devices play a large role in drama. They are also used in speech. Have you ever seen a messy room and thought "that room looks like a pigsty"? If so, you just used a simile! Literary devices can be found everywhere.

The **simile** is a commonly used literary device. It is a comparison using "like" or "as" to help describe something and is fairly easy to spot and use because of this construction.

Examples:

The *full moon* looked <u>like</u> an exquisite *pearl*.
The *classroom* was <u>as</u> cold <u>as</u> a *freezer*.

The first example compares the moon to a pearl. Pearls have a specific connotation associated with them: they are considered beautiful. Thus, the comparison conveys a certain meaning: that the moon is beautiful. As a reader, you understand this because you pick up on the connotation of the comparison. The second example compares a classroom to a freezer. This one requires you to rely on experience. As a reader, you know a freezer is extremely cold. Thus, the classroom must be extremely cold, as well.

Metaphors are similar to similes, but they do not use "like" or "as" when comparing. Instead, they say one thing *is* another thing as a point of comparison. While similes are easier to use, metaphors usually present a stronger image for the reader.

Examples:

The little *boy* was an *angel* all day.
Vivienne's *remark* was a *knife* in Glenn's heart.

The first example relies on connotation again. The word "angel" has a positive connotation. Therefore, the comparison implies that the little boy behaved well all day because he has been directly compared to an angel using metaphor. The second example appeals to the human experience of pain. While you have probably not been stabbed in the heart, you *have* experienced hurt. Thus, this comparison lets you as a reader understand, first, that what Vivienne said was cutting, or cruel, and, moreover, that it hurt Glenn very much. Did Vivienne literally stab Glenn in the heart? No—this is an example of **figurative language**, language that is not meant literally. Many but not all literary devices can be considered figurative language, and in this example, it has been used to convey the writer's meaning, that Glenn has been deeply hurt by what Vivienne said.

Personification is giving inanimate objects or ideas human characteristics. Using personification can usually give readers a powerful image in their minds because they can relate to the human characteristic being portrayed.

Examples:

The wind rushed through the *trees*, making them *whisper* quietly.
Victor's *nightmares dragged* him into a dark place, leaving him depressed.

Because of the personification, you understand that the trees' leaves are making a hushed, rustling noise like whispering. In the second example, the nightmares have been personified. They cannot actually drag anyone anywhere, but in the sentence, you understand that these bad dreams have made a strong impression on Victor. Additionally, connotation is at work again. "Dragged" can certainly have a negative connotation, and in conjunction with the words "nightmare," "dark," and "depressed," you know it is being used negatively.

Onomatopoeia is used when words sound like the sounds they are describing. They can be just a single word, creating a sound, or used as a verb to create the sound. The latter usually provides the reader with a stronger image than the former.

Examples:

Kasey _clacked_ across the room in her high heels.
The door _creaked_ slowly shut.
Crash!
Beep!

In the first example, the high heels are making a clacking sound. As a reader, it is almost like you can hear it. In the second example, the word creak makes a creaking sound. You know exactly what a door creaking closed sounds like, so this appeals to your experience of sound. The last two examples are just sounds—perhaps a plate falling to the floor or a computer making a beeping sound. All four are examples of onomatopoeia. A good way to remember onomatopoeia is to think of them as the *Batman* words. In the old *Batman* television show with Adam West, every time Batman had a fight with a villain onomatopoeia would appear on the screen: Pow! Bam! Bang! Onomatopoeia is also often used in comic books and graphic novels.

Sensory Imagery

Descriptive-narratives also provide description through **sensory imagery**. This is the use of vivid descriptions appealing to the reader's five senses: sight, sound, taste, touch, and smell. As a student writer, sometimes you make the mistake of only relying on sight to describe something, but sight is not the whole picture. Appealing to all five sentences will round out your imagery and present a stronger picture in your reader's mind.

> **Read Write! Tip**

Something important to notice is that the other four literary devices can fall under the umbrella of sensory imagery. For instance, the simile examples appeal to sight and touch. Onomatopoeia is always going to appeal to sound. Thus, an author uses simile, metaphor, personification, and onomatopoeia to strengthen their sensory imagery, just as you can when writing your own descriptive-narrative essay.

Read Write! Activity 9.1

Below is an excerpt from Helen Keller's autobiography, *The Story of My Life*. Read the excerpt and then answer the questions that follow. Be sure to read the short author biography as well.

Helen Keller (1880-1968) was an American author, speaker, and activist. After an early childhood illness, Keller became blind and deaf. However, with the help of her teacher, Anne Sullivan, Keller surmounted incredible odds and learned to communicate effectively with those around her. The story of Keller and Sullivan is told in the famous play, The Miracle Worker, *by William Gibson. Keller is considered by many to be inspirational because she thrived despite her disabilities in an era when deaf and blind people did not always prosper. The* Story of My Life *is one of Keller's 12 published books.*

Except from *The Story of My Life*

by Helen Keller

1   They tell me I walked the day I was a year old. My mother had just taken me out of the bath-tub and was holding me in her lap, when I was suddenly attracted by the flickering shadows of leaves that danced in the sunlight on the smooth floor. I slipped from my mother's lap and almost ran toward them. The impulse gone, I fell down and cried for her to take me up in her arms.

2   These happy days did not last long. One brief spring, musical with the song of robin and mocking-bird, one summer rich in fruit and roses, one autumn of

gold and crimson sped by and left their gifts at the feet of an eager, delighted child. Then, in the dreary month of February, came the illness which closed my eyes and ears and plunged me into the unconsciousness of a new-born baby. They called it acute congestion of the stomach and brain. The doctor thought I could not live. Early one morning, however, the fever left me as suddenly and mysteriously as it had come. There was great rejoicing in the family that morning, but no one, not even the doctor, knew that I should never see or hear again.

3   I fancy I still have confused recollections of that illness. I especially remember the tenderness with which my mother tried to soothe me in my waling hours of fret and pain, and the agony and bewilderment with which I awoke after a tossing half sleep, and turned my eyes, so dry and hot, to the wall away from the once-loved light, which came to me dim and yet more dim each day. But, except for these fleeting memories, if, indeed, they be memories, it all seems very unreal, like a nightmare. Gradually I got used to the silence and darkness that surrounded me and forgot that it had ever been different, until she came—my teacher—who was to set my spirit free. But during the first nineteen months of my life I had caught glimpses of broad, green fields, a luminous sky, trees and flowers which the darkness that followed could not wholly blot out. If we have once seen, "the day is ours, and what the day has shown."

1. Highlight the descriptive language in the passage above.

2. What is Keller's purpose in using such descriptive language?

    _____

    _____

    _____

3. What is the topic of the passage? _____

4. What is Keller's main idea? (Hint: it is implied.)

    _____

    _____

    _____

Dialogue

Something else writers can include in a narrative scene is dialogue. Dialogue is used when one person or several people in the story speak. Dialogue is not always necessary, but it is also sometimes essential to the story. If you include dialogue in your descriptive-narrative essay, it requires specific punctuation and format when it is used.

1. **When two or more people talk back and forth to one another, start a new paragraph each time you switch from one person to another.**

    Roberto said, "The day that you agreed to be my wife was the happiest day of my life. I am so happy that you chose to marry me. With you, I have everything that I will ever need."

    Josephina replied, "Roberto, I am grateful for your love."

    Roberto asked, "What would I do without you?"

    Josephina answered, "You will never need to find out because our love will last forever. If we are parted by death, we will see each other again someday."

2. **If only one person speaks, make the quotation part of the paragraph; do not indent it.**

    Roberto shows his love for his wife through the things he says and does. For example, the first words and the last words that Roberto says to his wife every day are these, "Josephina, I love you. I am so grateful that you agreed to be my wife." Although he says these words every day, Josephina never gets tired of hearing them because they daily reaffirm that her husband loves her. Besides declaring his love for her, Roberto shows his love by putting it into action. For example, he writes his wife love letters, runs her bath water, and brings home flowers and candy, not just on Valentine's Day, but at least once a week. Roberto definitely loves his wife.

3. **Periods and commas go inside of the closing quotation mark.**

    Roberto said, "I love only you."   "I love only you," Roberto said.

4. **If one person speaks for several sentences, only use one set of quotation marks. In other words, put the opening set of quotation marks at the beginning of the first sentence. Then, put the closing quotation marks at the end of the last sentence. DO NOT PUT OPENING AND CLOSING QUOTATION MARKS at the beginning and ending of each sentence.**

> In a disappointed tone that I will remember forever, Julie said, "I cannot believe that you cheated with my boyfriend. I thought that you were my friend. I will never trust you again."

5. **Make certain that if your dialogue/quote ends with a question mark, the A in asked is lowercased.**

> "Where are you going?" asked John.   John asked, "Where are you going?"

> ➢ **Read Write! Tip**

> Normally in formal, academic writing, you are asked to avoid second person (you) and contractions because they are considered informal. However, the descriptive-narrative has one place you can use second person and contractions, and that is within dialogue. As long as it is inside the quotation marks and someone is speaking, it is okay to use second person and contractions. This is because you want your characters' speech to sound natural, and the more informal wording requires that. Otherwise, your characters would sound stilted and fake.

Read Write! Activity 9.2

Below is an exchange among the narrator and his friends, Owen and Raul. Owen and Raul have just frightened the narrator as he waited for them to meet him near a spooky old house. There are 10 errors.

I launched myself out of the car, ready to fight. "What's your problem" I shouted?

Raul and Owen just kept laughing, and Raul said "you should have seen your face"!

Owen was slapping his knee, the big jerk. "you really thought something was there, didn't you?"

I had. My heart rate had skyrocketed, and I had probably jumped about ten feet in the air, not to mention that little scream. However, I was not about to admit that.

I knew it was you guys," I said.

"Sure, and I'm a millionaire" Owen said, rolling his eyes.

I crossed my arms. "Was this whole haunted thing just a joke?" I Asked.

They both became serious then, and Raul said, "Nah, come on. We really did see something last night. Let's go up to the house".

➢ **Think Write! Tip**

Usually descriptive-narrative essays are written in past tense because they are often about something that happened in your life in the past. Therefore, it is important to check verb tense as the descriptive-narrative essay is being written. It is very easy to shift into present tense when writing a descriptive-narrative because when you tell a story aloud, you oftentimes use present tense. However, when writing a descriptive-narrative, you need to make sure to stay in past tense if the event being written about happened in the past. After the descriptive-narrative is finished, it is important to go back and edit for **tense shifts,** which are times when you accidentally and unnecessarily change from one verb tense to another during a written work. You must always maintain a consistent tense no matter what mode is being written.

TRADTIONAL STORY STRUCTURE

All narratives, whether it is a professional reading or your own descriptive-narrative essay, will follow traditional story structure, which revolves around plot. **Plot** refers to the action of the story, and plot structure must clearly convey to the reader how the story takes place from beginning to end.

As previously mentioned, the beginning of the narrative requires exposition after the foreshadowing sentence. Traditional story structure then requires **rising action** during which the author continues to pace the story so as not to give the reader all of the details too early. The rising action in the story includes the conflict, and all of the suspense and/or questions about what is occurring or what will occur builds during this part of the story. Once all of the important details have been mentioned, the story will come to a **climax** or the high point in the story. For example, if your story is about a time when you had a near fatal car accident because you were texting while driving, the climax may be when your car impacted the other car and you had to be rushed to the emergency room where you were placed in the intensive care unit for several days. The rising action and climax are both included in the scene, and pacing and descriptive details are used to develop this section of the story.

After the climax, the **falling action** occurs. The most eventful part of the story has already transpired, and it is coming to a close. Referring back to the aforementioned car accident, the falling action may be that you were paralyzed for several months and had to endure a year of physical therapy. Falling action is usually summarized because it is not a part of the scene. After the falling action occurs, the story comes to a close by way of **resolution.** Every narrative you write should have an ending. In regards to the car accident, the resolution could be that you did not remain paralyzed and have gained a new sense of life; however, you now understand how important it is not to text while driving. The resolution is where the point of the narrative is explained to the reader.

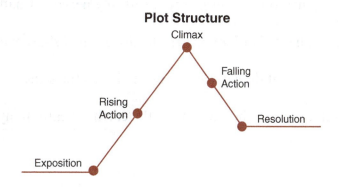

Plot Structure

READING DESCRIPTIVE-NARRATIVE

Now that you know the descriptive-narrative's elements and structure, you can use this knowledge to break down a descriptive-narrative text and understand it. Below are some additional tips for reading descriptive-narrative.

♦ Identify the narrator. Is the narrative told in first person or third person?
♦ Identify the 5WH of the narrative—who, what, where, when, why, and how. This will provide you with many important elements: the characters, the setting, and parts of the plot.
♦ Identify the conflict.
♦ Identify where the climax occurs. What is the high point of the story?
♦ Identify the resolution of the narrative.
♦ Identify the point of the narrative. From this, you can determine the main idea and theme of the story.

Read Write! Activity 9.3

Below is *The Tell-Tale Heart* by Edgar Allan Poe. Read the short story and be on the lookout for descriptive-narrative elements. Answer the questions that follow, and be sure to read the brief author biography, as well.

Image © Neftali, 2014. Used under license from Shutterstock, Inc.

> *Edgar Allan Poe (1809-1849) was a 19th century American author and poet. Many of his works were originally published in newspapers, and though not all of his writing was popular during his lifetime, many, such as the poem* The Raven, *were quite well received. Today Poe is most well-known for his horror, but he also wrote comedy and detective stories.* The Tell-Tale Heart, *which was published in 1843, is one of his most famous pieces.*

The Tell-Tale Heart

By Edgar Allan Poe

1   TRUE! — nervous — very, very dreadfully nervous I had been and am;

but why *will* you say that I am mad? The disease had sharpened my senses —

not destroyed — not dulled them. Above all was the sense of hearing acute.

I heard all things in the heaven and in the earth. I heard many things in hell.

How, then, am I mad? Hearken! and observe how healthily — how calmly I can tell you the whole story.

2   It is impossible to say how first the idea entered my brain; but once conceived, it haunted me day and night. Object there was none. Passion there was none. I loved the old man. He had never wronged me. He had never given me insult. For his gold I had no desire. I think it was his eye! yes, it was this! He had the eye of a vulture — a pale blue eye, with a film over it. Whenever it fell upon me, my blood ran cold; and so by degrees — very gradually —I made up my mind to take the life of the old man, and thus rid myself of the eye forever.

3   Now this is the point. You <u>fancy</u> me mad. Madmen know nothing. But you should have seen me. You should have seen how wisely I proceeded —with what caution —with what foresight —with what <u>dissimulation</u> I went to work! I was never kinder to the old man than during the whole week before I killed him. And every night, about midnight, I turned the latch of his door and opened it —oh so gently! And then, when I had made an opening sufficient for my head, I put in a dark lantern, all closed, closed, so that no light shone out, and then I thrust in my head. Oh, you would have laughed to see how cunningly I thrust it in! I moved it slowly —very, very slowly, so that I might not disturb the old man's sleep. It took me an hour to place my whole head within the opening so

far that I could see him as he lay upon his bed. Ha! —would a madman have been so wise as this? And then, when my head was well in the room, I undid the lantern cautiously —oh, so cautiously —cautiously (for the hinges creaked) —I undid it just so much that a single thin ray fell upon the vulture eye. And this I did for seven long nights — every night just at midnight —but I found the eye always closed; and so it was impossible to do the work; for it was not the old man who <u>vexed</u> me, but his Evil Eye. And every morning, when the day broke, I went boldly into the chamber, and spoke courageously to him, calling him by name in a hearty tone, and inquiring how he has passed the night. So you see he would have been a very profound old man, indeed, to suspect that every night, just at twelve, I looked in upon him while he slept.

4   Upon the eighth night I was more than usually cautious in opening the door. A watch's minute hand moves more quickly than did mine. Never before that night had I *felt* the extent of my own powers —of my <u>sagacity</u>. I could scarcely contain my feelings of triumph. To think that there I was, opening the door, little by little, and he not even to dream of my secret deeds or thoughts. I fairly chuckled at the idea; and perhaps he heard me; for he moved on the bed suddenly, as if startled. Now you may think that I drew back —but no. His room was as black as pitch with the thick darkness, (for the shutters were

close fastened, through fear of robbers,) and so I knew that he could not see

the opening of the door, and I kept pushing it on steadily, steadily.

5   I had my head in, and was about to open the lantern, when my thumb

slipped upon the tin fastening, and the old man sprang up in bed, crying out

— "Who's there?"

6   I kept quite still and said nothing. For a whole hour I did not move a

muscle, and in the meantime I did not hear him lie down. He was still sitting

up in the bed listening; —just as I have done, night after night, hearkening to

the <u>death watches</u> in the wall.

7   Presently I heard a slight groan, and I knew it was the groan of mortal

terror. It was not a groan of pain or of grief —oh, no! —it was the low <u>stifled</u>

sound that arises from the bottom of the soul when overcharged with awe.

I knew the sound well. Many a night, just at midnight, when all the world

slept, it has welled up from my own bosom, deepening, with its dreadful echo,

the terrors that distracted me. I say I knew it well. I knew what the old man

felt, and pitied him, although I chuckled at heart. I knew that he had been

lying awake ever since the first slight noise, when he had turned in the bed.

His fears had been ever since growing upon him. He had been trying to fancy

them causeless, but could not. He had been saying to himself — "It is nothing but the wind in the chimney —it is only a mouse crossing the floor," or "It is merely a cricket which has made a single chirp." Yes, he had been trying to comfort himself with these suppositions: but he had found all in vain. *All in vain;* because Death, in approaching him had stalked with his black shadow before him, and enveloped the victim. And it was the mournful influence of the unperceived shadow that caused him to feel —although he neither saw nor heard —to *feel* the presence of my head within the room.

8   When I had waited a long time, very patiently, without hearing him lie down, I resolved to open a little —a very, very little crevice in the lantern. So I opened it —you cannot imagine how stealthily, stealthily —until, at length a single dim ray, like the thread of the spider, shot from out the crevice and fell full upon the vulture eye.

9   It was open —wide, wide open —and I grew furious as I gazed upon it. I saw it with perfect distinctness —all a dull blue, with a hideous veil over it that chilled the very marrow in my bones; but I could see nothing else of the old man's face or person: for I had directed the ray as if by instinct, precisely upon the damned spot.

10   And have I not told you that what you mistake for madness is but over acuteness of the senses? —now, I say, there came to my ears a low, dull, quick sound, such as a watch makes when enveloped in cotton. I knew that sound

well, too. It was the beating of the old man's heart. It increased my fury, as the beating of a drum stimulates the soldier into courage.

11   But even yet I refrained and kept still. I scarcely breathed. I held the lantern motionless. I tried how steadily I could maintain the ray upon the eye. Meantime the hellish tattoo of the heart increased. It grew quicker and quicker, and louder and louder every instant. The old man's terror *must* have been extreme! It grew louder, I say, louder every moment! —do you mark me well? I have told you that I am nervous: so I am. And now at the dead hour of the night, amid the dreadful silence of that old house, so strange a noise as this excited me to uncontrollable terror. Yet, for some minutes longer I refrained and stood still. But the beating grew louder, louder! I thought the heart must burst. And now a new anxiety seized me —the sound would be heard by a neighbor! The old man's hour had come! With a loud yell, I threw open the lantern and leaped into the room. He shrieked once —once only. In an instant I dragged him to the floor, and pulled the heavy bed over him. I then smiled gaily, to find the deed so far done. But, for many minutes, the heart beat on with a muffled sound. This, however, did not vex me; it would not be heard through the wall. At length it ceased. The old man was dead. I removed the bed and examined the corpse. Yes, he

was stone, stone dead. I placed my hand upon the heart and held it there many minutes. There was no <u>pulsation</u>. He was stone dead. His eye would trouble me no more.

12   If still you think me mad, you will think so no longer when I describe the wise precautions I took for the concealment of the body. The night <u>waned</u>, and I worked hastily, but in silence. First of all I dismembered the corpse. I cut off the head and the arms and the legs.

13   I then took up three planks from the flooring of the chamber, and deposited all between the <u>scantlings</u>. I then replaced the boards so cleverly, so cunningly, that no human eye — not even *his* —could have detected any thing wrong. There was nothing to wash out —no stain of any kind —no blood-spot whatever. I had been too wary for that. A tub had caught all —ha! ha!

14   When I had made an end of these labors, it was four o'clock —still dark as midnight. As the bell sounded the hour, there came a knocking at the street door. I went down to open it with a light heart, —for what had I now to fear? There entered three men, who introduced themselves, with perfect <u>suavity</u>, as officers of the police. A shriek had been heard by a neighbor during the night; suspicion of foul play had been aroused; information had been lodged at the police office, and they (the officers) had been deputed to search the premises.

15   I smiled, —for what had I to fear? I <u>bade</u> the gentlemen welcome. The shriek, I said, was my own in a dream. The old man, I mentioned, was absent in the country. I took my visitors all over the house. I bade them search — search well. I led them, at length, to his chamber. I showed them his treasures, secure, undisturbed. In the enthusiasm of my confidence, I brought chairs into the room, and desired them here to rest from their fatigues, while I myself, in the wild <u>audacity</u> of my perfect triumph, placed my own seat upon the very spot beneath which <u>reposed</u> the corpse of the victim.

16   The officers were satisfied. My manner had convinced them. I was singularly at ease. They sat, and while I answered cheerily, they chatted of familiar things. But, ere long, I felt myself getting pale and wished them gone. My head ached, and I fancied a ringing in my ears: but still they sat and still chatted. The ringing became more distinct: —it continued and became more distinct: I talked more freely to get rid of the feeling: but it continued and gained definiteness —until, at length, I found that the noise was not within my ears.

17   No doubt I now grew very pale; —but I talked more fluently, and with a heightened voice. Yet the sound increased —and what could I do? It was a low, dull, quick sound —much such a sound as a watch makes when enveloped in cotton. I gasped for breath — and yet the officers heard it not.

I talked more quickly —more <u>vehemently</u>; but the noise steadily increased. I arose and argued about <u>trifles</u>, in a high key and with violent <u>gesticulations</u>; but the noise steadily increased. Why would they not be gone? I paced the floor to and fro with heavy strides, as if excited to fury by the observations of the men — but the noise steadily increased. Oh God! what could I do? I foamed —I raved —I swore! I swung the chair upon which I had been sitting, and grated it upon the boards, but the noise arose over all and continually increased. It grew louder —louder —louder! And still the men chatted pleasantly, and smiled. Was it possible they heard not? Almighty God! —no, no! They heard! —they suspected! —they *knew!* —they were making a mockery of my horror! —this I thought, and this I think. But anything was better than this agony! Anything was more tolerable than this <u>derision</u>! I could bear those hypocritical smiles no longer! I felt that I must scream or die! —and now —again! —hark! louder! louder! louder! *louder!* —

18   "Villains!" I shrieked, "<u>dissemble</u> no more! I admit the deed! —tear up the planks! —here, here! —it is the beating of his hideous heart!"

1. What can you infer about the narrator's mental state based on the passage?

   _____

   _____

   _____

2. Based on the context of paragraph 13, what can you infer is the meaning of "scantlings"?

   _____

   _____

   _____

3. Aside from "scantlings," underline three words you do not know the meaning of. Using context clues, decipher the meanings of the three words you have chosen.

   ♦ Word #1: _____

   Definition: _____

   _____

   _____

   ♦ Word #2: _____

   Definition: _____

   _____

   _____

   ♦ Word #3: _____

   Definition: _____

   _____

   _____

4. While there is not an explicit foreshadowing sentence in this story, the opening paragraph entices you to read further. What predictions did you make based on the introduction paragraph? Was the ending what you expected?

   _____

   _____

   _____

   _____

5. Highlight any descriptive language you find within the passage. How did Poe's use of descriptive language enhance the story?

_____

_____

_____

6. What is the mood of *The Tell-Tale Heart?* How does Poe develop the mood?

_____

_____

_____

7. Why do you think the narrator admits his crime to the police officers?

_____

_____

_____

8. What is the point of this short story? What is Poe trying to tell you as a reader?

_____

_____

_____

9. Read beyond the lines and think about the point thematically. Give the point universal meaning.

_____

_____

_____

WRITING DESCRIPTIVE-NARRATIVE

When you are asked to write a descriptive-narrative, you will follow the writing process. As you move through the steps, keep in mind the descriptive-narrative elements and traditional story structure.

Descriptive-Narrative Essay Prewriting

Because of the free form organization of the narrative essay, the prewriting strategy free writing may help you generate ideas more easily. As you free write, you can pour out your story onto the page and then go back and decide which points to develop more and which ones to leave out. However, any of the prewriting strategies discussed in chapter 3 would be appropriate here.

Descriptive-Narrative Thesis Statement

The thesis statement for the narrative essay consists of the foreshadowing sentence. This sentence, located at the end of the introduction, hints that something is about to happen. It should intrigue the readers and make them want to read the rest of the essay to find out what happens.

Descriptive-Narrative Body Paragraphs

As you saw in *The Tell-Tale Heart,* the descriptive-narrative contains more than three body paragraphs. In fact, it has as many body paragraphs as it needs to tell the story, to answer the 5WH, and to develop the conflict. In addition, the body paragraphs do not begin with traditional topic sentences or end with concluding sentences. The rules for body paragraphs are suspended for the descriptive-narrative because stories do not fit into the standard body paragraph format. You can make new body paragraphs when the action slightly changes, when some time elapses, when the paragraph is getting too long, or when dialogue is used.

Descriptive-Narrative Conclusion

In the conclusion paragraph, you should reveal the point of the story if it has not been done so already. If the point has been revealed, you should reiterate the point or the lesson learned.

Read Write! Activity 9.4

In Activity 9.3, you looked at *The Tell-Tale Heart* as a reader. Below is a descriptive-narrative essay entitled "Shoelaces." Read this essay below as a *writer*, looking at the descriptive-narrative elements and structure. Then, answer the questions that follow.

Shoelaces

1   At 16 and after over ten years of playing soccer, I figured I was a pretty smart player. After all, I was a starting forward on both my competitive team and the varsity team at my high school. I had pulled hat tricks, I could get past just about any sweeper, and I had the endurance and the strength to play the entire game without a substitute. However, I was soon to discover that I had at least one more lesson to learn.

2   On the Sunday before Thanksgiving of 1999, my team was playing our biggest rival in the competitive league, Velocity, at the soccer fields in Plano. We had never beaten them, and I had decided it was because Velocity had this huge sweeper, a blond girl who was about a mile tall, and none of our forwards could get past her. She was very intimidating, looming over us and casting a shadow as long as the field, but I had decided that today would be the day I would get past her. I would not be afraid of her anymore, and we would win.

3   The game began. I waited for my opportunity to challenge the sweeper, and finally it came. One of our defenders booted the ball over the half line where I was waiting, and I took off after it at top speed.

4   There she was, running after the ball at top speed too. She seemed even bigger than ever and moved a lot faster than I would have imagined she could. Her face was a mask of concentration, her blue eyes focused hard on the ball that was bouncing between us.

5   I narrowed my eyes. I was not going to be afraid of her. My team was counting on me to get that ball. I picked up my speed and pushed myself harder. As I did so I could hear the coach and my parents and other spectators cheering me on, and this just made me want it more.

6   We reached the ball at the exact same time. We both kicked it, our feet hitting the ball at the exact same moment. I kicked with the side of my foot, as though I were passing the ball, because I wanted to pull the ball slightly to the left. She kicked with her shoelaces to boot the ball as far away from her goal as she could. The forces at which we kicked, equally powerful, trapped the ball between us for a moment.

7   When this happened, our feet also stopped abruptly, but because of how I had placed my foot sideways, my knee kept going, ripping violently forward. A moment later the ball popped out from between us and flew toward their goal in the waning fall sunlight. I had won the ball, but I could not go after it because the force of my encounter with the giant sweeper had sent me somersaulting onto the ground.

8   As soon as I stopped, sprawled on Velocity's goal line, I knew something was wrong with my knee. At first it lost feeling. The numbness was strange and disconcerting, but then pain flared up suddenly, causing tears to form in my eyes. It felt as though something inside my knee had come unhinged. When I tried to walk, my knee would barely bend. I had to be carried to the car to be taken to the minor emergency room.

9   It turned out I had torn cartilage in my knee, and I eventually needed corrective surgery to bend it again. I was told that had I kicked the ball with my

shoelaces, it would not have happened. Kicking the ball with the side of my

foot had caused my knee to jerk sideways as well, and when my foot stopped

and my knee kept going, my meniscus tore. I continued to play soccer and I

continued to challenge other players, but never again did I use the side of my

foot when facing off with a defender; it was shoelaces from then on.

1. Underline the foreshadowing sentence.

2. How many body paragraphs are there? _____

3. Highlight any descriptive language used, including literary devices and figurative language.

4. What paragraph does the pacing slow down?

   _____

   _____

5. What paragraph ends the scene?

   _____

   _____

6. What is the conflict in this story?

   _____

   _____

7. What is the 5WH?

   Who: _____

   What: _____

   Where: _____

   When: _____

   Why: _____

   How: _____

8. Dialogue is not used in this narrative. Do you think adding dialogue would enhance or detract from the story? Why or why not?

_____

_____

9. What is the point of this narrative? What did the writer learn? Where is the point placed in the narrative?

_____

_____

> **Read Write! Tip**

In this chapter, you learned about the descriptive-narrative essay. It is important to know that description can also be a stand-alone rhetorical mode. A descriptive essay often follows the traditional five-paragraph essay and presents a thesis statement that includes a dominant impression. Descriptive essays usually describe people, places, or things. Rather than telling a story, they focus strictly on the descriptive elements, using literary devices, figurative language, and sensory imagery to paint a picture in the reader's mind. This mode is discussed more in Chapter 15: Reading and Writing Other Rhetorical Modes

Read Write! Review Questions: Reading and Writing Descriptive-Narrative

1. What is the purpose of descriptive-narrative writing?
2. Define scene and pacing.
3. What is the purpose of "showing, not telling"? Be sure to explain the purpose from the viewpoint of a reader and the viewpoint of a writer.
4. Define 5WH and explain their importance to a descriptive-narrative.
5. What is the importance of conflict in a descriptive-narrative? Explain its significance as both a reader and a writer.

Suggested Descriptive-Narrative Essay Topics

1. Write about a time you were frightened, experienced prejudice, or were angry. What did you take away from this encounter?
2. Write about a time that was embarrassing when it happened but is humorous now when you think about it.
3. Discuss a time when you were disappointed by someone close to you. How will you avoid this same situation or something similar from happening again?
4. Discuss a time you regret. What did you learn from the situation?
5. Write about a significant moment in your life: your graduation from high school, your wedding day, the birth of a child, or the funeral of someone close to you.
6. Tell the story of an inanimate object.

Read Write! Connection: Chapter 9

Access the *Read Write!* website and find *The Legend of Sleepy Hollow* by Washington Irving under Chapter 9: Reading and Writing Descriptive-Narrative. Break down the text into its narrative elements using PAUSE, paying close attention to mood and descriptive detail. Then, write a descriptive-narrative essay telling your own ghost story. Try to capture the same mood as Irving does in *The Legend of Sleepy Hollow*.

Chapter 10

Reading and Writing Comparison-Contrast

Key Terms

compare, contrast, block pattern, point-by-point pattern

© prochasson frederic/Shutterstock.com

Comparing and contrasting happens daily. People are constantly comparing and contrasting things like washing detergent, fast food, and clothing lines. They also compare and contrast political parties, universities, and religions. When you are asked to write a comparison-contrast essay, your professor most likely wants you to think about how two or more ideas are similar (comparing) or different (contrasting) or both similar and different (comparing and contrasting). For example, you may be given two different passages to read. After reading, you may then be asked to focus in depth regarding how different themes or ideas tie into the assigned texts. Because you will also be asked to offer your opinion about whatever is being discussed, most of the time these particular assignments require you to evaluate at a higher level of critical thinking. Your cognitive ability to actively analyze information thoroughly and correctly will determine the complexity of the global connections you make with academic material. Therefore, when you are assigned a compare-contrast reading passage or writing assignment, you must ask yourself some questions:

- ♦ What am I being asked to compare and/or contrast?
- ♦ What do I already know about the ideas being presented?
- ♦ What are the most important components regarding the ideas?

- What can I relate the ideas to outside of the academic realm?
- Can I summarize my thoughts about these ideas clearly enough that someone else understands my viewpoint?

COMPARISON-CONTRAST ELEMENTS

When you are asked to write an essay, make certain coherence or conveying a clear meaning to the reader is one of your main goals. To do this effectively, you must be sure to provide several details supporting the main idea of the body paragraphs and the essay as a whole. In compare-contrast writing, the supporting details are used to demonstrate likenesses and differences between ideas. In turn, when you are reading comparison-contrast, you should look to identify the topics and whether they are being compared, contrasted, or both, as well as the supporting details explicating the topics' likenesses and differences.

Organizational Patterns

The organizational pattern used for this rhetorical mode is also called comparison-contrast. Within this pattern, there are two ways the writing can be organized. The first is **block organization.** An author may use this method when he/she is writing shorter passages because this method allows the writer to fully express the likenesses or differences of one topic before moving to the next topic. Second is **point-by-point organization**. When utilizing this organizational pattern, the author may be writing a longer piece than just the traditional five-paragraph essay, and, as a result, the body of the essay is organized by discussing one point at a time and its relationship to each of the topics before moving on to the next point. There are several transitional words a writer can use to move smoothly through the passage. Below is a chart of transition words commonly used in compare-contrast writing.

Addition transitions **show additional ideas.**	Also, next, furthermore, another, finally, first, in addition, as well
Contrast transitions show **contrasting or differing ideas.**	However, although, even though, nevertheless, on the other hand, but, in spite of, in contrast, instead, yet
Example transitions **help to show examples or illustrate your ideas better.**	For example, for instance, including, such as, like

The Topic

What is the topic of the passage or essay? Knowing the answer to the aforementioned question when reading comparison-contrast may help you remember any prior knowledge or experiences you may have had regarding the topic and make reading and writing about the topic more meaningful. When you write comparison-contrast, you should make sure your topics are clearly stated.

The Title and Tone

Inferencing often starts when you read the title of a passage. You should be able to generate some ideas about what you may see as you begin to read and perhaps some hints about how the author will organize the passage may also become evident. As you read, you will become aware of how the author feels about the topics he/she is comparing and/or contrasting.

The Main Idea

When you read a comparison-contrast passage, the main idea may be stated directly or implied. If it is stated, the thesis may be general and not include a plan of development. If it is implied, be sure to analyze the supporting details to infer the main idea. The supporting details will be the ways the topics are similar, different, or both. When you write, you should express a clear thesis statement. This thesis statement may be general and broad, or it may include a plan of development.

The Introduction

Like the other rhetorical modes, when you write a comparison-contrast essay introduction you should be mindful of introducing the topic, provide background information about the topic, and provide a clear thesis/claim that informs the reader of what will be compared and/or contrasted. When you read, the introduction will help you determine the main idea, whether it is stated or implied.

Supporting Details

When you are reading a comparison-contrast passage, be sure to utilize PAUSE to make connections as you read. Be sure to write down or highlight things that catch your attention, and after reading, go back and analyze your annotations for a clearer understanding. Make special note of any comparison or contrast examples you encounter while reading. When you read or write a comparison-contrast essay, be sure to create a graphic organizer, such as a Venn diagram, that will aid in distinguishing the likenesses and differences.

READING COMPARISON-CONTRAST

Critical thinking is imperative when reading comparison-contrast passages. Again, PAUSE will enable you to think about a passage on a higher level of critical thinking. Look for the essential components that help your reading comprehension, such as main idea, transitional devices, and the organizational pattern. Make sure to summarize each paragraph so you can come back to it later and remember what you have read. Sometimes, an author may include his/her opinion in a comparison-contrast essay. After reading a comparison-contrast passage, be sure you are able to answer the following questions:

- ◆ What is the author comparing and/or contrasting?
- ◆ What organizational pattern is used?
- ◆ Are the ideas in the claim clearly supported?
- ◆ What are you supposed to do with the information you have just read?

Read Write Activity 10.1

Read the article "Seeing the Cycle of Life in My Baby Daughter's Eyes" by Haider Javed Warraich, M.D. Then, answer the questions that follow.

> Haider Javed Warraich, M.D., is a contributor to *The New York Times*.

Seeing the Cycle of Life in My Baby Daughter's Eyes

By Haider Javed Warraich, M.D.

1   Like many new fathers, I spend as much of my free time as I can get away with gazing into my baby daughter's eyes as she stutters and scans. I remember a day not long ago when I rocked my daughter, Eva, in my arms, and her eyes stopped and steadied as they looked back into mine. Her arms and legs ceased to rock and her entire body just relaxed. A chill went down my spine.

2   I felt that for the first time, she had really seen me. She was about 3 months old at the time. Within moments, though, her eyes left mine and started whirring around in their sockets again. While this was the first time I had shared such a moment of joy coupled with disappointment with her, I had experienced this many times with patients at the end of life.

3   Many have alluded to the symmetry of the beginning and the end of life. Most people, however, become parents long before they become caregivers. For me the order was reversed. For while I only recently became a father, medical training has made me much better acquainted with those at the opposite end of the spectrum.

4   The agony of death is more than just physical – it is an existential wound that gnaws away until there is slow, and frequently unwilling, acceptance of the inevitability of one's mortality. I sometimes see a similar pain in my baby girl's eyes as she makes another arduous journey – learning how to be alive. Frequently, as she cries when she is hungry, or cries when she is overfed, or cries as she tries to have a bowel movement, or just cries, it seems as if she is yearning to go back to the simple comforts of her mother's womb.

5   Changes in the medical system have brought the medicalization of the shallow slopes of our bell-curve-shaped lives. At the start of the century, most lives started and ended at home. However, while hospitals started to become the place where we took both our first breaths and our last in the 20th century, in recent years people have become eager to reverse both trends. Nutrition, too, has shifted from being completely natural, to being almost exclusively artificial formula for children and tube feeding and intravenous nutrition for the terminally ill, followed now by a realization that natural routes are best for both groups. What hasn't changed, and what binds the pediatric and the geriatric, is the obsession with their bowel movements.

6   As medical science has progressed, while we have extended life, we have transformed death from a singular event, into dying, an entire phase of our lives that can last from days to years. This is mirrored by an extension of childhood as well, with children being more dependent for a longer period of time than ever before in human history. Parenting therefore has become more demanding – and more expensive.

7   Caregiving for those at the end of life, as those who live it will attest, is equally arduous yet is barely recognized at a similar scale. In some ways, caregiving is similar to parenting – women do most of the heavy lifting. In fact, two-thirds of all caregivers are female. Yet, caregiving for the dying is different from parenting because it does not yet have a formally recognized role within the care of the patient. While there is no chance Eva would ever see her pediatrician without her parents, elderly patients, some with levels of dependency equal to that of a 3-month-old, present to the hospital or clinic all by themselves, all the time. Furthermore, while there is much debate about paying workers through maternity or paternity leave, a similar discussion does not exist around whether leave granted to those caring for parents or loved ones at the end of life, particularly those getting home hospice services, should be paid.

8   Part of the problem is also how differently we view infancy and old age. A daily struggle my wife and I face is how to hold back from oversharing pictures and videos of Eva on social media. We document her life meticulously, afraid of letting any single gesture slip away. Yet, not only do we siphon off old people to live outside of our immediate circles, but images of what the end looks like are scant, uncelebrated and frequently morbid. There is a significant disparity of empathy toward children versus the elderly. Children's shortcomings turn into viral YouTube videos, while those of the elderly are often derided and ridiculed by the very people charged with taking care of them.

9   In a more longitudinal sense, we care for our young the same way people have for thousands of years yet how we die has changed significantly over just the past few years and continues to be in flux. Advanced technology means that many people require much more assistance at home than before. Furthermore, while our lifespan has been extended dramatically, the years we spend with disability have also increased. Therefore, while we have had eons to define our roles as parents, the modern caregiver remains undefined and unrecognized, and thus, unsupported. Investing in children makes intuitive sense, but a similar case has not been built for taking care of the elderly.

10   As with raising a baby, the answer might come from the heart. What is

really needed is for us to love the old as we do the new and celebrate the end

as we do the beginning.

1. What are some changes the author mentions occurred at the beginning of the 20th century that are different today regarding birth and death?

   _____

   _____

   _____

2. What does the author compare "caregiving" to? What examples does he provide to support the comparison?

   _____

   _____

   _____

3. According to the author, what is the difference between people who take maternity/paternity leave after a child is born and caregivers who take leave to care for their dying parents?

   _____

   _____

   _____

4. What method does the author use to organize his ideas?

   _____

   _____

   _____

5. What is the author's tone throughout the passage? How does he feel about the elderly who are at the end of their lives?

_____

_____

_____

WRITING COMPARISON-CONTRAST

When you write a comparison-contrast essay, you should include at least three key points about the topics being compared and/or contrasted. Organize your writing so that the support is relevant and clearly conveys the intended meaning to the reader. Make sure to use formal Standard English and avoid mistakes mentioned in the Sweet Sixteen Rules of Writing.

Depending on the assignment, when you become the writer, you may be instructed to add a paragraph near the end of the essay that discloses your opinion on the topics being compared and/or contrasted. At this point, some elements of argument, which is covered in chapter 13, will be required. Remember, your opinion should not be notated using first or second person pronouns like "I" or "you." You will write this paragraph using third person pronouns.

> ➤ **Read Write! Tip**
>   The reason to avoid first or second person pronouns is so the focus remains on the topics and not the writer or the reader. Avoiding these pronouns will keep the writing objective as opposed to subjective.

Read Write! Activity10.2

Read "The Conflicting Ideals of Two Black Leaders" by Kenasia Johnson on page 248. After you have read the passage, return here to answer the questions.

1. What organizational pattern does the author use to develop the essay?

_____

_____

_____

_____

2. Are the topics being compared, contrasted, or both?

_____

_____

_____

_____

3. Is the essay written in block or point-by-point?

_____

_____

_____

_____

4. Is the main idea implied or stated?

_____

_____

_____

_____

5. Which three transitional devices does the author use within the body paragraphs to move from one topic to the other?

_____

_____

_____

_____

6. Does the author state an opinion? If so, what is her opinion?

_____

_____

_____

_____

Comparison-Contrast Prewriting

Use the prewriting strategies outlined in chapter 3 to help you generate ideas about the comparison-contrast topics. An excellent prewriting strategy to utilize is the Venn diagram, which provides a visual that uses intersecting circles to show the similarities and the differences between two or more topics.

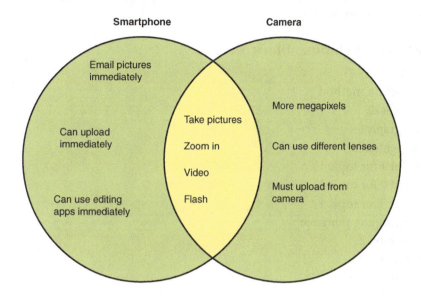

Comparison-Contrast Claim/Thesis Statement

The claim/thesis statement will disclose what will be compared and/or contrasted. You will not use first or second person pronouns in the thesis. You must make sure to use specific wording and not vague and obscure wording in the thesis statement. It may present a plan of development or be general.

Plan of Development Thesis Example

The pursuits of economic, political, and social rights for African-Americans were conflicting ideals for Washington and DuBois.

General Thesis Example

Ellie from *A Dog's Purpose* and the K-9 Comfort Dogs have many similarities and differences.

Comparison-Contrast Body Paragraphs

When you write the body paragraphs for a comparison-contrast essay, you must decide which method you will use to structure them. As mentioned earlier in the chapter, you may choose to use the block method or the point-by-point method. Be sure to stick with whichever method you choose so as not to confuse the reader or affect the coherency of the essay. You should use transitional words and phrases that will help the reader move smoothly from one piece of information to the next. Do not use first or second person pronouns; use only third person pronouns. Add a concluding sentence at the end of each body paragraph summarizing the main topic of the paragraph.

Comparison-Contrast Conclusion

The conclusion paragraph should summarize the comparison-contrast main idea. This paragraph should not offer any new information, but it should bring the essay to a close. Sometimes your professor may require you to add your opinion. This is where you will express how you feel about the comparison-contrast topics. Remember, even though it may be your opinion, you must refrain from using first or second person pronouns.

Comparison-Contrast Outline: Block Method

I. Introduction
   a. Introduction method
   b. Claim/thesis
II. Body Paragraph 1
   1. Topic Sentence
      a. Point 1 for topic 1
      b. Point 2 for topic 1
      c. Point 3 for topic 1
      d. Concluding sentence
III. Body Paragraph 2
   1. Topic Sentence
      a. Point 1 for topic 2
      b. Point 2 for topic 2
      c. Point 3 for topic 2
      d. Concluding sentence
IV. Conclusion Paragraph
   a. Thesis restatement
   b. Opinion (optional)
   c. Conclusion method

Comparison-Contrast Outline: Point-By-Point Method

I. Introduction
   a. Introduction method
   b. Claim/thesis statement containing the two topics that will be compared and/or contrasted and the three points that will be developed
II. Body 1
   1. Topic sentence for topic 1
      a. Supporting details for topic 1
      b. Supporting details for topic 2
      c. Concluding sentence
III. Body 2
   1. Topic sentence for main point 2
      a. Supporting details for topic 1
      b. Supporting details for topic 2
      c. Concluding sentence

IV. Body 3
1. Topic sentence for main point 3
   a. Supporting details for topic 1
   b. Supporting details for topic 2
   c. Concluding sentence
V. Conclusion
   a. Claim/thesis restatement
   b. Conclusion method

© Arcady/Shutterstock.com

Read Write! Review Questions: Reading and Writing Comparison-Contrast

1. What does it mean to compare and/or contrast topics?
2. What pattern should an author use when writing a comparison-contrast essay?
3. What is the "block" method of development?
4. What is the "point-by-point" method of development?
5. List some transitional devices that may be used when writing a comparison-contrast essay.
6. What type of graphic organizer could you use to generate ideas about comparison-contrast topics?

Suggested Comparison-Contrast Essay Topics

1. Compare and/or contrast community colleges and universities.
2. Compare and/or contrast Superman and Batman.
3. Compare and/or contrast online and traditional classes.
4. Compare and/or contrast football and soccer.
5. Compare and/or contrast cohabitation and marriage.
6. Compare and/or contrast Xbox and PlayStation.
7. Compare and/or contrast the NFL and NBA.
8. Compare and/or contrast Apple and Microsoft.

Read Write! Connection: Chapter 10

Choose two readings from the Further Readings section of this book to compare and/or contrast. How do the authors present their ideas differently? What writing techniques do they use that are the same? Write a short response detailing your analysis.

Chapter 11

Reading and Writing
Cause and Effect

Key Terms

cause, effect, reason, result, inference, tone

When you are asked to read or write a cause and effect passage or essay, your instructor wants you to gain an understanding of an incident. Mainly, you should be focused on the reason something happened and the results or consequences that followed. Therefore, when you find out the reason something happened, that is the "cause," and when you learn what the results are because of what happened, that is the "effect."

Why did Mom say she wanted to divorce Dad? Why did I not complete my homework? Why is it hard to balance school and work? The answer to all of these questions is connected to the "cause."

What would happen if Mom and Dad went to marriage counseling? What if I had done my homework a day in advance? What were the results when I worked less and enrolled into more hours at school? The answer to these questions is the "effect."

© Twin Design/Shutterstock.com

While reading cause and effect, most of the time the wording in the passage will hint to a cause and effect connection. Oftentimes, you will see signal words, such as "therefore," "because," "as a result of," "the cause of which," and similar phrases. As you read, be sure to annotate both the causes and effects in a passage and utilize the PAUSE strategy to actively engage with the text. Also, look for the organizational pattern that shares its name with the rhetorical mode covered in this chapter.

> ### Read Write! Tip
> Science and history textbooks often utilize the cause and effect organizational pattern. For example, a chemistry textbook might explain the causes and effects of a specific chemical reaction, and a history textbook may have you analyze the causes and effects of a war, such as World War I.

When you write a cause and effect essay, you must provide the reader with the cause(s) and effect(s) of an incident. For example, transitional devices like "so," "because," "as a result," "therefore," "due to," and similar phrases are all indicators that cause and effect exist. Thus, such transitional devices will play an important role in any cause and effect essay you write.

Something that is important to note is that cause and effect passages and essays can be about real incidents or hypothetical situations.

CAUSE AND EFFECT ELEMENTS

When you write any essay, you want to make certain that you maintain unity throughout the entire essay. It is important that you make a point and stick to it in order to convey meaning to the reader. In cause and effect writing, the supporting details expound upon the causes and/or effects of an occurrence.

Organizational Patterns

There are two organizational patterns that can be used in cause and effect writing: cause and effect, which means the passage is organized to show specific causes or effects or both, and emphatic, which means the passage is organized in order of emphasis or importance. This can be from most important to least important or vice versa. Below is a chart of transitional devices that can be utilized when reading or writing cause and effect.

Cause and effect transitions **show the cause and effect of something.**	Therefore, as a result, as a consequence of, because, since, consequently, so, thus, ultimately, in conclusion

At times, you may be asked to only dwell on the "cause" or the reason something happened, or you may be given the reasons something occurred and be asked to make an **inference** or draw a conclusion about the effect or the results. Then, there will be times when you are asked to do both. Keep in mind that including both causes and effects will lengthen the essay considerably.

Tone

The **tone** of a cause and effect essay or reading passage can be either humorous or serious; it depends on what is being discussed. Whether you are reading a cause and effect passage or writing a cause and effect essay, you must be able to identify the reasons and the results for an occurrence. Consider the following cause and effect questions:

♦ What is the cause for violence in low economic neighborhoods? *This is asking about the reasons.*

♦ What are the effects of parents working in the evening from 6 p.m. until 6 a.m.? *This is asking about the results.*

♦ What are some reasons teenagers run away from home? *This is asking about the causes.*

Image © Margoe Edwards, 2014. Used under license from Shutterstock, Inc.

READING CAUSE AND EFFECT

When you read a cause and effect passage, make sure to look for the reasons something occurred and what happened as a result of what occurred. You should utilize PAUSE as you read in order to decipher the causes and/or the effects. Also, you should summarize each paragraph so that you are sure you comprehend what the author is trying to convey and to ensure you are retaining the important details you will need later. Remember to look for signal words that will indicate when a cause or effect is being discussed, such as "as a result," "because," "the cause of," and similar phrases.

Read Write! Activity 11.1

Read the following cause and effect passage entitled "Voting: A Right Hindered." Then, answer the questions that follow.

Voting: A Right Hindered

1   Lillian Vaughn, an African-American woman, was walking home from work one evening in rural Georgia in 1958. She knew there was a local election occurring for mayor and decided that she would attempt to vote. Unfortunately, once at the voting booth, she overheard a city official laughing about how he would make sure her ballot was never counted. Demoralized, Lillian turned around without voting and headed home. During the 50s and 60s, many individuals of all races fought for the right for minorities to exercise their right to vote. Freedom riders traveled from the North to the South to educate misinformed citizens about the voting systems in place that made it legal for them to vote. Today, many people will vote in state and national elections for positions like governor of a state or President of the United States but refuse to vote in local elections. Many people do not vote in local elections because they feel due to unethical voting practices their vote will

not count, they do not know about local issues, and they are discouraged by new voting laws.

2   First, citizens refuse to vote in local elections for fear that their vote will not count. Recently, the media has depicted local officials practicing less than ethical voting practices. For example, ballots being found in the trash at some voting sites have raised concern among many voters. Some voters have given accounts of how as they were voting using the computerized system, glitches would emerge making it impossible for them to submit their ballots. Also, the treatment of voters once at the polls has deterred many citizens from taking the time to vote locally. Furthermore, it has been rumored that people in high positions are the only individuals whose votes really count. Before, during, and after the election, many citizens feel that decisions have already been made regarding local candidates and regardless, if they vote or not would essentially not matter. Voters refuse to participate and vote at the local polls because they believe their vote will not count.

3   Second, voters choose not to vote in local elections because they do not know enough about local issues. Some people have expressed that they are more interested in state and national government because what is decided on those levels is filtered down to the local levels. For example, when mandates

are created by the federal government about education, those mandates are then given to the states and then distributed locally. Some voters believe it is more important to vote for candidates on the state and national level hoping that these candidates will make a difference on the local level. Also, several citizens have complained that local candidates are not visible until it is an election year, hence making it difficult to discuss local issues in-depth. Additionally, to some voters, the issues on the local level do not seem as important as the issues on the state and national level. Due to lack of knowledge, many citizens opt not to vote in local elections.

4   Lastly, people exclude themselves from the voting process because of the new voting laws that are in place. For instance, several states have implemented a Voter ID law that requires citizens' state issued IDs match their voter registration IDs As a result, if they do not match, it may impede voters at the polls. Some people have voted for over 50 years using their drivers' licenses and now, if their middle initials are on their state issued IDs but are not on the voter registration IDs, the voters will be rejected at the polls because of this discrepancy. Furthermore, many voters refuse to vote locally because they think the new voting laws are in place to weed out certain people and deter them from voting. Voter suppression laws have been put in place to discourage

fraud at the polls, but many voters think it is just another way to suppress their right to vote, and consequently, they refuse to go to the polls. These new laws that are being practiced on the local level are the primary reason for the decrease in voter participation in local elections.

5   The right to vote is seen by some as one of the most important rights American citizens possess. The fact that many registered voters have given up voting in local elections has been an issue of concern. Voters refuse to vote locally because of rumored unethical practices that make them feel as if their vote will not count. Others will not vote because they do not know enough about local issues to make an intelligent decision about a candidate running for local office. Also, the fact that new laws have been put in place that actually hinder voters and cause them to cancel their voting plans in local elections are all issues many believe must be addressed and rectified if the democratic process is going to continue to be exercised successfully at the local level.

1. What is the main idea of the passage?

    _____

    _____

    _____

2. What three causes does the author list in the thesis statement?

    _____

    _____

    _____

3. What should the reader be able to infer from the title?

_____

_____

_____

4. List several transition words the author chooses to include in order to move the reader from one point to the next.

_____

_____

_____

5. What organizational pattern is used in this essay? Explain your answer.

_____

_____

_____

6. What do you think about voting for local candidates? Do you participate in local elections? Why or why not?

_____

_____

_____

_____

_____

_____

_____

_____

Read Write! Activity 11.2

Read Christopher Ingraham's "Here's How Legal Pot Changed Colorado and Washington" and then answer the questions that follow.

Christopher Ingraham is a reporter for *The Washington Post*. "How Marijuana Legalization in Colorado and Washington is Making the World a Better Place" was originally published on *The Post's* website on October 17, 2014.

How Marijuana Legalization in Colorado and

Washington is Making the World a Better Place

By Christopher Ingraham

1   No pressure, Colorado and Washington, but the world is scrutinizing your every move.

2   That was the take-home message of an event today at the Brookings Institution, discussing the international impact of the move toward marijuana legalization at the state-level in the U.S. Laws passed in Colorado and Washington, with other states presumably to come, create a tension with the U.S. obligations toward three major international treaties governing drug control. Historically the U.S. has been a strong advocate of all three conventions, which "commit the United States to punish and even criminalize activity related to recreational marijuana," according to Brookings' Wells Bennet.

3   The U.S. response to this tension has thusfar been to call for more "flexibility" in how countries interpret them. This policy was made explicit in recent remarks by Assistant Secretary of State William Brownfield, who last week at the United Nations said that "we have to be tolerant of different countries, in response to their own national circumstances and conditions, exploring and using different national drug control policies." He went on: "How could I, a

representative of the Government of the United States of America, be intolerant of a government that permits any experimentation with legalization of marijuana if two of the 50 states of the United States of America have chosen to walk down that road?"

4   As far as policy stances go this is an aggressively pragmatic solution. The federal government lacks the resources and perhaps the political will to crack down on the legalization states, but it also likely doesn't want to openly admit that it's allowing regulation regimes that openly contradict the provisions of major treaties. By saying that those treaties allow for interpretation, the government is attempting to carve out some space to allow legalization experiments to continue with minimal boat-rocking.

5   But as Wells Bennet and John Walsh of the Washington Office on Latin America write in a new Brookings report, that position will "rapidly become implausible and unsustainable if legalization spreads and succeeds." At today's event, Martin Jelsma of the Transnational Institute, an international think tank, agreed: "The U.S. is hesitant to acknowledge that the legal regulation [of marijuana] is a direct violation of the treaty system . . . you have reached the limit of what you can defend applying the most flexible interpretation of the treaty system."

6   As a result, the panelists at the event were in agreement that it's time to explore a multilateral reworking of the drug control treaties to better reflect current realities - particularly, to begin the process of re-scheduling marijuana, which international law currently considers one of the most dangerous drugs(despite decades of evidence to the contrary).

7   Sandeep Chawla, former deputy director of the U.N. Office on Drugs and Crime, called the current restrictions on marijuana "the weakest point of this whole control system, something that has been obvious for 30 years." He noted that one of the main obstacles to meaningful reform is layers of entrenched drug control bureaucracies at the international and national levels - just in the U.S., think of the **DEA**, **ONDCP** and **NIDA**, among others - for whom a relaxation of drug control laws represents an undermining of their reason for existence: "if you create a bureaucracy to solve a particular problem, when the problem is solved that bureaucracy is out of a job," he explained.

8   Lisa Sanchez, a program manager at México Unido Contra la Delincuencia, a Mexican non-profit devoted to promoting "security, legality and justice," underscored how legalization efforts in the U.S. are having powerful ripple effects across the globe: events in Colorado and Washington have "created political space for Latin American countries to have a real debate [about

drug policy]." She noted that motivations for reform in Latin America are somewhat different than U.S. motivations - one main driver is a need to address the epidemic of violence on those countries that is fueled directly by prohibitionist drug war policies.

9   Many countries are now taking a close look at what's happening in the states to learn lessons that can be applied to their own situations. And so far, the news coming out of Colorado and Washington is overwhelmingly positive: dire consequences predicted by reform opponents have failed to materialize. If anything, societal and economic indicators are moving in a positive direction post-legalization. Colorado marijuana tax revenues for fiscal year 2014-2015 are on track to surpass projections.

10   Countries, particularly in Latin America, are starting to apply these lessons in order to craft smarter policies that reduce violence and other societal harms brought about by the drug war. Uruguay, for instance, has moved toward full national legalization of marijuana, with an eye toward reducing the thriving black market there. Mexico's president has given signs he's open to changes in that country's marijuana laws to help combat cartel violence. The Organization of American States recently issued a statement in favor of dealing with drug use as a public health issue, rather than a criminal justice one.

11   Regardless the eventual direction of marijuana legalization in the U.S.,

steps toward reform here are already prompting other countries to seek out

more pragmatic solutions to their drug problems. In short, they're making

the world a better place.

1. Is the passage discussing causes, effects, or both?

2. What are the outcomes of the study discussed in the article?

3. Who is the intended audience?

4. What is the intended purpose?

5. Do you feel the writer made his point well? Why or why not? How could he improve it?

_____

_____

_____

_____

_____

_____

WRITING CAUSE AND EFFECT

When you write a cause and effect essay, you will include at least three causes or three effects. Depending on whether you discuss the causes, effects, or both causes and effects will determine how you organize your writing and the length of the essay. Be mindful that some writing assignments may ask you to take a position in addition to citing causes and effects. The conclusion should restate the thesis statement and bring the essay to a close. It is important that you stay on topic throughout the entire essay and do not offer new information in the conclusion.

Cause and Effect Prewriting

Before you begin a cause and effect essay, you should complete several prewriting strategies, such as free writing, listing, clustering, asking questions, outlining, and building a pyramid, to help you generate ideas

Cause and Effect Thesis Statement

The thesis statement states the topic, and provides three causes or effects that will be developed in the rest of the essay.

Cause and Effect Body Paragraphs

Each body paragraph will begin with a topic sentence that includes a transitional word and one of the causes or effects. Several supporting sentences will follow. Transitional words and phrases should be included throughout the paragraph in order to move from one piece of information to the next. A concluding sentence reiterating the cause or effect should summarize and bring closure to the paragraph.

Cause and Effect Conclusion

The conclusion paragraph lets the reader know that the cause and effect essay is coming to an end. Various techniques can be used to end the essay.

Cause and Effect Outline

    I. Introduction
       a. Introduction method
       b. Thesis statement containing the three topics that will be developed

II. Body 1
   a. Topic sentence for cause/effect 1
   b. Supporting details
   c. A concluding sentence
III. Body 2
   a. Topic sentence for cause/effect 2
   b. Supporting details
   c. A concluding sentence
IV. Body 3
   a. Topic sentence for cause/effect 3
   b. Supporting details
   c. A concluding sentence
V. Conclusion
   a. Thesis restatement
   b. Conclusion method

Read Write! Activity 11.3

Read the passage below entitled "7 Ways the U.S.A. Benefits from the Legalization of Gay Marriage" by Murray Lipp. Then answer the questions that follow.

Murray Lipp is the administrator of "Gay Marriage USA" on Facebook. This piece was originally published on *The Huffington Post* on June 2, 2013.

7 Ways the U.S.A. Benefits From the Legalization of Gay Marriage

By Murray Lipp

1   The legalization of same-sex marriage benefits both LGBT people and America as a nation. As two major Supreme Court decisions about same-sex marriage (Proposition 8 and DOMA) loom on the horizon, it's an opportune time to refocus attention on the many advantages associated with the pursuit and achievement of marriage equaility.

2   There are at least seven ways in which the legalization of gay marriage is beneficial for LGBT Americans and the United States of America.

Promotes Equality and Non-Discrimination in Society

3   Millions of LGBT people contribute daily to American life in a multitude of ways culturally, socially, financially, politically, vocationally, and spiritually. We are fundamental to this nation's continued growth and evolution and the U.S.A. would suffer greatly from the withdrawal of our many contributions. The legalization of same-sex marriage affirms the inherent worthiness of LGBT people as valued American citizens deserving of equal rights under the law.

4   This promotion of equality and non-discrimination plays an extremely important role in reducing homophobia and in affirming a minority group in society which has for so long endured significant discrimination and stigmatization. Legalizing same-sex marriage communicates to millions of people across the country that gay relationships are of equal value to straight relationships, thereby helping to reduce intergroup prejudice and supporting cultural diversity.

Fosters Psychological, Physical, and Social Wellbeing Amongst LGBT People

5   Same-sex couples are excluded from the institution of marriage in 38 states. Furthermore, the federal government denies legally married same-sex couples

more than 1000 federal rights and benefits associated with marriage. This discrimination and institutional exclusion negatively impacts LGBT people in a variety of tangible and practical ways. It can also cause psychological distress, social conflict and ill-health. Equal allocation of marriage rights and benefits to same-sex couples assists LGBT people in a practical sense and the elimination of relationship discrimination helps promote psychosocial and physical well-being.

6   It is to America's benefit when LGBT people are given the freedom to achieve their full potential in life without having to waste precious time and resources battling for basic equality. The act of discrimination is an essentially destructive societal behavior which, ultimately, brings negative consequences both to the oppressors and the oppressed. Ending discrimination in marriage laws goes some way to correcting this.

Promotes Family Stability and Validates LGBT Family Units

7   Today's children represent America's future and it is in the country's best interest to support their development, regardless of whom they are parented by. Marriage, as an institution, helps to foster the wellbeing of children by providing married couples with various rights, benefits and pro- tections which can strengthen relationship bonds and family units. Around

the nation there are millions of children being raised in households led by same-sex couples, many of whom are denied the right to legally marry in their home state.

8   The denial of equal marriage rights unfairly disadvantages children who are raised by same-sex couples residing in states where gay marriage is not legal or not recognized. This lack of support for LGBT families denies children within them the same type of protections afforded children in "traditional" families headed by married straight couples. It also sends a damaging message to children within LGBT families that their parents are inferior, second-class citizens who are not worthy of equal treatment in society. The legalization of gay marriage helps to address this injustice by supporting family stability and validating the worthiness of families led by same-sex couples.

Provides Economic and Business Opportunities

9   The legalization of same-sex marriage has consistently been shown to provide an economic boost to those states and countries that have embraced marriage equality. The marriage and wedding industry is a significant one. Allowing gay couples to marry provides businesses in this industry with a large and new market to access. Nearly $260 million was injected into the New York City economy in the year following the legalization of same-sex

marriage. Gay marriage tourism benefits those regions which permit same-sex marriage by attracting gay couples from other states and countries where it is not legal.

10   Most large businesses understand the importance of recognizing gay marriage because it enables them to more readily retain LGBT staff and customers. Not surprisingly, an increasing number of national and global companies are now expressing support for marriage equality and speaking out in favor of gay marriage.

Fosters True Freedom of Religion

11   Freedom of religion allows a person or group to pursue the practice of their religion without governmental interference. It also protects those who do not follow a religion by shielding them from being forced to live in accordance with religious beliefs and values they do not agree with. The legalization of same-sex marriage is consistent with freedom of religion in that it removes from marriage laws religious notions that may have initially shaped those laws. There is no hierarchy of religions in a society which truly honors freedom of religion. Accordingly, the religious views of no one particular group should be given preference in the development of marriage laws. While some religions don't support same-sex marriage, others certainly *do* support it. The most fair

and ethical approach — which treats all people equally regardless of religious affiliation — is to factor out religious points of view when crafting marriage laws within a secular context.

Assists With the De-politicization of LGBT Rights

12   The politicization of LGBT rights as a left vs right issue has been one of the many "culture wars" that has plagued American society in recent decades. The battle between pro-equality "liberals" and anti-equality "conservatives" continues to characterize the state by state legalization of same-sex marriage. Democratic politicians have successfully led legislative efforts to legalize gay marriage in nine states. President Obama's support of marriage equality, Bill Clinton's abandonment of the Defense of Marriage Act (DOMA), and Democratic voters' support of marriage equality contrast strikingly with the situation on the Republican side. Opposition to same-sex marriage remains a key part of the GOP platform and a majority of Republican politicians and GOP voters do not support marriage equality.

13   This unfortunate construction of marriage equality as a left vs right and Democratic vs Republican issue wrongly politicizes what is essentially a human rights matter. In this sense the legalization of same-sex marriage plays a central role in de-politicizing the quest for LGBT equality. It provides

Democrats and Republicans with an opportunity to refocus their efforts on addressing other problems in society and to stop wasting valuable resources on a manufactured culture war.

Strengthens National Identity and International Reputation

14   "Liberty and justice for all" is a phrase often used in descriptions of the U.S.A. which seek to capture the nation's collective psyche, spirit and identity. Historically, America has presented itself as a global leader in matters of freedom and democracy. It's unfortunate and ironic, however, that back on home soil one particular group of people is consistently denied full access to the "American dream." The fact that same-sex marriage is not legal in thirty-eight states of the U.S.A. and not recognized by the federal government has damaged America's international reputation in relation to LGBT rights.

15   Fifteen countries have moved ahead of the U.S.A. in providing federal marriage equality. The removal of anti-gay discrimination in all state and federal laws that apply to marriage would play a key role in enhancing America's international reputation in matters of social justice and in restoring our integrity as a global leader in the provision of civil and human rights. The tag of "liberty and justice for all" will become more believable

when same-sex couples are granted equal access to marriage laws across the country.

16   It is with hope and optimism that I anticipate the decisions to be soon made by U.S. Supreme Court in relation to Proposition 8 and DOMA. The sincere hope for equality advocates is that both laws will be struck down, that same-sex marriage will become legal in California once again, and that the federal government will no longer be allowed to deny rights and benefits to legally married same-sex couples.

17   It is time to stop playing politics and to stop "debating" whether LGBT Americans should have equal rights in society and whether same-sex relationships should be valued equally under the law. Allowing same-sex couples to marry harms no one. Conversely, it enhances the lives of millions of LGBT Americans and their families and also benefits broader society economically, cuturally, and politically. I look forward to the day when the provision of marriage equality is embraced and valued as a core feature of American culture and when "we the people" can rightly be claimed to include everyone.

1. What is being discussed: causes, effects, or both? How can you tell?

    _____

    _____

    _____

2. What is the purpose of the reading?

    _____

    _____

    _____

3. Who is the intended audience?

    _____

    _____

    _____

4. How is the passage organized?

    _____

    _____

    _____

5. In the context of section 6, what is a "culture war"?

    _____

    _____

    _____

6. On June 26, 2015, around two years after this piece was originally published, the Supreme Court ruled on same-sex marriage. Research this ruling online. What did you find? How does your research relate to this piece?

    _____

    _____

    _____

    _____

    _____

    _____

    _____

Read Write! Review Questions: Cause and Effect

1. When the reason something occurred is referred to, you are being asked to examine what?
2. When the effects of an incident are examined what is this referring to?
3. Define inference.
4. What are the signal words/transitional words for the organizational pattern used in cause and effect writing?
5. List some other signal words or transitional devices that may be used when writing a cause and effect essay.

Suggested Cause and Effect Essay Topics

1. What are some effects of an economic recession or depression?
2. What are the effects of cellphone use while driving?
3. What are the causes/effects of America's obesity epidemic?
4. What are the reasons for your chosen major?
5. What are some of the effects of completing a degree or certificate program?
6. What are some reasons a student might drop a college course?

Read Write! Connection: Chapter 11

Read the following ethical dilemma. Then, complete the following exercises working with cause and effect.

You have been employed at the same company as the assistant manager for three years. Lately, business has been slow, and management has approached you and asked you for suggestions on increasing business. As the assistant manager, you and other employees have noticed your immediate supervisor, the manager, is the reason the business is failing. The manager's behavior has been different lately. You have been wanting a promotion because you need the money. You are scheduled to meet with the owner to discuss the issue. What will you do?

♦ Without defaming the manager, write a hypothetical letter to the business owner about the causes for why the business is not doing well. Remember, words have a denotative and a connotative meaning. Your tone should remain neutral. Therefore, choose your words carefully.
♦ Write a one-page summary, including the causes and some possible results (solutions), for the problem.

> **Read Write! Tip**

The skills used in the Read Write! Connection can be applied in the workplace. In the professional world, you should refrain from using tactless language that defames others. Think of ways to convey your point without insulting others. In school, using tactless language could negatively affect your grade. In your career, you may be demoted, fired, or not hired in the first place.

Chapter 12
Reading and Writing Definition

Key Terms

definition, objective, subjective, extended definition

Defining words can make your reading and writing experiences become meaningful and allow you to be able to synthesize information effectively. The purpose of definition is to promote synthesis, analysis, and evaluation as they pertain to critical thinking. This particular mode or pattern requires critical thinking and a willingness to delve deeper into the meaning of various abstractions. This means you are reading beyond the lines and asking your audience to read your writing thematically. For example, if you think of a home at face value, you may think of the actual structure that was built on the block where you live; however, if you think critically about the word "home," words such as "safe," "unity," and "comfortable" may emerge in your mind.

Definition reading consists of the reader being able to read between the lines of a text for connotative meaning and analyze the words in order to extract the intangible concepts of a word beyond the lines. Definition writing is comprised of lengthy and an extended definition of words within the essay to ensure the reader fully recognizes there is more to words than their denotative meaning.

Definitions can be objective or subjective. If you define a word or concept by offering facts about that word, you are defining the word objectively. However, if you define the word or concept based on how you view the topic, then you are subjectively defining the word or concept.

PAUSE will be useful when you read definition passages. Likewise, as you write definition essays, following the prewriting and the writing processes carefully will be helpful.

Most times, you may be familiar with the formal definition or dictionary meaning of a word. Even if you are not familiar with the formal definition, it is easily accessible by looking the word up in a dictionary. In Chapter 8: Exemplification, the goal is to provide extended examples. Likewise, definition requires

Image © Masson, 2014. Used under license from Shutterstock, Inc.

the author to provide an extended definition. As mentioned above, words have a dictionary meaning; however, in academic writing, extended definitions are necessary to convey deeper meaning to the reader. When you write a definition essay, you should try to provide the most in depth meaning for your audience. Keep in mind, several words have different meanings. For example, you may be asked to define "emotional intelligence." At face value, you might look up the word emotional and then intelligence. By obtaining the meaning of both words, you may become familiar with the words. However, emotional intelligence is a theory that has a deeper meaning than the dictionary definition of the two words "emotional" and "intelligence." Thus, begins the journey of defining the theory of emotional intelligence, which will cause you to probe for a deeper understanding.

DEFINITION ELEMENTS

When you write any essay, you want to make certain that you provide numerous supporting details in your body paragraphs so that you are creating a sense of coherence for your reader. In definition writing, the supporting details are the extended definition used to convey a deeper meaning to your audience.

Organizational Patterns

There are several patterns of organization that can be used in definition writing. First is topical order where you provide extended examples by topic. Also, there is emphatic order, which means order of importance. There is problem and solutions ordering, as well, which means the passage is organized to first discuss the problem and secondly discuss a suggested solution. Finally, there is comparison-contrast; in this pattern, the passage is organized to discuss how two topics are similar or different or both.

Pay close attention to the transitional words and phrases the author uses to move smoothly through the passage from one piece of information to the next. When you write a definition essay, there are several transitional words you can use to navigate through and provide the audience with additional meaning. Below is a chart of transition words and phrases that work well for definition writing and that you will see when you read definition passages.

Addition transitions **show additional ideas.**	Also, next, furthermore, another, finally, first, in addition, as well
Contrast transitions **show contrasting or differing ideas.**	However, although, even though, nevertheless, on the other hand, but, in spite of, in contrast, instead, yet
Example transitions **help to show examples or illustrate your ideas better.**	For example, for instance, including, such as, like

When you are reading or writing definition, there are several concepts to consider. The questions below will help guide you whether you are reading or writing.

The Definition

What is being or will be defined? This question should prompt you to think about any prior knowledge you may have about the topic. Using the KWL template, located in the appendix, may be helpful during this process. Ultimately, it will allow you to tie those experiences to the passage making the definition more meaningful and concrete. It may also help you gain a different insight regarding the words or concepts being defined.

The Title

What inferences can you make by reading the title? Answering this question should enable you to generate ideas about what you may encounter as you begin reading, such as the author's tone. As you read and write a definition essay, you should consider the tone. The author's attitude towards a concept or definition of a word should become evident as you read a definition passage. Identifying the author's tone also answers the question of whether the author provides an objective or subjective definition. Likewise, when you write a definition essay, your audience should be able to determine your essay plan of development. Understanding the tone of a passage may help the audience make deeper connections regarding the concepts being defined. As you write a definition essay, tone can be incorporated during prewriting where you generate ideas about the topic and should remain consistent for the duration of the essay.

The Main Idea/Thesis Statement

As you read, understanding the formal definition of a word or concept will assist you in comprehending the deeper meaning the author is trying to convey. You should be able to identify the deeper meaning realizing it is the main idea.

When you write a thesis statement, you must make sure you clearly define a word or concept. You will acknowledge to the audience your plan of developing and supporting a deeper meaning throughout the essay.

Whether you are reading a definition passage or writing a definition essay, remember to continually gain or render a deeper meaning. After the thesis statement has been identified or constructed, the reader should be clear about what the author is attempting to define. Otherwise, the definition will not be effective and may even become confusing.

The Introduction

There are several methods of introduction that may be used in a definition reading passage or essay. Regardless to which method an author or you as a writer may choose, one main goal is to be able to identify and transpose a formal dictionary definition. This will lead to a broader definition in the thesis.

The Supporting Details

Do the topic sentences in the body paragraphs provide clarity and further define the author's main idea? Make connections by annotating as you read. Write down things that catch your attention while reading, and when you are finished, you can go back and analyze your notes for a clearer understanding. Use the PAUSE strategy in chapter 1 to do this effectively.

When you become the author, during prewriting be sure to look for ideas that do not overlap but do support the extended definition. Then, write topic sentences that directly relate to the ideas in the thesis statement.

The Conclusion

Does the conclusion of the passage reiterate the author's main idea? Does your essay restate the thesis? When you read a definition passage, by the time you get to the conclusion, you should have a very clear meaning of the deeper and more enhanced definition of a particular word or concept. When you write a definition essay, make sure the conclusion restates the thesis, reminding your audience of the main idea of the essay. Your audience should be clear about what you are trying to convey especially after reading the conclusion.

READING DEFINITION

When you read a definition passage, make sure you are reading thoroughly and utilizing PAUSE to look for an effective introduction as well as a main idea that states what word or concept will be defined. You should attempt to answer the prereading questions mentioned above. Annotate as you read in order to organize in your mind the author's ideas regarding the word or concept he/she has chosen. Also, you should summarize each paragraph. Read in such a way that you find yourself questioning the definition being offered in order to gain a clearer meaning. It may also be beneficial to paraphrase the passage in your own words so that you are clear about what the author is trying to convey.

After reading a definition passage, try to answer the following questions about the passage. Remember, these are the same questions your audience will attempt to answer after reading the extended definition you write.

- ♦ Do you understand the deeper meaning of the word or concept? Will your reader understand the deeper meaning you are trying to convey?
- ♦ Did you learn something new about the topic that could change your viewpoint?
- ♦ Do you want to know more about the topic?
- ♦ What are you supposed to do with the information you have just read?

Read Write! Activity 12.1

Read the following passage entitled "Ain't I A Woman?" by Sojourner Truth. Then, answer the questions that follow.

Sojourner Truth (1797–1883) was an African–American abolitionist and women's rights activist. Born into slavery, Truth escaped in 1835 and gained her freedom. The passage below is a speech on gender equality. It was delivered at the Ohio Women's Rights Convention in 1851.

Image © rook76, 2014. Used under license from Shutterstock, Inc.

Ain't I A Woman?

by Sojourner Truth

1 Well, children, where there is so much racket there must be something out of kilter. I think that 'twixt the negroes of the South and the women at the North, all talking about rights, the white men will be in a fix pretty soon. But what's all this here talking about?

2 That man over there says that women need to be helped into carriages, and lifted over ditches, and to have the best place everywhere. Nobody ever helps me into carriages, or over mud-puddles, or gives me any best place! And ain't I a woman? Look at me! Look at my arm! I have ploughed and planted, and gathered into barns, and no man could head me! And ain't I a woman? I could work as much and eat as much as a man - when I could get it - and bear the lash as well! And ain't I a woman? I have borne thirteen children, and seen most all sold off to slavery, and when I cried out with my mother's grief, none but Jesus heard me! And ain't I a woman?

3 Then they talk about this thing in the head; what's this they call it? [member of audience whispers, "intellect"] That's it, honey. What's that got to do with women's rights or negroes' rights? If my cup won't hold but a pint,

and yours holds a quart, wouldn't you be mean not to let me have my little half measure full?

4   Then that little man in black there, he says women can't have as much rights as men, 'cause Christ wasn't a woman! Where did your Christ come from? Where did your Christ come from? From God and a woman! Man had nothing to do with Him.

5   If the first woman God ever made was strong enough to turn the world upside down all alone, these women together ought to be able to turn it back, and get it right side up again! And now they are asking to do it, the men better let them.

6   Obliged to you for hearing me, and now old Sojourner ain't got nothing more to say.

1. What is the author defining in this speech?

_____

2. What is insinuated by the title? What inferences can you make? Why do you think this title was chosen?

_____

_____

_____

_____

_____

3. During a time of racial and gender inequality, what was the author trying to convey to the audience?

_____

_____

_____

4. What examples about womanhood does the author present?

_____

_____

_____

5. As the author offers an extended definition of the topic, do you think her reasons are strong enough to be substantial to the audience?

_____

_____

_____

_____

_____

_____

6. Is the author's definition of a woman subjective or objective? Provide examples from the passage to support your answer.

_____

_____

_____

_____

_____

_____

WRITING DEFINITION

When you write a definition essay, you will incorporate at least three different meanings of the word you are defining. Each meaning will be explained and developed in the body paragraphs of the essay. Specific support is needed so that the writer provides a deeper explanation of the word. Also, when you write, think about how you will expound on the definition incorporating an extended definition of the word or concept. The conclusion of a definition essay brings the essay to a close by restating the thesis.

Also, the writer may choose to use the summary conclusion method to summarize the point one last time for the reader.

Definition Prewriting

Before you begin a definition essay, you should complete several prewriting strategies, such as free writing, listing, clustering, asking questions, outlining, and building a pyramid, to help you generate ideas. You will also decide whether your definition will be objective based on facts or will it be subjective based on how you view the topic.

Definition Thesis Statement

The thesis statement states the word or concept that will be defined and provides three points that will be developed and extended in the rest of the essay.

Definition Body Paragraphs

Each body paragraph will begin with a topic sentence that includes a transitional word and one of the points from the thesis statement. Several supporting sentences will follow in order to extend the definition. Transitional words and phrases should be included throughout the paragraph in order to move from one piece of information or idea to the next. A concluding sentence reiterating the point should summarize and bring closure to the paragraph.

In definition essays, several modes can be used in order to extend the definition and convey the most meaning to the reader. First person pronouns like "I" or "we" may be used at your instructor's discretion. Likewise, third person pronouns may also be used. During prewriting, you will determine which pronouns will be most effective when you decide which organizational pattern will best convey the definition.

Definition Conclusion

The conclusion paragraph lets the reader know that the definition essay is coming to an end. Various techniques can be used to end the essay.

> ➢ **Read Write! Tip**
> Professional writers may use first and second person pronouns in their definition writing; however, as a student writer, your professor will inform you of what is acceptable for an essay assignment.

Definition Outline

The format of a definition essay is the same as a standard five-paragraph essay. Below is a basic outline.

I. Introduction
    a. Introduction method
    b. Thesis statement containing the three topics that will be developed in order to extend the definition

II. Body 1
   a. Topic sentence for main point 1
   b. Supporting details
   c. A concluding sentence
III. Body 2
   a. Topic sentence for main point 2
   b. Supporting details
   c. A concluding sentence
IV. Body 3
   a. Topic sentence for main point 3
   b. Supporting details
   c. A concluding sentence
V. Conclusion
   a. Thesis restatement
   b. Conclusion method

Read Write! Activity 12.2

Read the essay below entitled "Marriage: A Noun or a Verb?" Then, answer the questions that follow.

Marriage: A Noun or a Verb?

1   I came from a family where marriage is thought of as a sacred ritual. The rule in our family is once we cross over into the land of matrimony, it is expected that the bond will be forever. As a young girl, I often dreamed about my knight in shining armor and how he would find me, sweep me off my feet, and marry me. Everything would be pure bliss, and we would stay married happily ever after. After actually getting married and being married for nearly 20 years, I have come to realize marriage is far more than just a

union or legal contract. Marriage can be defined as "work" in the areas of affection, conversation, and companionship.

2   First of all, marriage can be defined as work in the area of affection. Many married couples who have been married for any length of time will usually at some point attribute a successful marriage to the continuous affection offered by both parties. Making it known often that they love and adore each other is an important factor in maintaining an affectionate relationship. For example, an "I love you" text may seem simple to most, but after couples become married, some of the things they did before they got married need to be remain ignited once they join in matrimony. Another way affection can be shown is through the sense of touch. Holding hands and a gentle kiss or hug can speak far louder than words and express a large amount of affection. Finding a way to be affectionate with each other is often time consuming, but the time spent showing adoration towards the other person may add years to the marriage from a long term perspective. It is a mistake for one spouse to assume the other "knows" he/she is loved; each spouse must be shown affection regularly. Working at showing affection is key in a marriage.

3   Secondly, married couples must work at maintaining communication. The art of conversation can strengthen a marriage bond tremendously.

Today, many married couples rarely see each other due to work schedules, and speaking face-to-face is sometimes impossible. Talking to each other is one of the surest ways to guarantee that each spouse is in a good place with himself/herself and within the marriage. Listening to each other, not in order to give advice or directives is what should be reciprocated between both parties within the marriage. In a marriage, timing is important when attempting to engage in conversation. For instance, a specific time when both spouses have enough time to listen and respond will ultimately result in them explaining how they feel and what needs must be met in order to strengthen the marriage. Thus, it is important to make time for conversation in the marriage as it most often is the first line of communication between spouses. Marriage is work because spouses must make an effort to communicate with one another on a regular basis.

4   Equally important in the work of a marriage is companionship. Being kind to each other is sometimes taken for granted. Kindness is essential in a marriage. Doing random acts of kindness on purpose shows a spouse that he/she is genuinely loved and cherished. Moreover, practicing the golden rule in a marriage is a sure way to strengthen the marriage bond. If one spouse treats the other the way he/she would like

to be treated, it is usually reciprocated without resistance. Again, time is of the essence in a marriage, and companionship calls for married couples to set aside time daily, weekly, or monthly that is specifically designated to improving the relationship. For example, planning a date night every Wednesday will remind both spouses that on Wednesday they are dedicated to each other and only an unexpected emergency can alter this time of companionship. As a result, it could lead to more time being spent producing an even stronger union. Most importantly, forgiveness is fuel for companionship. Inevitably, in a marriage, there will be disagreements where one spouse becomes offended. It is important to practice forgiving each other quickly and sincerely. Companionship is about improving attitudes and creating an atmosphere for a healthy marriage. Marriage can be defined as work because companionship requires the effort of both spouses.

5   Marriage is not just a concept. It takes strategic planning and work to create and maintain a healthy marriage. Being affectionate is very important in regards to letting the other spouse know how much each is needed and wanted in the relationship. Making time for conversation and companionship is also imperative to creating a strong relationship between married individuals. It takes more than a promise to keep a marriage strong. It takes work.

1. What word did the author define?

   _____

2. What definition does the author provide?

   _____

3. What three points does the author use as the basis for the definition?

   _____

   _____

   _____

4. What patterns of organization does the author use? How do you know?

   _____

   _____

   _____

5. Does the author write the definition objectively or subjectively?

   _____

   _____

   _____

6. Highlight the thesis restatement.

7. What transitional words does the author use to help the reader move smoothly through the essay?

   _____

8. What rhetorical mode from a previous chapter is used to write this definition essay?

   _____

Read Write! Review Questions: Reading and Writing Definition

1. What is the difference between an objective and a subjective definition?
2. True or False: There is only one organizational pattern that can be used in a definition essay.
3. True or False: Definition can be combined with other rhetorical modes.
4. List three transitions that can be used when writing a definition. How do you make connections as you read a definition?

Suggested Definition Essay Topics

1. Write an essay defining "discrimination."
2. Write an essay defining "love."
3. Write an essay defining "family."
4. Write an essay defining "American."
5. Write an essay defining "teacher."

Read Write! Connection: Chapter 12

Think of another word or concept like "marriage." Look the word up in the dictionary and read the objective, formal definition (find its denotative meaning). Write down as many ideas that come to mind about the word or concept. Think critically about how your definition coincides with the dictionary definition. Log on to your favorite social media site and post your subjective, extended definition. Record the responses you get. Do others agree or disagree with your definition?

Chapter 13
Reading and Writing Arguments

Key Terms

Argument, appeal, ethos, pathos, logos, tactful language, claim statement, fallacies, argument strategies

Arguments occur daily. In everyday life, disagreements ensue or happen, and they may be small or large and not necessarily controversial. For example, having an argument with your sister about whether or not strawberry ice cream is better than chocolate ice cream is not as controversial as an argument about whether or not third trimester abortions should be legal. Arguments are strong opinions about controversial topics. The author's goal is to try to convince the reader to take his/her side. In other words, arguments are meant to persuade the readers to agree with the author or at least question their own thinking about their opinions.

Image © Peter Polak, 2014. Used under license from Shutterstock, Inc.

Before you can read or think critically about an issue or a topic, you must determine what is expected from you as a student before and after reading. PAUSE will be useful when you read argument passages. Likewise, as you write argument essays, following the prewriting and the writing processes as you write will be helpful.

Similar to writing argument essays, when you read an argument, there are several factors you must consider, and there are specific elements you should look for. For example, you should determine the emotional appeal the author is incorporating into the argument. While reading, in order to effectively explicate an argument, you must follow the reading rules outlined in chapters 1, 3, and 5. Likewise, when you write an argument, you should be able to choose an appeal and incorporate it in your own writing. As your audience reads the arguments you write, they must be clear about the opinions you are trying to convey.

This chapter will discuss how to read and write arguments effectively. Your instructor may have several reasons for requiring you to read an argument. One reason might be to have you examine two or more views of an issue. Another reason could be to encourage you to choose a side of an issue or create a new viewpoint regarding an issue. Another important reason you will read arguments for class is so you can identify the strategies for effective arguing and include them in your own academic writing. Below are some factors to consider before, during, and after reading or writing an argument.

ARGUMENT ELEMENTS

When you write any essay, you want to make certain that you provide numerous supporting details in your body paragraphs so that you are creating a sense of coherence for your reader. In argument writing, the supporting details are the examples used to defend your stance.

Organizational Patterns

There are three organizational patterns that can be used in argument writing. The first is emphatic order, which means order of importance. The second is topical organization, which means your body paragraphs are organized by the three main points or the plan of development presented in the thesis statement. Last is problem and solution, which means the passage is organized to first discuss the problem and secondly discuss a suggested solution.

There are several transitional words you can use to navigate through the essay whether you are reading or writing it. Below is a chart of transition words and phrases often used in argument.

Time (chronological) transitions **show the order in which events occur(ed).**	first, next, before, after, then, as, during, immediately, later, meanwhile, now, often, previously, suddenly, when, while, second, third, last, finally
Addition transitions **show additional ideas.**	Also, next, furthermore, another, finally, first, in addition, as well
Cause and effect transitions **show the cause and effect of something.**	Therefore, as a result, as a consequence of, because, since, consequently, so, thus, ultimately, in conclusion
Contrast transitions **show contrasting or differing ideas.**	However, although, even though, nevertheless, on the other hand, but, in spite of, in contrast, instead, yet
Example transitions **help to show examples or illustrate your ideas better.**	For example, for instance, including, such as, like

The Appeals

There are three ways an author may choose to **appeal** to their audience in an argument: ethos, pathos, and logos. You should be able to recognize these appeals as you read various arguments, and when you write an argument essay, you should also incorporate one or more of these appeals.

Ethos, or the ethical appeal, is used to convince an audience of the author's credibility or reliability. When authors use ethos, they do so in order to convince the readers that they are a reliable and credible source of

Image © Peter Polak, 2014. Used under license from Shutterstock, Inc.

information on the topic at hand. They want the readers to believe they are "ethical" or right, for in doing so they gain the trust of the readers who may end up either changing their view or at least respecting the authors' viewpoints about an issue. This relates back to an author's credibility, which was discussed in chapter 5. When an author is trying to be persuasive, it is important to use the proper words and be seen as a reasonable person.

When you write arguments, you will use ethos to convince your audience that you are a credible and reliable writer. If your readers do not see you as credible, it will be hard to persuade them of anything, and your argument will fall flat. You will also need to choose your words purposefully and check your facts to avoid losing credibility. Remember that your credibility as a writer is discussed further in chapter 6. Another way you can use ethos is by continuously reiterating what the right thing is to do regarding the issue you are writing about. You will use moral and ethical beliefs as the foundation of your argument.

Pathos, or the emotional appeal, is used to persuade an audience by appealing to their emotions. When authors use pathos, they do so in order to make the reader feel a certain way. Emotions may range from sorrow to anger, but the emotional appeal is enhanced so that the readers feel a need to do something about the issue being discussed. The emotional appeal can be very powerful. Look at the following statement pulled from an essay on animal cruelty: "Every year, thousands of animals are abused and sometimes killed. Donating to the American Humane Society can help put a stop to this." How does such a statement make you feel? The idea of animals being hurt or killed is used purposefully to make you feel upset and persuade you to donate money to the cause.

When you write an argument essay, if you decide to utilize pathos, it is important to use words that suggest that the readers become emotional, whether this is stated directly or implied. You may also gather information based on your own experiences or the testimonials of others. Some examples of writing using the pathos appeal may be found in articles in magazines like *Reader's Digest* or *Essence Magazine*. The articles found in these magazines usually tug at the heart strings of readers by writing about societal matters, provoking emotional reactions from the audience.

Logos, or the appeal to logic, is used to influence an audience through logic or reason. When authors use logos, they do so in order to suggest to the readers "what makes sense." Another word for logic is sense or rational. Thus, the authors may use facts, statistics, and anecdotal historical facts. The authors will base their argument on what they have thought about and will ask the readers to think about an issue differently. It is important to use words that prompt the readers to think differently about an issue more so than they have ever thought before. For example, an author who appeals to logic may write: "Based on the survey given to students across the country and because bullying has increased over 50% in the last ten years, students should attend same gender high schools." Think about when you read a text that provides a plethora of statistics and facts to back up what it is saying—it is more convincing with this type of evidence to support the main idea.

When you write an argument relying on logos as the appeal to the audience, you will organize your writing based on what makes sense. You will provide the audience with supporting details that reiterate the logic of why your stance is the correct stance. You will use the strategies for arguing effectively to ensure that the audience is not insulted by your argument and the suggestion that "you" are right.

Strategies for Arguing Effectively

Good arguments utilize specific strategies to be as persuasive as possible. These strategies are listed below. While reading an argument, use PAUSE to annotate for these strategies to see if the author is arguing effectively. When you write an argument, be sure to incorporate the following strategies.

1. Be polite: Insulting the readers will lessen your chances of captivating an attentive audience.
2. Provide examples of how the opposing viewpoint and the author's are the same. This may put the readers at ease and consequently make them convert to the writer's viewpoint
3. Show where the author's and the opposing opinions are different: This will strengthen the argument.
4. Recognize the opposing argument: This will show that the author is a rational person.
5. Be able to identify or be prepared to offer a rebuttal or a counter argument if required. Remember to refer to the first strategy when refuting the opposition.

The Topic

What is the topic of the passage or essay? Answering this question should help you remember any experiences you may have encountered about the topic and ultimately allow you to tie those experiences to the passage when reading it, making it more meaningful and concrete. Remember that in an argument, the topic will be debatable. If there is nothing to debate, then what you are reading or writing is not an argument. As you read, be sure to identify the debatable topic, and then as you write, be sure you are able to incorporate a debatable topic into your own writing.

The Title and Tone

What can you infer about the argument by reading the title? Answering this question should enable you to generate ideas about what you may encounter as you begin reading, such as the author's tone. Many times, the tone of a passage may help the audience make a decision regarding their opinion about an issue. As you write arguments, you should consider the tone of your essay. This can be done during prewriting as you generate ideas about the topic and should remain consistent for the duration of the essay.

The Claim

The **claim** is the author's position or stance regarding the topic. When you write an argument, you will also make a claim. Knowing the author's position will help you comprehend what he/she is trying to convey to the reader. You should be able to identify the author's claim realizing it is the main idea of the argument. It may be stated or implied.

When you write a claim or thesis statement, you must make sure you take a clear stance and continually defend your position throughout the essay. Remember not to waiver from your stance. After the claim has been constructed, the audience should be clear about your stance and which side you will argue in the essay. Otherwise, the argument will not be effective. When you write the claim statement, consider using the words "should" and "should not." These words are often used in the claim statement of argument essays because they clearly state the writer's stance.

The claim statement, or thesis, will also contain a controlling idea, which is another term for the author's stance. Is the author for or against the topic being discussed? Remember, authors sometimes use different methods of introduction to catch the reader's interest. Be sure to read the introduction, including the claim, thoroughly in order to clearly identify the author's opinion.

When you write an argument essay, you must incorporate your opinion about the topic so that the reader will be clear about your stance. This should appear as a part of the thesis statement, or claim. Below is an example of a claim statement for an argument essay:

Parents should not spank their children because it causes emotional, mental, and physical harm.

Notice that this claim specifically includes three parts: the topic (spanking), the stance (that parents should not spank their children), and three supporting details that create a plan of development (emotional, mental, and physical harm).

The Introduction

Whether you are reading or writing, the introduction of an argument passage or essay should do the following: introduce the topic, give the reader background information about the topic, and provide the reader with a claim that specifically shows the author's stance about the topic.

Read Write! Activity 13.1

Below are two examples of introductions for the argument essay "Spare the Children." The first uses the "anecdote" method of introduction and the second uses the background information method. Then, answer the questions that follow.

Spare the Children

There were several children playing by the lake one Sunday afternoon. Everyone was having fun. One child fell into the lake and got his Sunday clothes drenched. He began crying profusely as he saw his father walking towards him. The boy's father took his belt off and began to spank him repeatedly. Afterwards, the boy looked around sobbing only to see his friends watching in a state of disbelief. Weeks after the incident occurred, the boy began to perform poorly at school and had reportedly been sent to the principal's office for fighting. When asked why he was behaving so badly, he had nothing to say. Eventually, he told the counselor at the school that he felt depressed. He admitted that his parents spanked him often and he wanted to run away. Parents should not spank their children because it causes emotional, mental, and physical harm

Spare the Children

For several centuries, parents have thought that corporal punishment was a way to discipline children. During biblical times, people believed that it was a mandate from God to not spare disobedient children from harsh physical punishment. Proponents of spanking have said that spanking children teaches children how to be respectful towards authority. Several parents believe that because they were spanked as children that they should instill the same values into their own children. Granted, some children who are spanked tend to change their negative behavior and refrain from repeating certain offenses; however, there are negative consequences that result from spanking children. In recent years, the question of whether or not spanking is a healthy and effective form of discipline has been on the minds of many people. Parents should not spank children because it causes emotional, mental and physical harm.

1. What type of appeal does the author use to get the reader's attention in each introduction? Write a phrase from each introduction to support your answer.

   _____

   _____

   _____

   _____

   _____

   _____

2. The strategies for arguing effectively were used in the second example. Identify the strategies and write the sentences that contains the strategies.

_____

_____

_____

_____

_____

_____

_____

_____

_____

_____

_____

3. Regardless of which introduction methods is used, based on the claim/thesis, as the essay develops, what will be addressed?

_____

_____

_____

_____

_____

_____

_____

_____

The Supporting Details

When you are reading argument, use PAUSE to make connections by annotating as you read. Write down things that catch your attention, and when you are finished, you can go back and analyze your notes for a clearer understanding. Make special note of any use of the appeals you identify.

When you become the writer, be sure to look for ideas that do not overlap but do support your opinion about the topic during prewriting and drafting. Then, write topic sentences that directly relate to the ideas in the thesis statement by linking back to the claim.

Many authors will conclude each body paragraph reiterating their stance. So should you when you write the body paragraphs of your argument. A concluding sentence will let the reader know you are finished discussing a particular point and are moving to the next point.

Fallacies

Fallacies are errors in logic. As you read an argument, you should duly note any such flaws or myths that weaken the argument. There are many different types of fallacies; when you encounter them, you will find that they erode the author's credibility and persuasiveness. Thus, you should avoid logical fallacies as you write your own argument to avoid losing credibility with your readers.

READING ARGUMENT

When you are reading an argument, evaluate and analyze the passage by taking the essay apart using PAUSE. Once you identify small connections, you will then be able to put the argument back together for a clearer meaning. Pay close attention to the transitional words and phrases the author uses to move smoothly through the passage from one piece of information to the next. These will signal the organizational pattern.

Also, make sure you are reading thoroughly and looking for an effective introduction that contains a claim statement that states the author's stance or main idea. You should attempt to locate the argument elements mentioned above and annotate as you read in order to organize the author's thoughts and reasons for the stance presented. Also, you should summarize each paragraph. Read in such a way that you find yourself questioning the issues being debated in order to gain a clearer meaning. It may also be beneficial to paraphrase the passage in your own words so that you are clear about what the author is trying to convey. As you read, look for fallacies, such as generalizations, or any other factors that may deter the reader from accepting the stance of the author.

Image © ARENA Creative, 2014. Used under license from Shutterstock, Inc.

After reading an argument, try to answer the following questions about the passage. Remember, these are the same questions your audience will attempt to answer after reading the arguments you write.

- ♦ Do you agree with the author's claim?
- ♦ Did you learn something new about the topic that could change your viewpoint?
- ♦ Do you want to know more about the topic?
- ♦ What are you supposed to do with the information you have just read?

Read Write! Activity 13.2

Read the essay below entitled "College Costs" by student Karelly Hernandez. Then, answer the questions that follow.

College Costs

by Karelly Hernandez

1   With every passing year, the costs for college seem to increase. As the costs increases, colleges are able to provide better supplies and an excellent faculty since the students help pay for them. Having a higher tuition is great because students will be guaranteed an excellent education. However, college costs should be lowered because more students will attend college, fewer students will be in debt, and students should not have to pay for their education.

2   First, more students will be able to attend college if the price is lowered. Many students are not able to attend college because of how much it costs. They want to have a higher education, but their financial problems will not allow them to be able to attend without owing a large amount of money at the end. Instead, they decide it will be better on them financially if they just get a job and save money until it is the right time for them to go to college. Usually, after waiting until they have enough money, many people tend to give up on ever attending college and just get a regular, low paying job. However, if the tuition is lowered, more students will be able to attend and afford the college that they want to go to. The success rate of high school students attending college will be high. When a college cost is lower, it seems more appealing to students. When a college appeals to students,

they will feel an urge to attend and become a college graduate. As college students graduate, they will leave their old jobs behind and get better jobs. These jobs will be the ones that they have been studying so hard for, and they will feel a sense of accomplishment. A lower college cost will help students get a higher education and achieve what they have been yearning to accomplish since they were children.

3   Secondly, if the cost for college is lowered, there will be less student debt. Students who have trouble paying for college seek every way to get financial aid. Usually, students apply for scholarships and student loans to help them pay for the classes they need to take. Many students who apply for student loans have trouble paying for them and eventually are $19,000 or more in debt. However, if college costs are lowered, students will not have to worry about being in debt. Students who are in debt are usually more stressed out than the people who are not in debt. If the tuition rate is lowered, they will not have to worry about trying to find a way to get money to pay the government back. People tend to have more problems if they are in debt than those who are not. While being in debt, all that goes through a student's mind is paying back his/her loans. When they are not in debt, students are focused. They are focused on what they are trying to achieve and become successful. All they focus on is school and being as successful as they can be. Being in debt will just get in the

way of students being happy and enjoying what they have accomplished. If students are in debt, their whole life will be focused on trying to pay off the loans. Students want to be able to afford a college without having any problems with the government.

4   Lastly, college costs should be lowered because students should not have to pay for their education. Education plays an important role in becoming successful. Many people want to be successful but cannot because college is too expensive. Although everybody wants to be a successful person, many people cannot be who they want to become because they are not able to attend college. Many people believe that college is starting to become unaffordable, and soon they will not be able to attend. If colleges become unaffordable, there will be fewer successful people in the world. Students should have the right to have a good education without having to pay for it. Having to pay for their education adds more stress to a student's life. If students are expected to be successful, why should they pay for what they are expected to do? It will be easier for students if they do not have to pay for college because they will not have to worry about owing money or not having the money to pay for the classes they need.

5   Many students want to be successful, but they cannot afford college. College costs should be lowered, so it can be affordable. If the college cost is lowered, there will be less student debt. Students who want to be successful should not have to pay for college. Education is an important thing in a person's life and should not be overly expensive.

1. Which appeal does the author use primarily to convince the reader? List some words that prove the appeal you chose is accurate.

   _____

   _____

   _____

2. What are the three major supporting details the author uses to back up her claim?

   _____

   _____

   _____

3. What should the reader be able to infer about the title? After reading the claim, what should the reader be able to deduce?

   _____

   _____

4. What connections can be made that prove the author's stance?

   _____

   _____

   _____

   _____

   _____

   _____

5. List several transition words the author chooses to include in order to move the reader from one point to the next.

_____

_____

_____

6. Do you agree with the author? Did your viewpoint change while you read the passage?

_____

_____

_____

_____

_____

_____

_____

_____

Read Write! Activity 13.3

Read the following article "The Argument Against Headphones" by Virginia Heffernan. Then write a response discussing whether you agree or disagree.

Virginia Heffernan is a contributing writer for *The New York Times*.

"Against Headphones"

by Virginia Heffernan

1   One in five teenagers in America can't hear rustles or whispers, according to a study published in August in The Journal of the American Medical Association. These teenagers exhibit what's known as slight hearing loss,

which means they often can't make out consonants like T's or K's, or the plinking of raindrops. The word "talk" can sound like "aw." The number of teenagers with hearing loss — from slight to severe — has jumped 33 percent since 1994.

2   Given the current ubiquity of personal media players — the iPod appeared almost a decade ago — many researchers attribute this widespread hearing loss to exposure to sound played loudly and regularly through headphones. (Earbuds, in particular, don't cancel as much noise from outside as do headphones that rest on or around the ear, so earbud users typically listen at higher volume to drown out interference.) Indeed, the August report reinforces the findings of a 2008 European study of people who habitually blast MP3 players, including iPods and smartphones. According to that report, headphone users who listen to music at high volumes for more than an hour a day risk permanent hearing loss after five years.

3   Maybe the danger of digital culture to young people is not that they have hummingbird attention spans but that they are going deaf.

4   The history of headphones has always been one of unexpected uses and equally unexpected consequences. Headphones were invented more than a century ago. According to some accounts, modern headphones were the

brainchild of Nathaniel Baldwin, a tinkerer from Utah who grew frustrated when he couldn't hear Mormon sermons over the noise of the crowds at the vast Salt Lake Tabernacle. Baldwin's device, which was designed first as an amplifier, came to incorporate two sound receivers connected by an operator's headband. Within each earphone was, according to legend, a *mile* of coiled copper wiring and a mica diaphragm to register the wire's signals with vibrations. When the Navy put in an order for 100 such Baldy Phones in 1910, Baldwin abandoned his kitchen workbench, hastily opened a factory and built the prosperous Baldwin Radio Company. His innovations were the basis of "sound powered" telephones, or phones that required no electricity, which were used during World War II.

5   It's not incidental that Baldwin imagined headphones first as a way to block out crowd noise and hear sermons. Workers and soldiers have long used them to mute the din of machinery or artillery while receiving one-way orders from someone with a microphone. From the beginning, it seems, headphones have been a technology of submission (to commands) and denial (of commotion). When World War II ended, submission-and-denial was exactly what returning veterans craved when they found themselves surrounded by the clamor and demands of the open-plan family rooms of the postwar suburbs. By then,

they knew what device provided it. In the '50s, John C. Koss invented a set of stereo headphones designed explicitly for personal music consumption. In that decade, according to Keir Keightley, a professor of media studies at the University of Western Ontario, middle-class men began shutting out their families with giant headphones and hi-fi equipment. Further, they recalled the sonar systems they saw at war.

6   The Walkman appeared in 1979, the invention of Sony, and headphones became part of a walking outfit. Headphones and earbuds are now used with MP3 players, mobile phones, tablet computers and laptops.

7   Most discussions of the transformation of music by digital technology focus on the production end. But headphones transform sound for the consumer too. Headphones are packed with technology. When an audio current passes through the device's voice coil, it creates an alternating magnetic field that moves a stiff, light diaphragm. This produces sound. If you think about all the recordings, production tricks, conversions and compressions required to turn human voices and acoustic instruments into MP3 signals, and *then* add the coil-magnet-diaphragm magic in our headphones, it's amazing that the intensely engineered frankensounds that hit our eardrums when we listen to iPhones are still called music.

8 Whatever you call it, children are listening to *something* on all these headphones — though "listening" is too limited a concept for all that headphones allow them to do. Indeed, the device seems to solve a real problem by simultaneously letting them have private auditory experiences and keeping shared spaces quiet. But the downside is plain, too: it's antisocial. As Llewellyn Hinkes Jones put it not long ago in The Atlantic: "The shared experience of listening with others is not unlike the cultural rituals of communal eating. Music may not have the primal necessity of food, but it is something people commonly ingest together."

9 Headphones work best for people who need or want to hear one sound story and no other; who don't want to have to choose which sounds to listen to and which to ignore; and who don't want their sounds overheard. Under these circumstances, headphones are extremely useful — and necessary for sound professionals, like intelligence and radio workers — but it's a strange fact of our times that this rarefied experience of sound has become so common and widespread. In the name of living a sensory life, it's worth letting sounds exist in their audio habitat more often, even if that means contending with interruptions and background sound.

10   Make it a New Year's resolution, then, to use headphones less. Allow kids and spouses periodically to play music, audiobooks, videos, movie, television and radio audibly. Listen to what they're listening to, and make them listen to your stuff. Escapism is great, and submission and denial, too, have their places. But sound thrives amid other sounds. And protecting our kids' hearing is not just as important as protecting their brains; it *is* protecting their brains.

WRITING ARGUMENT

When you write an argument, you will incorporate at least three reasons that you will support in the body of the essay. Each of the three body paragraphs will develop one of the points from the claim or thesis statement. Specific support is needed so that you express your argument in a well-thought out manner. Also, when you write, avoid using generalizations or insulting language because that will cause the reader to stop reading and dismiss the argument as irrational. The conclusion of an argument essay or passage brings the essay to a close by using a restatement of the claim. The call-to-action method is often used to end the argument essay. This conclusion method calls the readers to get out of their seats and do something about the topic.

> ➤ **Read Write! Tip**
> Recall in chapter 4 that you may be asked to write more than five paragraphs in your essay. In the argument essay, you may be required to add a fourth body paragraph addressing a counterclaim and providing a rebuttal. A counterclaim is a point that acknowledges the opposition, and the rebuttal counters the opposition, bringing the argument back to your viewpoint and should prove why your argument is stronger.

Argument Prewriting

Before you begin an argumentative essay, you should complete several prewriting strategies, such as free writing, listing, clustering, asking questions, outlining, and building a pyramid, to help you generate ideas.

Argument Claim/Thesis Statement

The thesis statement states the topic, offers the author's stance, and provides three reasons that will be developed in the rest of the essay.

Argument Body Paragraphs

Each body paragraph will begin with a topic sentence that includes a transitional word and one of the points from the claim/thesis statement. Several supporting sentences will follow in order to support the argument. Transitional words and phrases should be included throughout the paragraph in order to move from one piece of information to the next. A concluding sentence reiterating the stance should summarize and bring closure to the paragraph.

In argument essays, no first person pronouns like "I" or "we" are used in the claim statement or anywhere in the essay. Therefore, you absolutely cannot use any of the following phrases, "I think . . . ," "In my opinion, . . . ," or "I feel . . ." Using any of these phrases weakens your argument because the entire essay expresses your opinions. Instead, you should simply state the topic, your opinion about the topic, and three reasons.

Argument Conclusion

The conclusion should restate the claim/thesis, including the three main points used as a plan of development in the claim/thesis statement. Also, remember not to offer any new information in the conclusion paragraph.

> ➢ **Read Write! Tip**
> Professional writers may use first person pronouns in their persuasive writing; however, as a student writer, your professor will usually ask you to avoid first person pronouns when writing an argument. Recall that you cannot use second person pronouns (you, your, yours) either.

Argument Outline

The format of an argument essay is the same as a standard five-paragraph essay. Below is a basic outline.

I.   Introduction
    a. Introduction method
    b. Claim/Thesis statement containing the three topics that will be developed

II. Body 1
    a. Topic sentence for main point 1
    b. Supporting details
    c. A concluding sentence

III. Body 2
    a. Topic sentence for main point 2
    b. Supporting details
    c. A concluding sentence

IV. Body 3
    a. Topic sentence for main point 3
    b. Supporting details
    c. A concluding sentence

V.   Conclusion
    a. Claim/Thesis restatement
    b. Conclusion method

Read Write! Activity 13.4

Read the argument essay "Spare the Children" below. Then, answer the questions that follow.

Spare the Children

1   For several centuries, parents have thought that corporal punishment was a way to discipline children. During biblical times, people believed that it was a mandate from God to not spare disobedient children from harsh physical punishment. Proponents of spanking have said that spanking children teaches them how to be respectful towards authority. Several parents believe that because they were spanked as children that they should instill the same values into their own children. Granted, some children who are spanked tend to change their negative behavior and refrain from repeating certain offenses; however, there are negative consequences that result from spanking children. In recent years, the question of whether or not spanking is a healthy and effective form of discipline has been on the minds of many people. Parents should not spank children because it causes emotional, mental and physical harm.

2   First of all, when parents decide to spank their children, it could lead to emotional scarring. In addition to the physical scars a spanking can leave on a child's body, the emotional scars are far worse. Children who are spanked will often hide their emotions inside which will eventually lead to

them acting out in some other way. For example, when it comes to problem solving, they may resort to hitting and yelling as opposed to communicating effectively with others. They have been taught, through spanking, when someone does something wrong it is most important to make them feel a painful experience in order to reinforce positive behavior. Also, long term emotional problems may set in as a result of spanking. Children who are spanked tend to become less likely to tell the truth, fearing that they will be subjected to severe physical punishment. These emotional shortcomings often lead to children growing up and turning to a life of crime. Spanking causes feelings of self-worthlessness. For instance, children who are faced with childhood issues feel they cannot go to their parents for comfort fearing they may be punished for voicing their feelings and opinions. There are several options available to discipline a child for misbehavior, and spanking should never be an option.

3   Secondly, parents who spank their children are in danger of causing them to be harmed mentally. Children tend to have aggressive behaviors and are less likely to become an asset to society. Aside from the emotional stress spanking causes, mentally a child's brain and decision making skills are equally affected. Instead of being able to solve problems critically, weighing all of the

consequences surrounding their behavior, children who are spanked usually have one way of dealing with problems: violence. Also, children who are spanked do not perform well in school. They are apprehensive and untrusting of other adults who are in their lives fearing they will retaliate physically if they make a mistake or misbehave. Thus, children who are spanked at a young age tend to disregard authority outside the home resulting in juvenile delinquency and a lifetime of bad behavior. The mental harm spanking a child could cause is a reason to choose another discipline method other than spanking.

4   Most importantly, spanking children damages them physically. For instance, child abuse cases are at an all-time increase. Parents justify spanking their children so severely because it was that way when they were children. Many parents believe if a child's body is not covered with scars and bruises that the spanking was ineffective. Relying on what they were taught as children, some parents do not even know when the spanking should conclude, and consequently, many children are left battered to fend for themselves. Emergency rooms are filled with children who have been spanked too severely and they often have to get family services involved which could lead to the deterioration of the family unit. Spanking should be avoided in order prevent physical injuries to a child.

5   The use of physical punishment as a means of discipline is ineffective. Spanking causes children to be emotionally unstable while they are children and when they enter adulthood. Mentally, spanking causes children to view themselves as inferior to others which leads to acting out and aggressive behavior. The physical scarring that spanking yields is the cause of many children being taken away from their families. There is much to consider when it comes to disciplining children, and spanking should not be an option.

1. What does the author continuously say about spanking?

   _____

   _____

   _____

2. What three points does the author use as the foundation of the argument?

   _____

   _____

   _____

3. What pattern of organization does the author use? How do you know?

   _____

   _____

   _____

4. Highlight the thesis restatement.

5. What transitional words does the author use to help the reader move smoothly through the essay?

_____

_____

_____

_____

Read Write! Activity 13.5

Find two opposing arguments about the same topic and then use PAUSE to break them down. As you do so, be sure to take special note of any appeal(s) and argument strategies discussed in this chapter that the authors use to persuade the reader. Then, write a short summary of each argument. Be sure to write using your own words without taking away the authors' meaning from the passages.

_____

_____

Read Write! Review Questions: Reading and Writing Argument

1. List three strategies an author could use and that you should use when writing an argument.

2. True or False: The claim statement and the main idea of an argument should be different.

3. When you read and write the conclusion of an argument, what must be evident?

4. What must you continuously do when you write the body paragraphs of an argument? What should the supporting details of an argument written by another author do?

_____

_____

Suggested Argument Essay Topics

1. Should concealed handguns be allowed on college campuses?
2. Should college professors date their students?
3. Should colleges enforce dress codes?
4. Should couples be required to attend six months of premarital counselling before getting married?
5. Should ex-felons be able to vote?
6. Should gay and lesbian couples be allowed to adopt children?

7. Should corporal punishment be allowed in public schools?
8. Should third trimester abortions be legal?

_____

_____

Read Write! Connection: Chapter 13

Go on a social media site and read a post about a controversial issue. Verify whether the strategies for arguing effectively are included in the post. Then, decide whether or not the author supports their stance. Finally, determine how you feel about the post. Do you agree or disagree with the author? Why or why not?

_____

Chapter 14
Summarizing

Key Term

summary

When you are asked to summarize a book you have read, a movie you have seen, or even a speech you have listened to, what is expected is that you read, watch, or listen to a book, movie, or speech and turn it into a smaller version mentioning only the details that are relevant and important. It is not necessary that you recount all details in their entirety; it is only necessary that you make clear to the reader who, what, when, where, why, and how the most important details occurred. After reading a summary, you should know the gist—the main idea or the essential part—of what occurs in the book, movie, chapter, essay, or speech without having to read, see, or hear it in its entirety. A **summary**, therefore, is a condensed version of a longer piece that captures the author's main idea and key points in the order that they appear.

When you are reading or writing a summary, you can compare it to packing for a trip. Most people who go on trips usually pack things they will not even need. They throw everything and anything into their suitcases. For example, if they are going on a trip for seven days, they bring 15 outfits, six pairs of shoes, and three jackets. However, if they have de-

cided not to check their luggage and do carry on, then they must pack wisely and only bring essential items, such as four outfits that can be mixed and matched, one pair of shoes, and one jacket. Careful thought must be given to what is brought; otherwise, they risk packing too much and having to check and pay for their overstuffed bag.

Like when a traveler packs his/her carry on, careful thought must be given to what is put into a summary. If too much is included, then the reader might as well have read the original writing, watched the whole movie, or listened to the entire speech. However, if not enough information or the wrong information is provided, then the summary is useless.

When you *write* a summary, you must only include the key information; the nonessential details should be left out. Have you ever heard a police officer say, "Just the facts, please, only give me the facts"? The officer is only after the key details regarding the accident. He/she does not need to know that you were listening to your favorite Bruno Mars song when you were rear ended sitting at the red light. That detail can be left out; the officer is interested in, however, whether or not you were wearing your seat belt. Therefore, when you write a summary, you leave out your thoughts and opinions, focusing only on the main idea and the relevant supporting details.

When you *read* a summary, whether one you have written or someone else has written, you are getting the abbreviated edition of a longer piece of work. As you learned in Chapter 1: The Reading Process, a summary aids in your reading comprehension and study skills because it requires you to sift through the material, locate key information, and state it mostly in your own words. When you read a summary someone else has written, such as in a chapter summary in your biology textbook, the author will recap, or restate, the most important points that were made in the chapter. Reading summaries or creating questions from summaries will ensure that you are studying the most important information that may appear on quizzes or tests.

BENEFITS OF SUMMARZING

Summarizing effectively will enhance the following:

♦ *Reading comprehension*: As you read the article, passage, essay, or text, you are using the PAUSE strategy to extract the main idea and the supporting ideas.
♦ *Study skills:* Turning headings, major components, and key terms into questions reinforces learning and enables you to anticipate quiz and exam questions and identify the main idea. When summarizing, however, you are focusing only on answering the questions that will help you identify the main idea.
♦ *Critical thinking skills:* Since you cannot include everything in your summary, you must sort through information and classify it as either relevant or irrelevant.
♦ *Writing skills:* Condensing the author's main idea and supporting details into succinct sentences without changing the original intent strengthens your writing.
♦ *Organizational skills:* Not only must the main idea be included but so must the author's supporting details; these must be restated in the original order that they appear.

SUMMARIES AS MULTIPLE CHOICE QUESTIONS

On some exams, you may be asked to pick out the choice that best summarizes the passage. As you read the choices, you want to select the one that overall conveys the main idea of the passage. You can eliminate the choices that do not adequately restate the main idea because they have misinterpreted it, focused on a minor detail, or contain information that is not stated in the passage.

> **Read Write! Tip**

Before you read the choices that best summarize the passage, mentally formulate your own brief summary. Then, select the choice that is similar to what you would have written.

Read Write! Activity 14.1

Before reading the passage about heroes below, reflect on the idea of heroes by answering the following questions:

1. Who are some of your heroes or sheroes? What makes them heroic to you?

   _____

   _____

   _____

   _____

   _____

2. The book that the passages come from was published in 1907. It only contains male heroes, such as Hercules, Robin Hood, King David, and two presidents: George Washington and Abraham Lincoln. List three female heroes in addition to any you listed in question 1.

   _____

   _____

   _____

   _____

   _____

Read Write! Activity 14.2

Below are several paragraphs taken from *Heroes Every Child Should Know: Tales for Young People of the World's Heroes in all Ages*, which was edited by Hamilton Wright Mabie. Read each paragraph carefully, utilizing PAUSE. Then, circle the answer that best summarizes each one.

Hamilton Wright Mabie (1846-1916) was a lawyer, essayist, critic, and editor of several anthologies for children.

Excerpt from *Heroes Every Child Should Know*

Edited by Hamilton Wright Mabie

Paragraph #1:

If there had been no real heroes, there would have been created imaginary ones, for men cannot live without them. The hero is just as necessary as the farmer, the sailor, the carpenter and the doctor; society could not get on without him. There have been a great many different kinds of heroes, for in every age and among every people the hero has stood for the qualities that were most admired and sought after by the bravest and best; and all ages and peoples have imagined or produced heroes as inevitably as they have made ploughs for turning the soil or ships for getting through the water or weapons with which to fight their enemies. To be some kind of a hero has been the ambition of spirited boys from the beginning of history; and if you want to know what the men and women of a country care for most, you must study their heroes. To the boy the hero stands for the highest success: to the grown man and woman he stands for the deepest and richest life.

A. Heroes, whether real or imaginary, have always been necessary in society. They are individuals who encourage others to strive to be the best they can be. There has always been a cause or a reason for heroes. Heroes are important to mankind because they represent supreme success.

B. Real heroes are people who have a great work ethic and a story to tell. Most heroes are fictitious characters who inspire us to be successful in life. Boys and girls love heroes. Heroes can be fictitious or fake. They will always exist.

C. Ambitious people aim to be heroes. They want to be loved by everyone because it makes them feel important. Heroes are important to those who love and respect them. Heroes tell much about the people who created them.

D. None of the above

Paragraph #2

It was not long before men saw that strong men could not work for themselves without working for others, and there came in very early the idea of service as part of the idea of heroism, and the demi-gods, who were among the earliest heroes, were servants as well as masters. Hercules, the most powerful of the heroes to Greek and Roman boys, was set to do the most difficult things not for himself but for others. He destroyed lions, hydras, wild boars, birds with brazen beaks and wings, mad bulls, many-headed monsters, horses which fed on human flesh, dragons, he mastered the three-headed dog Cerberus, he tore asunder the rocks at the Strait of Gibraltar which bear his name to open a channel between the Mediterranean and the Atlantic. He fought the Centaur and brought back Alcestis, the wife of Admetus, from the pale regions of death where she had gone to save her husband's life. In all these labors, which were so great that works of extraordinary magnitude have since been called Herculean, the brave, patient, suffering hero, was helping other people rather than helping himself.

A. Demi-gods had to know how to serve others. Hercules rescued Alcestis while she was trying to save her husband's life. Heroes like Hercules have to be able to serve as well as lead.

B. Hercules served others more than himself. Although he possessed amazing strength and is noted for his amazing feats, the positive attributes he possessed set him apart from other mythical heroes.

C. Greek and Roman boys always viewed the demi-gods as heroes. Their goal as they were growing up was to be both a servant and a master. The boys knew it was important to labor in order to be seen as a hero. They looked up to Hercules for this reason.

D. It is selfish to think of only oneself. Greek and Roman demi-gods learned the importance of helping others. They fought bravely to show the power they possessed but were always reminded to help others more than they helped themselves.

Paragraph #3

The men whose bravery and great deeds are described in these pages have been selected not because they are faultless in character and life, but because they were brave, generous, self-forgetful, self-sacrificing and capable of splendid deeds. Men love and honor them not only because they owe them a great deal of gratitude, but because they see in their heroes the kind of men they would like to be; for the possibilities of the heroic are in almost all men. Stories of the heroes have often made other men strong and brave and true in the face of great perils and tasks, and this book is put forth in the faith that it will not only pass on the fame of the heroes of the past but help make heroes in the present.

A. Most heroes are faultless, and that is what makes them stand apart. The strength they possess along with their giving attitudes makes others want to live up to their standards. Heroes are needed in order to show others how to live.

B. Only the best and strongest individuals can be considered heroes. The fact that they possess humanlike qualities allows regular individuals to see hope in one day becoming a hero.

C. People who aspire to be heroes should view the task of a hero as one that is not completed by many. They are expected to encourage others. When they fail, it is indeed a huge blow to mankind.

D. Heroes are labeled as such because even though they have human qualities, they allow the positive attributes of giving and selflessness to define their character in order to be an encouragement to others. Their stories allow others to see that they can be heroes, too.

FORMAL SUMMARIZING

In addition to selecting the best choice that summarizes the passages or writing a summary as part of PAUSE, you may be asked to write a more formal summary.

Structure of a Formal Summary

Your professor may ask you to submit a summary for a grade or to ensure that you are understanding what you are reading. Formal summaries vary in length based on the length of the original work. For example, if you are summarizing a book, your essay may be three to five pages in length. If you are summarizing a movie, it could range from one to two pages. If you are summarizing a three- to five-page essay or article, then your summary should range between one to two pages. Always check with your instructor for the exact length requirement.

Formal summaries contain the following:

♦ The title of the passage—placed in quotation marks if it is an article, essay, a speech, or a student's paper; italicized if typed or underlined if handwriting the title of books or movies
♦ The author's name if known—use the author's first and last name the first time it is mentioned in your summary. After that, refer to the author by his/her last name only.
♦ The main idea of the passage stated in your own words

- The major supporting details also stated in your own words
- If you do use any of the author's exact words, they should be used sparingly and placed in quotation marks.
- Present tense verbs are typically used when writing a summary—the author discusses . . . the writer explains . . . the essay addresses . . .

Now that you know the structure of a summary, you can use this knowledge to break down a passage, an article, an essay, a movie, a speech, or a text in anticipation of summarizing it.

Writing a Formal Summary

1. Read the passage prior to writing your summary. Use the prereading and annotating strategies. Reread and further annotate as needed or create a graphic organizer.
2. Use one of the prewriting strategies, such as outlining. Prewriting will allow you to generate your thoughts for your summary.
3. Write your first draft.
4. Begin your summary by stating the title of the passage and the author's name. Then, state the main idea in one or more sentences depending on the length of the summary.
5. State the major supporting details in the order they were listed in the original source, leaving out irrelevant ideas. The length requirement will determine if these supporting details are explained in one paragraph or in several paragraphs.
6. Review your summary to determine if it presents an overview of the original source and if any more information is needed. Add more information and revise as needed.
7. Unlike other writings, summaries do not have a separate concluding paragraph or require restatement of the main idea. However, if in the conclusion the author includes important information, such as something that happens in the future, a reason one outcome is more likely than another, or why one subject is preferred over the other, then that should be addressed in your summary, as well.
8. Proofread your summary, checking for clarity and use of present tense verbs. Remember to only use the author's first and last name at the beginning of the summary, and after that first reference, refer to the author by his/her last name only for the duration of the summary.
9. Cite your sources as required by your instructor. Some instructors may require you to write a separate Works Cited page. Refer to Chapter 7: Using Sources in Your Writing for more information regarding how to do this.

Image © biletskiy, 2014. Used under license from Shutterstock, Inc.

Image © Stephen B. Goodwin, 2014. Used under license from Shutterstock, Inc.

Read the essay "The Conflicting Ideals of Two Black Leaders" by Kenasia M. Johnson. Notice that the essay has been annotated prior to being summarized. The main idea has been highlighted in yellow, the major supporting ideas have been bolded, and other key details have been underlined.

> Kenasia Johnson is a 22-year-old ABC News producer. At the age of 18, she obtained an Associate of Arts from the Richland Collegiate Academy at Richland College in Dallas, TX. She majored in Broadcast Journalism at The University of North Texas and earned her bachelor's degree at age 20. She will start graduate school in fall 2017.

The Conflicting Ideals of Two Black Leaders

by Kenasia Johnson

1   Throughout African-American history, the ability to be heard by mainstream America in order to have various issues addressed has been a major challenge. Many prominent black leaders like **Booker T. Washington** and **W.E.B. DuBois** attempted to find solutions to gaining prosperity amongst African-Americans. Although Washington and DuBois had the same common goal—to enhance the success of African-Americans, both men had strikingly different views of the way to meet those goals. The pursuits of economic, political and social rights for African-Americans were conflicting ideals for Washington and DuBois.

2   The forecast for **economic growth** for African-Americans in the late 19th and early 20th century was not promising. Many freedmen were not receiving the wages they worked for, and land was not fairly given out to blacks.

Washington believed that the best way for African-Americans to prosper as a race was to give up all social and political rights and focus on economic growth. In his infamous Atlanta Compromise Speech of 1895, Washington makes the following statement, "We shall prosper in proportion as we learn to dignify and glorify common labor and put brains and skill into the common occupations of life . . ." Washington suggested that African-Americans must take the freedoms that they want from mainstream society in small increments. He believed that blacks cannot ask for everything all at once. Once the black man can appreciate the value of labor, then will mainstream society be willing to consider the other liberties blacks have continually strived for. Washington's counterpart, W.E.B. DuBois gave great criticism to the influential leader's view of the prosperity of African-Americans. DuBois questioned Washington's philosophy on economic growth by asking how can blacks ever progress in America if they have to sacrifice what should be "inalienable rights" to all citizens. In DuBois' essay, "The Souls of Black Folk: Of Booker T. Washington and Others," he viewed the surrender of political and social rights by African-Americans as an act of submissiveness. DuBois states, "He [meaning Washington] insists on thrift and self-respect, but at the same time counsels a silent submission to civic inferiority such as is bound to sap the manhood of any race in the long run." <u>DuBois suggested that the</u> <u>only way that blacks could ever gain economic growth was to have a voice</u> <u>in politics</u>. Both Washington and DuBois had a different vision of the way African-Americans should gain economic success in mainstream America.

3   Not only did the two men differ in how African-Americans should strive for economic success, but they also differ in **the role of politics**. <u>Washington</u> <u>had great belief that due to the circumstances that blacks were in, they should</u> <u>give up **political matters**</u> such as the right to vote and accept **segregation**. He insisted that African-Americans show mainstream society that they were loyal and hardworking citizens. Towards the middle of his "Atlanta Compromise" speech, Washington makes the statement, "It is at the bottom of life we must begin and not the top. Nor should we permit our grievances to overshadow our opportunities." <u>Washington urged that blacks advocate a gradual approach to</u> <u>political growth</u> to avoid retaliation from mainstream America. In contrast, <u>DuBois believed that African-Americans should demand their political rights</u>. He did not believe that blacks should just accept discrimination. DuBois states his view on the right to vote by saying, "It is utterly impossible, under modern competitive methods, for workmen and property-owners to defend their rights and exist without the right of suffrage." <u>DuBois suggested that having</u>

the ability to vote and be involved in politics can serve as a "self-defense" mechanism for African-Americans. Their views of political rights were of great conflict between Washington and DuBois.

4   The most controversial issue that Washington and DuBois had opposing views on was the **social rights value of education**. During slavery, African-Americans were prohibited to learn how to read or write. Education was not accessible to most slaves. After reconstruction, many African-Americans wanted to attain an education and become literate like their white counter-parts. Washington believed that an industrial education would greatly benefit blacks. The Tuskegee Institute founded by Washington and other prominent black leaders taught African-Americans practical skills, such as basic farming and economics. Washington ends his "Atlanta Compromise" speech by saying, "The opportunity to earn a dollar in a factory just now is worth infinitely more than the opportunity to spend a dollar in an opera house." Washington suggested that an industrial education should be the focus for African-Americans if they want to progress as a race. DuBois questioned Washington's close-minded view of blacks to strive for an industrial education. In his "Souls of Black Folks" essay, DuBois shows tough criticism towards Washington's philosophy of education. DuBois states, "He advocates

common-school and industrial training, and depreciates institutions of higher learning." DuBois implied that Washington is not considering that some blacks may have abilities that are suitable for liberal arts schools. DuBois <u>does not agree that an industrialized institution is the only way that African-Americans can showcase their talents</u>. DuBois then suggested that Washington is contradicting himself when he states, "But neither the Negro common-schools, nor Tuskegee itself could remain open a day were it not for teachers trained in Negro colleges." DuBois challenged Washington by saying the people who are teaching in "industrial" schools typically come from a liberal arts background and would be just as beneficial in society as blacks who went to trade schools.

5   Washington and DuBois' goal for the advancement of African-Americans economically, politically, and socially played a vital role in American history. Both leaders ironically had the same goal, but with drastically different ways of obtaining it. <u>DuBois was not close-minded to the idea of blacks having an economic, political and social agenda all at once</u>. He believed that each agenda could coherently exist. Unlike Washington, DuBois believed that African-Americans were capable of much more than just working industrial jobs. DuBois saw great potential in his people to obtain not only an industrial

education but also a liberal arts education. <u>DuBois' philosophy on how blacks could succeed as a race would be the more practical</u>. Washington and DuBois both served not only as great black leaders in America, but as the voice for many African-Americans who went through constant struggles to gain **equality and acceptance in mainstream society**.

Courtesy of Kenasia M. Johnson

Summary Example

A Summary of "The Conflicting Ideals of Two Black Leaders"

In Kenasia Johnson's essay "The Conflicting Ideals of Two Black Leaders," she discusses the opposing viewpoints of two famous African-American leaders: Booker T. Washington and W.E.B. DuBois. Both men desired the success of African-Americans. However, they differed on how to go about achieving it in regards to three key factors: economics, politics, and social rights.

One way they differed is in regards to economic rights. Johnson states that Washington wanted African-Americans to postpone pursuing their political and social rights and focus on their economic rights. In Washington's "Atlanta

Compromise" speech of 1895, he states that their rights must be asked for slowly one at a time to avoid a backslash. If African-Americans show that they are willing to work hard, then in time, they will receive additional rights. According to Johnson, Dubois, on the other hand, states in "The Souls of Black Folk: Of Booker T. Washington and Others," that the three are too closely related to petition for them one at a time.

Johnson states that another way that the two leaders differed is in their view of the role that politics should play. Washington wanted African-Americans to give up asking for the right to vote and to go along with segregation. DuBois, however, believed that African-Americans must petition for their political rights as a means to protect their economic rights.

The third way the two men differed involved their view on the social rights of education. Washington wanted blacks to pursue learning a trade while DuBois believed African-Americans should pursue both learning a trade and a higher education.

Johnson concludes her essay by recapping the three ways the men differed in how blacks could gain their rights and be accepted in mainstream society. The author ends by stating that DuBois' viewpoints on how African-Americans could be successful was the "more practical."

WRITING A RESPONSE TO A READING

Sometimes in addition to writing a summary, you will be asked to respond to what you have read. In other words, the assignment may require you to evaluate what you have read by including your reaction to the reading, your thoughts about it, or how well you feel the writer conveyed his/her message.

Reading Response Example

A Reading Response to "The Conflicting Ideals of Two Black Leaders"

The author Kenasia Johnson uses the comparison-contrast pattern, focusing on contrast as she discusses the diametrical opposed viewpoints of Booker T. Washington and W.E.B. DuBois in her essay "The Conflicting Viewpoints of Two Black Leaders." Johnson maintains a balanced approached to the two men throughout her essay until the conclusion, where she states her belief that DuBois' plan would better serve African-Americans.

Although I have not read the two articles that Johnson references in her essay, I am familiar with the two famous black leaders. During black history month last year, a mock debate was organized with a history professor portraying Washington, a government professor portraying DuBois, and another history professor serving as a moderator. The moderator asked a series of questions to her colleagues who were portraying the two leaders. After reading Johnson's essay, their responses and their attire make more sense. For example, the professor portraying Washington wore overalls and talked about the value of learning a trade and having patience. On the other hand, the professor who portrayed DuBois wore a suit with a bow tie and spoke of the urgency of African-Americans receiving their economic, political, and social rights.

Although I understand Washington wanting to move slowly to avoid upsetting mainstream America because of the danger of physical violence, like Johnson, I believe that DuBois' desire to have African-Americans pursue all of their rights is the better course of action. While things have changed greatly today for African-Americans, other minorities, and women, America still has work to do. For example, in spite of there being black billionaires and women at the helm of Fortune 500 companies, the majority of African-Americans and other minorities still live in poverty, and women do not earn as much as men. Furthermore, in spite of having a black president and women serving in Congress, new voter I.D laws threaten many Americans' right to vote. Finally, although there are black graduates of technical, liberal arts, medical, and law schools, students who attend high schools in affluent neighborhoods are more likely to go to college than those from poorer neighborhoods. I wonder what Washington and DuBois would think of our country today.

Read Write! Review Questions: Summarizing

1. What is a summary?
2. What details should a writer include in a summary?
3. What should a writer do before summarizing?
4. List at least two things a writer should not add to a summary.
5. True or False: When writing a reading response, you may include your thoughts and opinions.

Read Write! Connection: Chapter 14

Read the following social media post written by an African-American and write a one or two sentence summary. Then, write a response regarding your thoughts on the use of the N word and other derogatory words, like the B word.

Free speech is not expensive. It's FREE. . . . The race that originated the N word won way back then because the word served its purpose. (Degrade and demoralize) NOW...The only race who has the real problem with the N word is the BLACK race. . . . most other races train their children to either 1.NEVER use it OR 2. never use it in public. . . . the problem is. : WE decided to turn a word (the "gga" spelling) that has been used for decades as a PRIVATE "term of endearment" (whether it is right or wrong) into a PUBLIC spectacle. . . . #theywonagain #dontlikeitkeepscrolling

Chapter 15
Reading and Writing Other Rhetorical Modes

Key Terms

Process, Classification, Description, Combined Modes

In chapters 8–14, you learned how to read and write exemplification, descriptive-narrative, comparison-contrast, cause and effect, definition, argument, and a formal summary. This chapter will briefly introduce you to the following rhetorical modes:

- Process
- Classification
- Description
- Combined Modes

PROCESS

A **process** essay explains how something works or how something is done. Every day you use processes as you navigate through your life. Several processes are often done unconsciously and in no formal order, such as getting ready for school in the morning or deciding what you and your friends will do for fun over the weekend. There are some processes, however, that you must do in a particular order following specific directions, such as changing a car tire or performing a tonsillectomy.

When you *read* a process essay, you should focus on the steps that the author provides. These should be clear so that they can be replicated by anyone who attempts to follow them. Below are some additional tips for reading process passages.

- What can you infer about the passage from reading the title?
- Is the text written in second person or third person? In process essay writing, it is acceptable to use second person.
- What is the tone of the reading? Is it serious or humorous? Is it consistent throughout?
- What is the main idea of the passage? Where is it located?
- Is the passage written in the standard five-paragraph essay format? If so, does it contain a plan of development (the three main points listed) or is it a general thesis where there are more than three points that are not listed?

♦ What is the organizational pattern of the text?

♦ Is the author credible? Do you trust the advice being offered?

♦ Were you able to follow the steps or did you become frustrated?

♦ What additional clarification of the steps could have been provided?

When you *write* a process essay on how something is done, you should choose a topic that you know a great deal about because you are considered "the expert," meaning your essay must contain all of the information needed for your reader to follow your advice. You must include in your list of steps tips to help the reader know if he/she is doing the procedure correctly, why it is important to follow this advice, what happens if this advice is not followed, what precautions should be taken, and what problems could occur. Besides providing steps that are clear and easy to follow, you have the added responsibility of making the process writing interesting to your reader, as well. Remember, in process essay writing, it is usually acceptable to use second person; however, check with your instructor to be sure or for more specific guidelines.

Image © Monkey Business Images, 2014. Used under license from Shutterstock, Inc.

Below is a process essay entitled "How to Become a Successful Student in College" by student Jennifer Loredo. Use PAUSE to break this essay down to its basic elements in preparation to write your own.

How to become a Successful Student in College

by Jennifer Loredo

1   How can you become a successful student? Can you study more often, participate in class, or maybe pay more attention? You may have your faults that prevent you from being successful in college. However, once you find out what they are, make a plan to strengthen any weak areas that are affecting you. You can be a successful student by attending class, paying attention, and doing your work.

2   First, your attendance is very important to be successful in college. You should attend class because you will miss class work if you do not attend. If you miss class work, your grade will go down. If your final grade falls below a 70, you will fail that class for the semester. If you fail that semester, you will have to repeat the same class the next semester. If you do the same thing that semester, you will have to pay double on the third try. You pay for the classes, so you should go to get what you paid for. Put everything aside the night before class so that you are not rushing the next day, and go to class. In addition, if your friends invite you out to a party during the week and you know you have an 8 a.m. class, you must either say no or go for just a little while, deciding in advance what time you will leave. If your friends give you a hard time about leaving, remind them that you are in college. If they still give you a hard time, you may be able to only spend time with them on the weekends after all of your work for class is done. You must not let anything get in your way of going to class; otherwise, you are affecting your future. You are the only one who can change it. Ultimately, attendance is very important to your success in college.

3   Secondly, paying attention in class plays a big role in your success in college. If you do not pay attention in your class, how will you understand

any work that you need to do? For example, your instructor is explaining a big assignment and you are playing on your phone. You did not hear the instructions or the due date. How will you get your work done and turned in on time? Consequently, you will have to ask one of your peers because he/she was paying attention. However, now you are depending on someone else to give you all the key information that you need instead of getting it first-hand yourself. You should leave your phone in the car or a locker so you will pay attention. Paying attention in class is very important to your success in college.

4   Finally, you must do all your assignments. If you go through all the trouble to enroll, apply for financial aid, and buy your books, you should make time to do your work. When you do your work, you show concern for your education. If you choose not to do your work, you will get zeroes. Do you want your transcripts to show a GPA below your potential? Most students do not want that. When you get your assignment, make certain you understand it before you leave class. Next, if you have an hour break between classes, instead of conversing with friends, see if you can get started on it or even finish it. If you do not have enough time to do it between classes, let it be the first thing you do when you get home. Finally, do your homework before you hang out with friends or go out. Homework must be a priority.

5   Attending class, paying attention, and doing your work are important to your success in college. Do not enroll and waste your money or time if you cannot take college life seriously. College is necessary if you want to provide your family and yourself with a good future.

Suggested Process Essay Topics

1. How to make a good impression on a first date
2. How to be named Employee of the Month
3. How to break up with someone (make it serious or humorous)

CLASSIFICATION

A *classification* essay places ideas into categories or groups. For example, you may classify music into various genres, such as *classical, country, pop, hip hop,* or *rock.* In addition, you could classify students by how they approach work given in class: *the serious student, the some timey,* and the *slacker.* Also, you could classify students by their behavior: the *brown noser, the studious, the charmer, the lazy,* and *the clown.* The purpose of classification writing is to make people, things, or ideas more understandable by placing them into categories or groups.

As you *read* a classification essay, you should look for the signal words, addition and example transitions, that signal the pattern. Below are some additional tips for reading classification passages.

- ♦ What can you infer from reading the title?
- ♦ Is the text told in first person or third person?
- ♦ What is the main idea of the passage? Where is it located?
- ♦ What is the organizational pattern of the text?
- ♦ Do the examples provided in the passage explain or clarify the various categories?
- ♦ What other categories could have been included?
- ♦ Does the author have a bias towards one category or the other?
- ♦ Does the author make any comments that make the passage or any aspect of it memorable?

When you *write* a classification essay, you should follow the writing process. As you complete the steps, focus on making sure that your categories do not overlap and that you provide specific, clear examples that clarify or explain the categories.

Below is a classification essay entitled "Types of Exercisers." Use PAUSE to break this essay down to its basic elements in preparation to write your own.

Types of Exercisers

1   I am aware that exercise plays a crucial part in the health and well-being of individuals. Consequently, I try to partake in various activities, such as playing tennis, walking, jogging, and swimming. Though my experience with exercise is limited, I have observed various types of exercisers who are distinguishable by their commitment to fitness.

2   The first type is the "gung ho" exerciser. These individuals are dedicated to exercising daily, 365 days a year. I see them running in the heat of summer and in the cold of winter. Nothing keeps them from working out. Like the postal workers who deliver mail in all types of weather, the "gung hoers" work out in the rain, the sleet, and the snow; nothing keeps them from exercising. Although I doubt I will ever be in this category, I respect their commitment; they are my exercise heroes.

3   The second type of exerciser is the seasonal exerciser. Their commitment is strong at certain times of the year, but then it fizzles out and becomes nonexistent. At the beginning of each year, the seasonal exercisers are signing up at gyms, purchasing new tennis shoes, and scheduling aerobic classes.

They are determined that this year they will be successful with their New Year's resolution to get off of the couch and onto the court. Although they have well-laid plans, they are back on the couch sooner than later. However, once summer arrives, they return to the gym, lace back up their tennis shoes, and pull out their aerobic mats. They may manage to go for a month or maybe two, but after they return from their summer vacation, they heed the call of the couch once again and promise to start fresh in the upcoming new year.

4   The third type is the occasional exerciser. These individuals are committed more than the seasonal exercisers but not as much as the "gung ho." They exercise consistently whether it is once or twice a week or once or twice a month. Their dedication ensures that they schedule workouts into their routines and that they keep their commitments to sweat, stretch, or swim. The occasional exerciser strives to do more but is determined not to do less.

5   The fourth type is the good intentions exerciser. These individuals rally their coworkers to walk during lunch time or right after work, but for some reason, they are always missing when it is time to work out. They are swamped with work or have to rush home to attend their child's recital. Something always gets in the way of their ability to exercise. However,

they proudly wear their sporty workout clothes and expensive sneakers. They dress for workout success, but they never seem to succeed at actually working out.

6   Being committed to exercising is tough. Therefore, I respect the "gung ho" exercisers who will not let anything get in their way. I also respect the seasonal exercisers who start strong and then slip back into old habits, for at least they are trying. The occasional exercisers are where I would like to see myself; they are committed to working out. Just as soon as I find the time in my hectic schedule, I will start working out, but in the meantime, check out my new treadmill; it makes an excellent clothes rack.

Suggested Classification Essay Topics

1. Classify types of teachers.
2. Classify types of cell phone users.
3. Classify types of neighbors.
4. Classify types of coworkers.
5. Classify types of pet owners.

DESCRIPTION

In chapter 9, descriptive-narrative was addressed. However, description can be its own rhetorical mode. The purpose of description is to create an image in a reader's mind using only words.

When *reading* a descriptive essay, you should focus on the dominant impression, or mood, which is the overall feeling of what is being described, and literary devices, which are the supporting details. You should be able to picture the topic in your mind as you read.

When *writing* description, you develop an essay that has a dominant impression. The use of sensory imagery, which appeals to the five senses, and literary devices distinguish this mode. The more sensory imagery used, the stronger the descriptive essay will be. When you write a descriptive essay, you are not telling a story; you are only describing something.

Below is a descriptive essay entitled "Crimson and Burnt Orange." Use PAUSE to break this essay down to its basic elements in preparation to write your own.

Crimson and Burnt Orange

1   In early October every year, the Red River Rivalry is held at the original Cotton Bowl in Fair Park in Dallas, Texas. This football game between the University of Oklahoma and the University of Texas is highly anticipated every year by Sooner and Longhorn fans alike. It is played in Dallas because it is considered "neutral ground" for the two teams, each traveling approximately 200 miles to reach Fair Park. Tickets can cost hundreds of dollars, and people scalp them for even more. The Red River Rivalry is fun because of the fans, the stadium, and the fair.

2   First, the fans make the Red River Rivalry an entertaining experience. They come dressed in their teams' colors: Sooners in crimson and cream and Longhorns in burnt orange and white. The Sooners are a red river flowing into the stadium, and the Longhorns look like a wildfire. Everyone is loud and raucous, shouting school chants and taunting and jeering at the opposing team. Inside, the fans are all crowded in like sardines, packed shoulder to shoulder, but that is part of the fun. They eat nachos smothered in bright orange cheese and drink hoppy smelling beer and bottled water that is cool

on the tongue. When the Sooners score, the OU fans roar with triumph, and the Ruf/Neks, OU's men's spirit group, fire their shotguns with a loud crack. If the Longhorns score, the fans scream and shout with joy, and the Texas Cowboys, UT's men's spirit group, let UT's canon, Smokey, boom. Some of the biggest fans of the teams are the two university marching bands. The horns flash in the sun, and the cymbals are shiny gold coins. The drummers pound the snares and basses, creating a pulsing beat. The music of both bands parades around the stadium merrily, weaving in and out of the crowd like a dancer. The fans sway and move like a sea of grass in the wind. The exuberant fans make the Red River Rivalry a blast.

3   Next, the stadium and its field are integral parts of the enjoyment of the Red River Rivalry. The Cotton Bowl is big and old, and it is amazing to know that Sooner and Longhorn fans have gathered there for over a century of football games. The seating is split 50/50, so half the stadium is crimson and half is burnt orange. The seats are shiny and silver and filled with a diverse group of people. Some seats are practically in the clouds while others are right on the sideline. Inside, delicious smells from the concession stands waft through the corridors, and lines for the water fountain and bathroom stretch for miles, but it is worth it in the end. Next, the field below is painted

as green as an emerald with bright white lines to mark the boundaries of the game. The south end zone is a deep red, and the north end zone is a rusty orange. The replay screen up in the south end zone is a giant, looming over the OU side of the field and casting a shadow that helps fans find relief from the sun. Down on the field, the players fight to win the game. Footballs arc like rainbows across the green grass, and the running backs are cheetahs rushing across the field to catch them. The defense plows through the offense, trying to sack the quarterback. The fans roar with approval, and the sound echoes off the stadium's high walls. The Cotton Bowl is a fun place for the Red River Rivalry.

4   Finally, no matter who wins the game, fans flow out of the stadium to enjoy the State Fair of Texas. It seems everyone is always starving after the game, and a "victory corny dog" is a must. The breading is crisp and greasy and delicious, and a streak of tangy mustard tops it all off. There are other things to try as well: turkey legs, brisket, Indian tacos, and gyros. The smell of grease hangs in the air like a fog, making the stomach growl. For a sweet treat, some fans get a sticky caramel apple or a deep fried dessert, like a fried Oreo or Twinkie. Others go for funnel cakes covered in powdered sugar like fairy dust. After filling themselves up, then fans can head indoors to check

out shows and get out of the heat. A myriad of cars are housed in one building, looking like an auto salesman's show room. Another building houses a petting zoo. The llamas are soft like cotton, and the piglets oink and squeal. Afterward, it is time for rides. The Ferris wheel, called the Texas Star, presides over the state fair like a queen, wheeling lazily in the dusky fall sunlight. There are small roller coasters and rockets, tilting ships and gentle carousels. The rides bob up and down, crash and whiz and whirl, playing music like wind-up toys, old gramophones, and huge boom boxes. Brakes hiss as the rides stop, and seat belts click as people unbuckle them to get off. As the sun dips beneath the horizon, the fair lights blink on. They are a rainbow of colors, twinkling like stars in the night sky. The fair is one of the best parts of the Red River Rivalry.

5   The Red River Rivalry is a must see for all Sooners and Longhorns. It is an event like no other and has to be experienced firsthand. The fans, the stadium, and the fair make it a fabulous time. In the future, Oklahoma and Texas teams and fans alike will continue to gather at the Cotton Bowl every October to battle it out.

COMBINED RHETORICAL MODES

Although the rhetorical modes can be used alone, sometimes authors incorporate various modes. For example, chapter 9 combined description and narration. In addition, classification essays may include elements of definition to explain each category and then incorporate elements of exemplification to develop or support each of the categories. Furthermore, cause and effect essays may use elements of argument. Although various modes may be used, the author primarily uses one; however, readers should be aware that various modes can be used to help them understand what they are reading. For an example of an essay that combines modes, read the essay "Choose Wisely," written by Michelle Stewart-Thomas, located in Part V: Further Readings on page 356. "Ain't I A Woman?" by Sojourner Truth, located in chapter 14, is another example of combined rhetorical modes.

PART IV
The Mechanics Handbook

Chapter 16

Subject and Verbs

Key Terms

subject, compound subject, verb, compound verb, action verb, linking verb, helping verb, prepositions, prepositional phrases, infinitives

Subjects and Verbs are the building blocks of sentences. Therefore, it is essential that you know what they are, how to identify them, and what role they play in creating polished writing that is easy to comprehend and conveys a clear message.

SUBJECTS

Subject: who or what the sentence is about. It is the person, place, thing, or idea that the sentence is about. Subjects can be nouns, pronouns, or gerunds (-ing words that are acting as nouns).

Example:

- ♦ Ricardo likes to read mystery novels.
- ♦ The rapper performed a mixture of his old and new songs.
- ♦ Her dog is a pit bull.
- ♦ They are kind people.
- ♦ Swimming allows me to release my stress.

Read Write! Activity 16.1

Circle the subject in the following sentences.

1. Beyoncé is a megastar from Houston, Texas.
2. She is married to Shawn Carter aka Jay Z.
3. Beyoncé's album *Lemonade* won Grammys for best urban contemporary album and best music video.
4. However, it did not win album of the year.
5. The members of Destiny's Child were Beyoncé, Kelly Rowland, and Michelle Williams.

Compound subject: more than one subject in a sentence. A compound subject can be two, three, four, or more subjects in a sentence.

Example:

- Ricardo and Malika are very good student writers.
- The rapper and the gospel singer collaborated on a hit song.
- Her dog is a pit bull, but it is very friendly.
- The furniture, clothes, trunks, and boxes have been put in storage.
- Reading, drawing, and playing video games are Jasmine's spring break plans.

Read Write! Activity 16.2

Circle the compound subjects in the following sentences. Do not include coordinating conjunctions—FANBOYS—for, and, nor, but, or, yet, so.

1. Alaska and Hawaii were the last two states to become part of the United States.
2. In addition, they are the only states that are not part of the contiguous United States; contiguous means sharing a border.
3. Alaska is located northwest of Canada, and Hawaii is located in the Pacific Ocean.
4. Alaska became the 49th state on Saturday, January 3, 1959, and Hawaii became the 50th state on Friday, August 21, 1959.
5. Presidential candidate and former governor of Alaska Sarah Palin put her state in the spotlight, and former President Barack Obama did the same for Hawaii, where he was born.
6. Alaska's mountains, glaciers, and national parks are enjoyed by thousands of tourists every year.
7. The gorgeous beaches, the active volcanos, the lush greenery, the rich culture, and Pearl Harbor attract tourists annually to Hawaii.

VERBS

Verb: the action or state of being of the subject. It is what the subject is doing in a sentence (walk, talk, think, sing, etc.) or it links the subject to its state of being (is, are, was, were, am, be, being, became, become, seem, feel, has, have, had, like).

When identifying verbs, look for words that have a present and a past tense form to them or can have –ing added to them (*sing*—present tense, *sang*—past tense, *singing*—*ing* form). However, be aware that not all verbs can have –ing added to them.

Examples:

- Ricardo likes to read mystery novels.
- The rapper performed a mixture of his old and new songs during his concert.
- Her dog is a pit bull.
- They are kind people.
- Swimming allows me to release my stress.

Read Write! Activity 16.3

Underline the verb in the following sentences.

1. Students need to decide what kind of college to attend.
2. For example, there are two-year and four-year colleges.
3. Some students want to live near home.
4. However, other students choose to go to college out of state.
5. For all students, college is a huge investment in time and money.

Compound verb: more than one action of the subject in a sentence. There can be two or more verbs in a compound verb.

Examples:

- The old woman grabbed her cane and walked slowly.
- She leaned heavily on her cane and limped painfully.
- A young man came over and helped her to cross the street.
- She took his arm, thanked him, and started off with him.

Read Write! Activity 16.4

Underline the compound verbs in the following sentences.

1. The quarterback evaded two defenders and ran into the end zone.
2. The fans screamed and high-fived each other in joy.
3. The opposing team's coach cussed at his players, threw down his clip board, and stomped his foot.
4. The journalists reported and tweeted about the coach's bad behavior, causing it to go viral.
5. After the game, the coach apologized for his behavior, paid a fine, and enrolled in an anger management course.

> ➤ **Read Write! Tip**
>   There are actually two different definitions of "verb" in English. Though the two definitions are similar, they are not exactly the same.

Verb: action or state of being (parts of speech)
Verb: action of the subject (elements of the sentence)

When a writer is dealing with subjects, the "elements of the sentence" definition is the one that is needed and what is covered in this chapter. The other definition is the general "parts of speech" definition. Sentences can have many verbs in them, but not all of those verbs are going to function as the action of the subject.

Verb Types

There are several different types of verbs in the English language. Identifying verbs is easier when a writer is aware of the different verb types.

Action verb: a word that shows true action, like "jump" or "dance." It is something that can actually be done. There are many action verbs in the English language.

Examples:

- Sean programs the computer.
- The tree branches swayed gracefully in the wind.
- Sarah danced on the table.

Linking verb: a word that connects a subject to its state of being. The most common linking verb is "be" and all its forms (am, is, are, was, were, being, been). Other verbs can function as linking verbs as well.

Examples:

- Kasey attends Texas State University.
- The office was a huge mess.
- Oscar became happy when he found out he made the soccer team.
- Paolo grew solemn when he heard the bad news.

Helping verb: a verb type used to create verb tenses. The most common helping verbs are "have" and "be" and all their forms, though other verbs can also function as helping verbs, such as could, should, and would and all their forms. When a writer is asked to find the complete verb, it is necessary to include the helping verb as part of the action of the subject. This can make the verb two or even three words long. Always include the helping verb as well as the main verb when identifying complete verbs.

Examples:

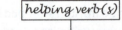

- The pirate had buried his treasure on Sea Monkey Island.

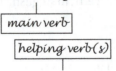

- Santa Monica Pier was built right on the Pacific Ocean.

- The Lyrid meteor shower will be occuring after midnight tonight.

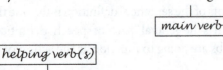

- Sharnell has been taking dance lessons for 10 years.

> ➤ **Read Write! Tip**
>
> Helping verbs and their main verbs can also function as linking verbs. In the example above about Santa Monica Pier, "was built" is functioning as a linking verb.

Read Write! Activity 16.5

Underline the complete verbs in the following sentences.

1. Miguel has been considering either a career in law or in the medical field.
2. He is planning to attend the University of Texas in Austin.
3. His parents are hoping for a scholarship for their son.
4. Miguel has earned all A's in all his classes and has received numerous awards.
5. The superstar student and his proud parents will be checking the mailbox daily for news about a scholarship.

THINGS TO WATCH OUT FOR WHEN IDENTIFYING SUBJECTS AND VERBS

When sentences get more complicated, it becomes more difficult to identify the subject and the verb. A few things writers need to watch out for are the word "not," prepositions, prepositional phrases, and infinitives.

Not: "Not" is not a verb. Therefore, it should not be included as part of the verb. It modifies the verb by making it negative, but when identifying verbs, do not include the word "not" as a part of the action of the subject.

Examples:

- Richard was not planning to attend the seminar.
- William is not from California.
- Raul should not leave his room for an hour.
- The pants were not the right size.
- The airplane will not arrive until later tonight.

Read Write! Activity 16.6

Circle the subject and underline the verb.

1. Bethany's dryer is not working properly.
2. Unfortunately, she will not be able to replace it until next month.
3. After purchasing a new dryer, Bethany should not have to go to the laundry mat anymore.

Preposition: a part of speech that shows relationships between nouns and pronouns. Many times, though not always, these are directional or location words. Below is a list of commonly used prepositions.

Commonly Used Prepositions

about	above	across	after
along	among	around	as
at	before	behind	below
beneath	beside(s)	between	beyond
by	despite	down	during
except	for	from	in
inside	into	near	of
off	on	onto	out
outside	over	than	through
to	toward(s)	under	underneath
until	up	upon	with
within	without		

Prepositional phrase: phrases that consist of a preposition, its object, and any words in between that connect them. Prepositional phrases usually take a three word construction, but they can also be two, four, or more words.

Examples:

- Jumping on the trampoline can be good exercise.
- The case of trophies is located in the front hall.
- The house by the car lot is brand new.

Prepositional phrases can make it difficult to identify the subject. What is important to know is that **the subject is *not* found in a prepositional phrase** no matter how the sentence is put together. Therefore, to stay on track, cross out all prepositional phrases when looking for subjects and verbs. If they are eliminated, they will not be there to be confusing.

Examples:

- Jumping ~~on the trampoline~~ can be good exercise.
- The case ~~of trophies~~ is located in the front hall.
- The house ~~by the car lot~~ is brand new.

Once the prepositional phrases are crossed out, the subjects of the above sentences quickly become clear: "jumping," "case," and "house." The words "trampoline," "trophies," and "lot" are no longer confusing because they have been eliminated.

Read Write! Activity 16.7

Cross out all prepositional phrases in the following sentences. Then, circle the subjects and underline the verbs. Two sentences have compound verbs.

1. On Tuesdays and Thursdays, Jason attends classes from 8 a.m. to 12:20 p.m.
2. During her shift at the library, Lisa checks in the books and returns them to the shelves.
3. Jogging in the park and on the beach keeps Harry in excellent physical shape.
4. The roses under the bridge and by the bench are in full bloom.
5. Each of the candidates put on a name tag, introduced himself/herself to the other people at the networking event, and gave a brief presentation about his/her plans for the company to the executives.

Infinitive: a verbal created by "to + a verb." Examples include to run, to jump, and to play. Any verb with the word "to" in front of it becomes an infinitive.

Infinitives can make it difficult to properly identify verbs because they look very similar to verbs. However, they are not verbs but verbals, verb forms that function as nouns or modifiers instead of verbs in a sentence. Infinitives cannot function as the action of the subject in a sentence. It can be helpful to cross out infinitives as well as prepositional phrases.

Examples:

♦ Vivienne has gone to pick up her son from daycare.
♦ Erin is going to attend college this fall.
♦ Ronald wants to sled down the hill after school.

> **Think Write! Activity Tip**

The first step to always take when asked to identify subjects and verbs is to cross out prepositional phrases and infinitives. Then, either the subject or the verb can be found first. However, if it becomes difficult to find the subject, identify the verb first. Then, it usually becomes clear who or what is doing the action.

Read Write! Activity 16.8

Cross out all infinitives. Then, circle the subjects and underline the verbs.

1. Hakeem likes to solve math problems and to conduct scientific experiments.
2. Erin forgot to get her parents' permission to go skiing.
3. Roberto likes to play the drums, to sing, and to write music.

Read Write! Activity 16.9

Cross out any prepositional phrases and infinitives in the following sentences. Then, circle the subject and underline the verb in each sentence. Watch out for compound subjects and compound verbs.

1. The students and two of their professors are planning to go on a trip to New York.
2. In the Big Apple, they will dine on a variety of food and visit all of the major tourist sites.
3. One of the places is the 9/11 Memorial and Museum; several of the students lost family members in the attack on the Twin Towers and want to pay their respects.
4. The group of nearly 40 people will travel by bus from Atlanta to New York City and will stay in a dorm on a local college to save money on hotels.
5. Traveling to New York and reading the names of the victims etched on the memorial is going to be an emotional experience for all of the students and the professors.

Chapter 17
Subject-Verb Agreement

Key Terms

subject-verb agreement, prepositional phrases, infinitives, indefinite pronouns

Subject-Verb Agreement plays an important role in creating mechanically sound sentences.

SUBJECT-VERB AGREEMENT

In Chapter 16: Subjects and Verbs, you learned how to identify subjects and verbs. Now that you have a good grasp on identifying these key sentence components, understanding subject-verb agreement will be easier.

The Rule of Subject-Verb Agreement

Subjects and their verbs must match in number. Therefore, singular subjects take singular verbs, and plural subjects take plural verbs. Look at the chart below showing all the forms of the verb "laugh" in every person in present tense.

		Singular		Plural
(first person)	I	laugh	We	laugh
(second person)	You	laugh	You	laugh
(third person)	He/She/It	laughs	They	laugh

Notice that the only change that happens to the verb occurs in third person singular where an "s" is added. Generally, third person singular and plural in present tense are where the most common subject-verb agreement errors occur. The mix up usually comes with the added "s".

> **Think Write! Tip**

Subject-verb agreement usually only causes errors in present tense. Most past tense verbs only have one form, like adding "-ed." However, there is an exception. In past tense, "be" becomes "was" for third person singular and "were" for third person plural. Generally, this is the only place in past tense that subject-verb agreement can get difficult.

Subject-verb agreement can get confusing because it is the opposite of what writers are used to thinking. When an "s" is added to a noun, it makes the noun plural. However, if an "s" is added to a present tense verb, it makes it third person singular. Look at the chart below.

Singular Nouns	Singular Verbs	Plural Nouns	Plural Verbs
The girl	laughs	The girls	laugh
The baby	cries	The babies	cry
The track star	runs	The track stars	run

This can get baffling, so one way to keep from getting confused is to remember this: if the subject has an "s" on it, then the verb usually will not have an "s" on it. Keep in mind, however, that some words, like class and recess, already end in "s" but are considered singular. For these kinds of words, the trick above cannot be used; instead read and choose the verb form carefully.

Read Write! Activity 17.1

Choose the correct verb form for the subjects in the sentences below.

1. Jesus, a two-year-old toddler, (giggles/giggle) every time his dad (smiles/smile) at him.
2. The soldiers (is/are) in basic training for four more weeks.
3. The fire fighter (works/work) as a personal chef on her days off.
4. Victoria's Siamese cats (enjoys/enjoy) chasing dogs twice their size.
5. *The Simpsons* (is/are) a popular television show.

Prepositional Phrases

Recall that prepositional phrases are phrases that consist of a preposition, its object, and any words in between that connect them.

Remember that they can make it hard to find the subject; they also make it hard to choose the correct verb if the subject is identified wrong. Therefore, always cross out prepositional phrases when identifying subjects and verbs *and* when working with subject-verb agreement.

Examples:

- The party goers ~~at the apartment club house~~ were cited ~~for disturbing the peace~~.
- Each ~~of the party goers~~ has to appear ~~before a judge on next Monday~~.

> **Think Write! Tip**

While there are many prepositions, the one that you must focus on the most when dealing with subject-verb agreement is "of." Otherwise, you will choose the wrong verb.

Infinitives

Recall that infinitives are verbals that are created by "to + a verb." They should also be crossed out when working with subject-verb agreement so that they are not mistaken for the verbs in a sentence.

Example:

The computerized baby doll has been programmed ~~to cry~~, ~~to walk~~, ~~to eat~~, ~~to talk~~, and ~~to sleep~~.

Read Write! Activity 17.2

Cross out any prepositional phrases and infinitives in the following sentence. Then, choose the correct verb form to go with the subjects.

1. The apples in the orchard (needs/need) to be picked soon.
2. The set on the stage (was/were) built by the technical theatre club.
3. Each of the students (needs/need) to study for the upcoming exam.
4. One of the members of the audience in the balcony (has/have) won a new car.
5. The fax machine and the printer in the home office (is/are) acting up today.

The Subject and the Verb Reversed

In all of the sentences presented so far, the subject has come first in the sentence. However, it is possible for the verb to come before the subject depending on how the sentence is constructed. For example, questions will also reverse the order of the subject and the verb. Sentences that begin with "here" or "there" can also reverse the subject and verb order. It is possible to reverse this order other ways as well, just depending on how the sentence is constructed.

Examples:

♦ Do <u>you</u> believe in miracles?
♦ How are the <u>twins</u> getting to school this morning?
♦ Here is today's <u>edition</u> under the car.
♦ There is the <u>one</u> from yesterday, as well.
♦ In the bushes is last week's <u>edition</u>.

Read Write! Activity 17.3

The following sentences have the subjects and the verbs reversed. Cross out any prepositional phrases. Then, choose the correct verb form to go with the subject.

1. In the backyard by the rose bush (is/are) a huge ant hill.
2. There (is/are) ten students from China in the class.
3. Here (is/are) my key to my locker; I (has/have) been looking everywhere for it.
4. (Is/Are) Raul and Maria in the middle of something, or can I (talks/talk) to them now?
5. (Has/Have) Liza made up her mind about her costume for the party?

Compound Subjects

Compound subjects also make it difficult to ensure subjects and verbs are agreeing. Compound subjects are either going to be joined by the conjunction "and" or the conjunction "or".

Compound subjects joined by "and" are considered plural. They will always take a plural verb.

Examples:

♦ Running **and** skiing <u>are</u> Daniel's favorite leisure activities.
♦ The car **and** the boat <u>were parked</u> in the driveway.

Compound subjects joined by "or" can be considered singular or plural, depending on the subjects. If both of the compound subjects are singular, the verb will be singular, as in the examples below.

Examples:

♦ Running **or** skiing <u>is</u> Daniel's favorite leisure activities.
♦ The car **or** the boat <u>was parked</u> in the driveway.

If both of the subjects are plural, the verb will be plural, as in the examples below.

Examples:

♦ The moms **or** the dads <u>pick</u> up the children from school.
♦ The lions **or** the tigers <u>eat</u> all the meat.

This becomes complicated if the compound subject is comprised of a singular subject and a plural subject. When this occurs, match the verb to the subject sitting closest to it in the sentence.

Examples:

♦ The breadsticks **or** the salad <u>comes</u> with the meal.

In the first example, salad, which is singular, is closest to the verb. Therefore, the singular verb "comes" goes with it.

♦ The salad **or** the breadsticks <u>come</u> with the meal.

In the second example, breadsticks, which is plural, is closest to the verb. Therefore, the plural verb "come" goes with it.

Read Write! Activity 17.4

Choose the correct verb form for the following compound subjects. Be aware of which conjunction is connecting the compound subjects and do not forget to cross out prepositional phrases.

1. The boxer and his trainers (is/are) excited about the upcoming fight.
2. The fans and the boxer (is/are) excited about the upcoming fight.

3. A pen or pencils (is/are) required for the exam.
4. Pencils or a pen (is/are) required for the exam.
5. The two lamps or the overhead light (needs/need) to be turned on.

Indefinite Pronouns as Subjects

Indefinite pronouns do not refer to a specific person, thing, or amount. They cause problems in subject-verb agreement because certain indefinite pronouns can be either singular or plural, depending on the sentence. Others are always singular or always plural.

These four indefinite pronouns are always plural. Therefore, they will always take a plural verb.

Both	Few	Many	Several

Examples:

♦ A **few** of the churchgoers **bring** potluck meals every Sunday.
♦ **Many** of the colleges **offer** specialized history classes.

These 16 indefinite pronouns are always singular. Therefore, they will always take a singular verb.

Everyone	Anyone	Someone	No one
Everybody	Anybody	Somebody	Nobody
Everything	Anything	Something	Nothing
Each	Either	Neither	One

Examples:

♦ **Neither** of the children **wants** to do afternoon chores.
♦ **Each** of the chores only **takes** a minute.

These five indefinite pronouns can be singular or plural. Whether or not they take a singular or plural verb depends on the context of the sentence.

All	Any	most	None	Some

Examples:

♦ **Any** of the boys **are** welcome to attend.
  ♦ In this sentence, we know that "all" is plural because of "boys," so we use "are" instead of "is."
♦ **None** of the homework **was** picked up.
  ♦ In this sentence, we know that "none" is singular because of "homework," so we use "was" instead of "were."

Read Write! Activity 17.5

Cross out any prepositional phrases or infinitives. Then choose the correct verb form for the following sentences containing indefinite pronouns.

1. Someone always (sneaks/sneak) into the break room and (drinks/drink) all of the coffee.
2. Each of the desks (needs/need) to have the graffiti removed from it.
3. No one in the family (wants/want) to tell grandpa to mind his own business.
4. Many of the professional athletes (has/have) started charities to benefit various causes.
5. In the game Clue, any of the players (is/are) possibly the culprit.

Read Write! Activity 17.6

Cross out any prepositional phrases and infinitives. Then, circle the subject and underline the complete verb in each sentence.

1. Each of the stores is having a huge sale to attract customers.
2. There is something for everyone on sale.
3. On sale are clothes, shoes, computers, jewelry, and furniture.
4. The salesclerks or the manager of the store on the corner has been blogging about the event to attract customers.
5. Several customers plan to arrive at midnight and get in line to be the first in the stores.

Read Write! Activity 17.7

The following paragraph has five subject-verb agreement errors in it. Cross out any prepositional phrases and infinitives. Then, make corrections to subject-verb agreement.

The Terrible Mail Carrier

For four months, the neighbors have been gathering at 7 p.m. to resort the mail. Their mail carrier constantly deliver the mail to the wrong address. Each of the homeowners in the neighborhood have complained about the situation and has demanded the mail carrier be fired. The mail carrier or his supervisors at the post office needs to do something soon. There is rumors of a plan to picket the post office on Monday. "Why should we has to put up with this bad service?" demanded one of the homeowners. "We are not going to put up with it anymore!"

Chapter 18

Sentence Patterns

Key Terms

independent clause, dependent clause, subordinating conjunctions, sentence patterns (simple, compound, complex, compound-complex)

As a writer, you want to use a variety of sentence patterns to engage your reader and to keep your writing from being boring.

Before discussing sentence patterns, it is important to understand what a clause is and that they are used to create the different sentence patterns.

TYPES OF CLAUSES

There are two types of clauses: independent clauses and dependent clauses.

Independent Clause

Independent clauses are complete sentences that can stand on their own; they have a subject and a verb, and they express a complete thought.

Examples of Independent Clauses:

♦ The restaurant was loud and crowded.
♦ They lost everything.
♦ Raquel and David plan to take a vacation to Jamaica in July.

Dependent Clause

Even though **dependent clauses** have a subject and a verb, they do not express a complete thought. Therefore, they depend on the independent clauses they are connected to for them to make sense. They are not complete sentences on their own because they contain subordinating conjunctions.

Subordinating Conjunctions are dependent words, like "because," "since," or "when." When these kinds of words are added to a sentence, they create dependent clauses. If these clauses tried to stand on their own as complete sentences, they could not because they would be considered fragments.

Examples of Dependent Clauses (Fragments):

- Because it was Valentine's Day.
- When the tornado hit their small town in Oklahoma.
- After they receive their tax refund.

However, when dependent clauses are added to independent clauses, they become complete sentences and create two of the four sentence patterns.

Examples:

- The restaurant was loud and crowded because it was Valentine's Day.
- When the tornado hit their small town in Oklahoma, they lost everything.
- After they receive their tax fund, Raquel and David plan to take a vacation to Jamaica in July.

Being able to distinguish an independent clause from a dependent clause will help you identify and create the different sentence patterns.

SENTENCE PATTERNS

There are four **sentence patterns** or sentence types to use to enhance your writing: simple, compound, complex, and compound-complex.

Simple Sentences

The **simple** sentence is the basic sentence form; it is a single independent clause. It stands on its own and expresses one idea. It can have one subject and one verb, or it can contain compound subjects and/or compound verbs.

Examples:

- The telephone rang continuously all afternoon.
- Nicole got a job at the casino and rose through the ranks to a high paying position.
- Chan and Lewis decided to dress as a horse for Halloween.
- Sophie loves to chase the laser pointer.

> **Read Write! Tip**

Typical simple sentences do not contain semicolons, coordinating conjunctions (FANBOYS) that join two or more sentences, or dependent clauses.

Read Write! Activity 18.1

Place a check mark on the blank in front of the three simple sentences below.

_____ 1. When it is dark outside.
_____ 2. The adult brothers and sisters chipped in to buy their parents a new car.
_____ 3. Ice skating, skiing, and snowboarding are Alicia's favorite winter sports.
_____ 4. Although the book shelf was starting to bend in the middle.
_____ 5. Christopher enjoys spending time with his grandparents.

Compound Sentences

Compound sentences contain two or more independent clauses and are created using coordination. There are two ways to coordinate ideas and create compound sentences.

Comma and a coordinating conjunction: Independent clauses can be combined by joining them with a comma and a coordinating conjunction. There are seven coordinating conjunctions, and you can memorize them using the acronym FANBOYS.

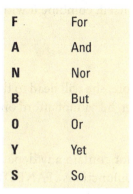

F	For
A	And
N	Nor
B	But
O	Or
Y	Yet
S	So

Compound sentences using the FANBOYS have a subject and a verb on both sides of the comma and the coordinating conjunctions.

Examples:

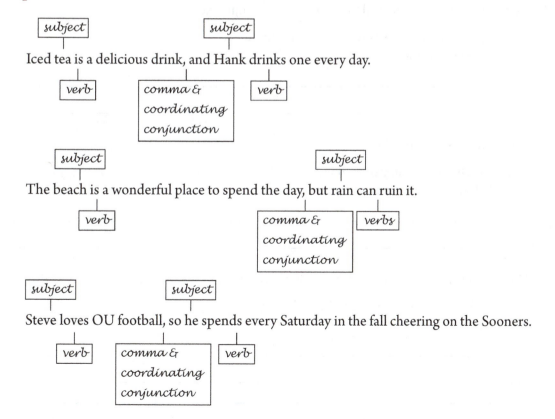

Semicolon: A semicolon can also be used to create compound sentences. Use it to combine two independent clauses that go together by simply placing the semicolon at the end of the first clause. Do not capitalize the first letter of the second clause unless it is a proper noun or the pronoun I.

Examples:

♦ The snow is getting so deep; we will have to shovel the walk tomorrow.
♦ *Macbeth* is my favorite Shakespeare play; I love the witches' chants.

In addition to using a semicolon by itself, combine it with a conjunctive adverb (transition), and a comma.

Examples:

♦ Meredith needs a new car; therefore, she will head to the car lot this weekend.
♦ Lorenzo wants a new car; however, he cannot afford one.

> **Read Write! Tip**
Compound sentences do not contain any dependent clauses; they are simple sentences combined using coordinating conjunctions (FANBOYS) or semicolons.

Read Write! Activity 18.2

Combine each pair of simple sentences into a compound sentence as directed.

1. Combine using a comma and the coordinating conjunction *so*.

   The mayor was convicted of stealing campaign funds.
   He resigned in disgrace.

   _____

   _____

2. Combine using a semicolon.

   The cordless mouse stopped working.
   It needed some new batteries.

   _____

   _____

3. Combine using a semicolon and the conjunctive adverb (transition word) *however* and a comma.

   The fire alarm went off in the middle of the night.
   It was a false alarm.

   _____

   _____

Complex Sentences

A **complex** sentence has two parts: an independent clause and at least one dependent clause.

Example:

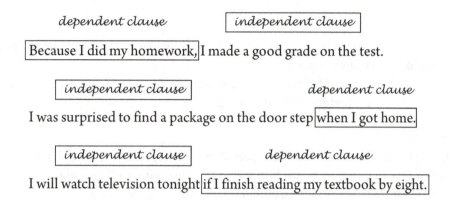

dependent clause   *independent clause*

Because I did my homework, I made a good grade on the test.

independent clause   *dependent clause*

I was surprised to find a package on the door step when I got home.

independent clause   *dependent clause*

I will watch television tonight if I finish reading my textbook by eight.

In the examples above, "because I did my homework," "when I got home," and "if I finish reading my textbook by eight" are the dependent clauses because they cannot stand on their own. If the independent clauses are taken away, incomplete thoughts are left, which are sentence fragments.

There are many subordinating conjunctions to use to create complex sentences. Below is a list of the common ones. Remember, however, that there are many more.

Common Subordinating Conjunctions

after	before	once	although
as	as long as	as though	because
even if	even though	if	that
while	since	unless	until
when	whenever	where	wherever

Complex sentences can be put together in numerous ways. However, if the dependent clause starts the sentence, use a comma before the independent clause begins because the dependent clause is considered introductory.

Examples:

♦ If Melanie goes to the Halloween party, she will need a costume.
♦ When the tree blew over, it fell on Edwin's car.
♦ Although I like cake, I prefer ice cream.

These same sentences can be more or less reversed. If the dependent clause comes at the end of the complex sentence, no comma is needed.

Examples:

- Melanie will need a costume if she goes to the Halloween party.
- The tree fell on Edwin's car when the tree blew over.
- I prefer ice cream although I like cake.

In addition, these sentences can be written to contain more than one dependent clause.

Examples:

- Because she does not want to stand out by wearing her regular clothes, Melanie will need a costume if she goes to the Halloween party.
- When the tree blew over, it fell on Edwin's car because he does not have a garage to park it in.
- Although I like cake, I prefer ice cream because I have a variety of flavors to choose from.

> **Read Write! Tip**
>
> Complex sentences can contain more than one dependent clause that begins with one of the subordinating conjunctions, but they can only contain ONE independent clause, so no FANBOYS or semicolons joining independent clauses can be used.

Read Write! Activity 18.3

Add an independent clause to the following dependent clauses to create complex sentences. First, insert the independent clause that you create after the dependent clause. Then, rewrite the independent clause again so that now it begins the complex sentence.

Example:

Although the farmer put up scarecrows, the crows ate up the crops.
The crows ate up the crops although the farmer put up scarecrows.

1. If the rain does not stop soon, _____ .
   _____ if the rain does not stop soon.

2. When I have extra spending money, _____ .
   _____ when I have extra spending money.

3. Because the concert was cancelled, _____ .
   _____ because the concert was cancelled.

Read Write! Activity 18.4

Identify each sentence as compound or complex. Write your answer at the end of each sentence.

1. The children were excited about going to the circus in the afternoon, so their teacher had a hard time getting them to do their work in the morning.

2. When it was time to get on the bus to go to the circus, the students jumped for joy.
3. At the circus, the students clapped loudly for the acrobats; they also cheered for the lions, tigers, elephants, and monkeys.
4. Although the students had eaten lunch at school, they consumed large amounts of popcorn and cotton candy and drank numerous sodas.
5. The students were happy, stuffed, and exhausted when the circus ended.

Compound-Complex Sentences

Compound-complex sentences must meet the requirements of both compound AND complex sentences. Therefore, they must contain at least two independent clauses and at least one dependent clause.

Examples:

♦ Ann traveled to Malaysia; **while she was away,** her daughter's apartment was burglarized.
♦ **Although the weather is lovely right now,** it is supposed to rain later, so I brought my umbrella.
♦ The chorus book was expensive to purchase, but Nellie had the money because she had just gotten paid.

It is possible to put compound-complex sentences together several ways. The dependent clause and independent clauses can be put together whichever way the writer prefers or whichever way sounds best. However, be careful when writing compound-complex sentences because they can be tricky. Therefore, these are the least written kinds of sentences.

> **Read Write! Tip**
> Compound-complex sentences must contain at least two independent clauses and at least one dependent clause. Therefore, look for coordinating conjunctions (FANBOYS) or a semicolon AND at least one dependent clause that begins with one of the subordinating conjunctions (because, when, after, etc.)

Read Write! Activity 18.5

Identify each sentence as a simple, compound, complex, or compound-complex; write your answer at the end of each sentence.

1. Simple sentences do not contain any FANBOYS joining two sentences, semicolons, or dependent words.
2. Compound sentences are two sentences connected with one of the FANBOYS, or a semicolon is used to join two sentences.
3. When complex sentences are created, a word like *because, when, if,* or *although* must be used.
4. Because compound-complex sentences have two or more sentences in them, and they have a dependent word, they are trickier to write.
5. Each of the sentences above explains its sentence pattern.

Read Write! Activity 18.6

Identify each sentence as simple, compound, complex, or compound-complex; write your answer at the end of each sentence. There are two simple, three compound, three complex, and two compound-complex sentences.

1. The meteorologist predicted rain, sleet, and snow.
2. When the biologist was asked to give the key note address at the medical convention, she gladly accepted.
3. The psychologist was tired of patients cancelling their appointments, so he instituted a cancellation fee.
4. The archeologist requested funding to travel to Egypt; when it was granted, she was ecstatic.
5. After the gynecologist completed her paper work, she signed out for the evening.
6. The oncologist presented a lecture about the increase in cancer cases in a local community.
7. The endocrinologist was awarded a grant to research juvenile diabetes; he hopes to find a cure.
8. The sociologist conducted a study to determine if bullies are born or if they are made.
9. The geologist plans to turn over his extensive rock collection to the museum, but he is also considering selling it.
10. When the criminologist discovered a diary written by the accused murder, she immediately turned it over to the police, and they gave it to the prosecutor.

Read Write! Activity 18.7

Determine the sentence pattern for the following sentences. On the line preceding them, place an "S" for the four simple sentences, a "C" for the one compound sentence, a "CX" for the three complex sentences, and a "CC" for the two compound-complex sentences.

© PhotoRoman/Shutterstock.com

What am I?

1. _____ I am a symbol of the United States of America. 2. _____ While there are small, hand-held versions of me, there are also ginormous ones of me. 3. _____ Regardless of my size, I am always rectangular, and my colors are red, white, and blue. 4. _____ When I was first created, I only had thirteen alternating red and white horizontal stripes on me and thirteen stars; these geometric shapes represented the original thirteen colonies of my place of birth. 5. _____ Over time, 37 more stars were added for a total of 50. 6. _____ Although I have my own day in June, I am proudly displayed on other holidays, as well. 7. _____ I have a busy schedule because I attend parades, inaugurations, political conventions, and other events. 8. _____ At funerals, I am folded and presented to family members for their loved one's service to the country. 9. _____ Songs, oaths, and poems have been written about me. 10. _____ I must be burned when I become too old to do my job, but until then, I proudly wave over the land of the free and the home of the brave.

Chapter 19
Sentence Fragments

Key Term

sentence fragment, missing piece fragments, dependent clause fragment, example and exception fragments, verbal fragments

Complete sentences are key to polished writing. Complete sentences allow for understanding, but fragments can make it hard for the reader to comprehend the message the writer is trying to get across.

DEFINITION OF A SENTENCE FRAGMENT

A **sentence fragment** is an incomplete sentence. It is missing something. A complete sentence is made up of a subject, a verb, and a complete thought. When one of these parts is missing, a fragment occurs. Sentence fragments cannot stand by themselves.

FOUR TYPES OF SENTENCE FRAGMENTS

Missing piece fragments occur when a key part of a sentence is missing, like a subject or a verb.

Examples:

- ♦ The movers loading everything into the truck.
- ♦ Is so tiring to watch.

Read Write! Activity 19.1

For each pair, determine whether the following sentences are complete thoughts or not. If they are, put a "C" for correct on the line preceding them. If they are not, put an "F" for fragment.

1. a. _____ The crowd booing and growing impatient for the concert to start.
   b. _____ The crowd began to boo and grew impatient for the concert to start.

2. a. _____ Loves the warm weather in the summertime.
    b. _____ Joachim loves the warm weather.
3. a. _____ Taking college courses in the summer allows students to graduate sooner.
    b. _____ Taking several college courses in the summer at a community college.

Dependent clause fragments occur when a dependent clause has been separated from an independent clause it should be attached to.

Examples:

♦ Because it is past midnight. Kevin is going to bed.
♦ All of the spectators left their seats and ran into the stadium. After it started to rain.
♦ I need to stop by the bank. Which is on the way to the museum.

> ➢ **Read Write! Tip**
> Generally speaking, a sentence that starts with the word "which" is going to be a fragment. The only exception to this is if the sentence is a question.
> Not a fragment: Which way is the museum?

Read Write! Activity 19.2

Attach the dependent clause to the independent clause. If the dependent clause comes before the independent clause, insert a comma. However, if the dependent clause comes after the independent clause, do not insert a comma. An exception to this rule are the words "which" and "where"; they require commas in front of them when they are in the middle of the sentence. Edit for capitalization as needed when combining the sentences.

1. Because a blizzard is expected. Schools and businesses are closing early.
2. Although the child cut back on eating candy. He still had five new cavities.
3. One of my favorite stores is Target. Which always has good sales.
4. When the strike ended. The workers had better wages and safer working conditions.
5. The talent show was cancelled. Because not enough tickets were sold.

Example and exception fragments occur when words and phrases like "for example," "for instance," "like," "such as," "with," "except," "especially," and "without" are used.

Examples:

♦ Brian has many hobbies. For example, bird watching.
♦ I want so many rooms in my dream house. Like a library, conservatory, dining room, gym, and bowling alley.
♦ I enjoy eating a variety of candy. Such as Snickers and Reese's Peanut Butter Cups.

Verbal fragments occur when a writer has accidently used a verbal instead of a verb in the sentence. There are three types of verbals.

- Infinitives: to + a verb
  - <u>To prepare</u> for the marathon. Allison ran every day after work.
- Gerunds: verb + ing
  - Maribeth ran down the street. <u>Singing</u> at the top of her lungs.
- Participle: past tense/participle form of the verb
  - No one saw the hidden recording device. <u>Tucked</u> away in Elmer's pocket.

Below are steps a writer can take to identify sentence fragments.

Step 1: Identify the subject of the sentence; if there is not one, it is a fragment.
Step 2: If the sentence appears to have a subject, find the verb that goes with that subject; if the subject is not completing an action or in a state of being, it is a fragment.
Step 3: If it appears as though the sentence has a subject and a verb, the last thing to do is check if the sentence is a complete thought. Be on the lookout for dependent clauses. Recall, that they do contain a subject and a verb, but they do not express a complete thought. Here is an example of a Dependent Clause: **When it is dark outside**. If it stops abruptly, the sentence is a fragment. A good way to test this is to read the sentence aloud.

CORRECTING FRAGMENTS

There are two ways to correct fragments:

- Add words, like a subject or a verb.
- Connect the fragment to a nearby sentence that it makes sense with.

Examples:

Jose walking the dog. Later went to pick up his dry cleaning. And then out to dinner.

The first sentence needs a verb added: Jose *was* walking the dog, or you could change walking to the past tense walked.

The second sentence needs a subject added: Later *he* went to pick up his dry cleaning.

The third sentence should be connected to the second sentence: Later *he* went to pick up his dry cleaning and then out to dinner.

The coordinating conjunctions (FANBOYS) should almost *never* start sentences. While professional writers, like journalists and novelists, are known to start sentences with coordinating conjunctions, it should not be done in formal, academic writing for school.

They are used to connect two sentences and therefore go in the middle of sentences.

Wrong: The recital began. And the dancer leapt into the air.

Correct: The recital began, and the dancer leapt into the air.

Only one of the FANBOYS is an exception to this rule, and that is "so" when it is functioning as an adverb and not a conjunction.

Example:

So far I have gotten juice and pretzels.

In this sentence, "so" is being used as an adverb to modify the word "far," so this is not a fragment.

"For Example" and "For Instance": The Exceptions to the Connection Rule

"For example" and "for instance" often create fragments. When correcting fragments with "for example" and "for instance" in them, do not connect them to the sentence that comes before them. Instead, add words to create a new sentence beginning with "for example" or "for instance."

Examples:

♦ Buddy has many toys. For example, tennis balls, Kongs, and chew ropes.

Do not connect the "for example" sentence to the part about Buddy. In this instance, add words to create a complete sentence, like the example below.

♦ Buddy has many toys. For example, he has tennis balls, Kongs, and chew ropes in his toy basket.

Do not be afraid to add or take away words as needed to help the sentence make sense. The only thing that should not be done is changing the meaning of the sentence.

Read Write! Activity 19.3

Determine whether or not the following sentences are complete thoughts or not. If they are, put a "C" for correct on the line preceding them. If they are not, put an "F" for fragment.

1. _____ The batter stepping up to bat.
2. _____ Eying the pitcher to psych him out.
3. _____ The pitcher threw a curve ball.
4. _____ The batter swinging as hard as he could.
5. _____ Although he kept his eye on the ball.
6. _____ He missed it, and the umpire yelled, "Strike one!"
7. _____ The fans began to say mean things to the batter.
8. _____ Such as "Batter out!" and "Back to the minor's league you go!"
9. _____ When the pitcher threw another curve ball.
10. _____ The batter swung, hit the ball, silenced the crowd, and scored a home run.

Read Write! Activity 19.4

Underline the ten fragments in the following paragraph. Then, make corrections by adding words, deleting words, or connecting the fragments to nearby sentences they make sense with. Write your corrections in between the lines

Happily Ever After?

My sister determined to get me dating again after my breakup with my last boyfriend. The two of us spent hours nightly on dating sites. Looking for the perfect guy for me. Finally, after two months of talking to a guy online. He and I agreed to go out on a date. We wanted to meet at a relatively quiet location. Such as a coffee shop or a small café. He told me he would be wearing blue jeans and a blue polo shirt. I said that I would be wearing a blue sundress. When I arrived at Starbuck's. I saw him immediately. He smiling at me. I walked over to his table. Which had a bouquet of roses on it for me. Because we had so many things in common. Such as favorite color, hobbies, musical groups, and goals in life. We ended up talking for three hours. And have been happily dating for a year now.

Chapter 20

Run-ons and Comma Splices

Key Terms

run-on, comma splice

RUN-ON AND COMMA SPLICE DEFINITIONS

Two sentence errors that you must be on the lookout for and avoid are run-ons and comma splices. A **run-on** sentence occurs when two or more complete sentences (independent clauses) are joined together with no punctuation between them.

♦ Julius has been reviewing his biology notes he is ready for the final exam.

A **comma splice** occurs when two complete sentences (independent clauses) are improperly joined with just a comma. In other words, a comma is trying to be a period or a semicolon.

♦ Julius has been reviewing his biology notes, he is ready for the final exam.

As you look for run-ons and comma splices, you must ask yourself the following important question: *Can I put a period somewhere and make two separate sentences?* If the answer is yes, then the sentence is a run-on or a comma splice.

Ask the question for the sentence below: *Can I put a period somewhere and make two separate sentences?*

♦ The python slithered through the swamp it was seeking its dinner.

The answer is yes; the sentence is a run-on. A period can be placed after swamp.

♦ The python slithered through the swamp. It was seeking its dinner.

What about the sentence below? ***Can I put a period somewhere and make two separate sentences?***

♦ The band members were drunk and loud.

The answer is no. *The band members were drunk* is a sentence, but *and loud* is NOT a sentence. Therefore, the sentence must stay altogether.

Try one more. ***Can I put a period somewhere and make two separate sentences?***

♦ My watch needs a new battery, it keeps losing 10 minutes every day.

The answer is yes; the sentence is a comma splice. The comma needs to be replaced with a period.

♦ My watch needs a new battery. It keeps losing 10 minutes every day.

Although inserting a period is not the only way to correct run-ons and comma splices, it is the question to ask as you analyze each of your sentences to determine whether it is a run-on or a comma splice.

FOUR WAYS TO CORRECT RUN-ONS AND COMMA SPLICES

Make two separate sentences using a period.

♦ Julius has been reviewing his biology notes. He is ready for the final exam.

Read Write! Activity 20.1

Determine whether the following sentences are run-ons or comma splices. If they are run-ons, put "RO" on the line preceding them. If they are comma splices, put "CS." Then, insert a period to make two separate sentences. Add capitalization as needed.

1. _____ The two muscled men entered the ring, the crowd began to roar.
2. _____ The opponents hurled insults at each other, the smaller of the two put his opponent in a head lock.
3. _____ Wrestling is a popular sport it is very exciting to watch.
4. _____ Some people believe it is fake, others say it is real.
5. _____ Some aspects of wrestling may be scripted the injuries are real.

Connect using a semicolon by itself or a semicolon, a conjunctive adverb (transitional word), and a comma.

♦ Julius has been reviewing his biology notes; he is ready for the final exam.
♦ Julius has been reviewing his biology notes; therefore, he is ready for the final exam.

Chart of Most Frequently Used Conjunctive Adverbs (Transitions)

Transition	Meaning	Example Sentence
; therefore,	As a result	Julia is very friendly; therefore, she has numerous friends.
; consequently,	As a result	I studied for the exam; consequently, I made an A on it.
; however,	Contrast	I want to lose weight; however, I do not make the time to exercise.
; nevertheless,	Contrast	Angel's leg has been bothering him; nevertheless, he is determined to participate in the walkathon.
; then,	Shows time order	Lisa finished her homework; then, she went out to dinner with her friends.
; furthermore, ; in addition, ; moreover, ; thus,	Shows addition	The tornado destroyed houses; furthermore, it uprooted trees.

Read Write! Activity 20.2

Correct the following run-ons by inserting a semicolon.

Example

```
                    ;
The baby's fever broke  his parents were very relieved.
                    ^
```

1. The professor felt her students needed more time to complete the project she gave them two more days.
2. My son earns extra money by selling items on eBay he buys things cheap and sells them high.
3. The barber cut his client's hair too short the client refused to pay.

Read Write! Activity 20.3

Correct the run-ons by filling in the blank with a semicolon, a *conjunctive* adverb (transitional word), and a comma. Try not to use the same transitional word more than once.

Example

```
                      ; therefore,
The baby's fever broke  his parents were very relieved.
                      ^
```

1. During the storm, the electricity went out _____ we had to sit in the dark for six hours.
2. To pass the time, we played music on our cell phones _____ our batteries eventually died.
3. Then, we were bored _____ we went to sleep.
4. The storm knocked out the power _____ it destroyed 14 homes.

Connect using a comma and one of the coordinating conjunctions (FANBOYS):

The comma goes in front of the conjunction and follows this pattern:

a complete sentence + a comma and one of the FANBOYS + a complete sentence

♦ Julius has been reviewing his biology notes, so he is ready for the final exam.

Chart of the Seven Coordinating Conjunctions (FANBOYS)

Coordinating Conjunction	Meaning	Example Sentence
, for	Because, shows cause	The pen did not work, for it was out of ink.
, and	Shows addition	The reality show is a hit, and it continues to attract new viewers.
, nor	Not either one	The babysitter did not answer the house phone, nor did he answer his cell phone.
, but	Contrast	Lisa loves to shop, but she only buys items on sale.
, or	Provides an alternative or choice/option	Blake will vacation in San Antonio in the summer, or he will go to Denver in the winter.
, yet	Contrast	The white board was brand new, yet it would not erase like the old one.
, so	As a result, shows effect	Ling makes the best apple pie, so she wins the dessert contest every year.

Read Write! Activity 20.4

Determine whether the sentences are run-ons or comma splices. If they are run-ons, put "RO" on the line preceding them. If they are comma splices, put "CS."

Then, correct the run-ons or the comma splices by adding a comma and a coordinating conjunction (FANBOYS).

Example

                          so
The baby's fever broke, his parents were very relieved.
                          ^

1. _____ The children had fun playing outside they cried when it was time to come inside.

2. _____ Michael and Michelle are identical twins, they have completely different personalities.

3. _____ Isabel's care package from her parents will arrive on Tuesday, it will arrive on Wednesday.

4. _____ The new car kept breaking down the dealership refused to take it back.

5. _____ The announcer fired the gun the race began.

Connect using a subordinating conjunction (dependent word).

♦ Because Julius has been reviewing his biology notes, he is ready for the final exam.
♦ Julius is ready for the final exam because he has been reviewing his notes.

Notice that subordinating conjunctions can be placed at the beginning of the sentence or in the middle of the sentence. When the subordinating conjunction begins the sentence, never put a comma right after it; the comma goes where the dependent clause ends.

Chart of Most Frequently Used Subordinating Conjunctions

Subordinating Conjunction	Meaning	Example Sentence
Although	Contrast	• Although I want to lose weight, I do not make the time to exercise. • I do not make the time to exercise although I want to lose weight.
Even though	Contrast	• Even though Morgan apologized three times, Lilly will not take him back. • Lilly will not take Morgan back even though he has apologized three times.
Because	As a result	• Because Julia is very friendly, she has numerous friends • Julia has numerous friends because she is very friendly.
Since	As a result	• Since the time change occurred, Walter has been feeling tired. • Walter has been feeling tired since the time change.
When	Time specific	• When my alarm goes off, I always hit snooze. • I always hit snooze when my alarm goes off.
While	At the same time	• While you are taking a nap, I will do my homework. • I will do my homework while you are taking a nap.
If	Conditional, depends on something else	• If my car breaks down again, I will buy a new one. • I will buy a new car if mine breaks down again.

See Chapter 18: Sentence Patterns for an additional list of subordinate conjunctions.

Read Write! Activity 20.5

Determine whether the sentences are run-ons or comma splices. If they are run-ons, put "RO" on the line preceding them. If they are comma splices, put "CS." Then, correct the sentences using a subordinating word as directed. Remember when the subordinating word is the first word of the sentence, place a comma where the dependent clause ends.

1. _____ My library books were overdue I had to pay a fine.

   Use *Because* at the beginning of the sentence.

   _____

   _____

   Use *because* in the middle of the sentence. (HINT: You will have to rearrange the sentence to have it make sense.)

   _____

   _____

2. _____ Liza has free time, she likes to watch a movie.

   Use *When* at the beginning of the sentence.

   _____

   _____

   Use *when* in the middle of the sentence. (Rearrange the sentence.)

   _____

   _____

3. _____ Raymond mowed the lawn Paul trimmed the hedges.

   Use *While* at the beginning of the sentence.

   _____

   _____

   Use *while* in the middle of the sentence.

   _____

   _____

Read Write! Activity 20.6

Determine whether the following sentences are correct or not. If the sentence is correct, put a "C" on the line preceding it. If the sentence is not, put an "RO" for run-on or a "CS" for comma splice. Three sentences are correct, three are run-ons, and four are comma splices.

1. _____ The Statue of Liberty is in New York it was a gift from France.
2. _____ The Statue of Liberty is in New York, it was a gift from France.
3. _____ Rachel did not study for the quiz she failed it.
4. _____ Because Rachel did not have time to study, she failed the quiz.
5. _____ Rachel failed the quiz because she did not study for it.
6. _____ The price of gas went down, many families plan to take a road trip for the holiday.
7. _____ Jose's grandparents live in Mexico, they have been married for 40 years.
8. _____ His family is planning a huge anniversary party for them; his grandparents plan to renew their wedding vows at the celebration.
9. _____ Run-Ons and comma splices can be tricky, writers must look out for them.
10. _____ Students who want to master run-ons and comma splices must review the above charts it is crucial that they memorize the different ways to correct these sentence errors.

Read Write! Activity 20.7

Correct the following run-on the different ways as directed. Punctuate carefully as needed.

The elevator was out of service we had to take the stairs.

1. Correct using *so.*

_____

_____

2. Correct using *therefore.*

_____

_____

3. Use *because* at the beginning of the sentence.

_____

_____

Correct the following comma splice the four different ways as directed.

The beach is deserted at night, it is packed during the day.

4. Correct using *but.*

_____

_____

5. Correct using *however.*

_____

_____

6. Use *Although* at the beginning of the sentence.

_____

_____

7. Use *although* in the middle of the sentence.

_____

_____

_____

Read Write! Activity 20.8

Determine whether the following sentences are correct or not. If they are, put a "C" for correct on the line preceding them. If they are not, put an "RO" for run-on or a "CS" for comma splice.

Living like the Wealthy for a Week

1. _____ Two years ago I got the chance to live for a week as the one-percenters live, my cousin Darla, along with 12 other family members and myself, rented a three-story mansion in Puerto Vallarta, Mexico. 2. _____ We each paid $500 it was worth it. 3. _____ Our home for the week had seven bedrooms, nine bathrooms, a large kitchen, a game room, a huge dining room/living room, four balconies, a private garden, and a swimming pool. 4. _____ Besides the great amenities, we had a private staff we had a butler, a cook, and two housekeepers. 5. _____ The butler not only took care of our needs at the house, but he also assisted with making reservations

at restaurants when we wanted to dine out and with arranging transportation to take us to various tourist sites. 6. _____ One of my favorite outings was to a private island that we reached by a chartered boat, the water was so beautiful and clear. 7. _____ On another day, we stayed at home about eight of us took turns having a private massage from one of the two masseuses whom the butler arranged to come pamper us. 8. _____ After my massage, I swam in the pool, then I took a long nap. 9. _____ I had a wonderful time in Mexico I wanted to stay forever. 10. _____ I will never forget this trip.

Chapter 21

Pronoun Usage

Key terms

pronoun, pronoun case (subjective, objective, possessive, reflexive, intensive), antecedent, pronoun-antecedent agreement

PRONOUNS

Working with pronouns and their antecedents is similar to working with subjects and verbs. However, before beginning, it is important to understand how to use pronouns before working with pronoun-antecedent agreement.

Pronouns: pronouns are words that replace a noun.

Pronoun Case

Pronouns have different **pronoun cases**, meaning you use specific pronouns for specific purposes when writing or speaking. These include subjective case, objective case, possessive case, reflexive case, and intensive case.

Subjective case: pronouns that can be used as the subject of a sentence

Person	Singular	Plural
First	I	We
Second	You	You
Third	He/She/It	They

Examples:

- ♦ I always remember to brush my teeth before bed.
- ♦ We cannot wait to take our spring break trip to the Bahamas.
- ♦ They are brand new shoes.

Objective case: pronouns that can be used as the object of a sentence

Person	Singular	Plural
First	Me	Us
Second	You	You
Third	Him/her/it	Them

Examples:

- The key ring belongs to her.
- The book was written for them.
- He brought the donuts for us.

Possessive case: pronouns that show ownership

Person	Singular	Plural
First	My/mine	Our/ours
Second	Your/yours	Your/yours
Third	His/her/hers/its	Their/theirs

Examples:

- "Smells Like Teen Spirit" is his favorite song.
- Her closet is very disorganized.
- Your essay was very well written.
- That carport is theirs.

Reflexive and intensive case: reflexive pronouns show action that was performed by someone to himself/herself. Intensive pronouns are used for emphasize and are identical to reflexive pronouns.

Person	Singular	Plural
First	Myself	Ourselves
Second	Yourself	Yourselves
Third	Himself/herself/itself	Themselves

Reflexive Examples:

- Julia looked herself over in the mirror before leaving for work.
- Christina and Samantha bought themselves silly hats to wear for the costume party.

Intensive Examples:

- The superintendent herself delivered the graduation speech.
- The house itself is quite beautiful.

Who vs. Whom

"Who" and "whom" create pronoun case problems. This is because "who" is subjective while "whom" is objective. Below is a trick to know when to use "who" and when to use "whom."

- ♦ If the sentence can be rephrased to use one of the objective pronouns, like him/her/them, then use "whom". If the sentence can be rearranged to use one of the subjective pronouns, like he/she/it/they, then choose "who."
- ♦ For example, the novel title *For Whom the Bell Tolls* can be rearranged to say "the bell tolls for him". Therefore, "whom" is required.
- ♦ On the other hand, the book title *The Girl Who Played with Fire* can be rearranged to say "she played with fire". Therefore, "who" is needed this time.
- ♦ It works with questions as well. If the question can be answered with an objective pronoun, use "whom." If the question is answered with a subjective pronoun, use "who."
  - ♦ Whom is the gift for? The gift is for him.
  - ♦ Who is in the office? He is in the office.

Read Write! Activity 21.1

Choose who or whom to correct the sentences below.

1. (Who/Whom) is going to tell him that he is fired?
2. (Who/Whom) will the proceeds from the bake sale go to?
3. To (who/whom) should I direct this telephone call?
4. The woman (who/whom) has long red hair wants to dye her hair blonde and cut it.
5. Beverly, (who/whom) I know, is a very honest and trustworthy person.

PRONOUN-ANTECEDENT AGREEMENT

Pronoun-antecedent agreement is an important rule to memorize for polished writing. It is similar to subject-verb agreement, and some of the same rules can be applied.

Antecedent: the word the pronoun replaces.

The Rule of Pronoun-Antecedent Agreement

Pronoun-Antecedent Agreement means that pronouns and their antecedents must agree in number and gender. Therefore, if the antecedent is plural, the pronoun must be plural, and if the antecedent is feminine, for example, the pronoun must be feminine, as well.

Examples:

- ♦ **The flag** was tossed high in the air, but *it* got caught by the wind and carried off.
  - ♦ The "flag" is the antecedent; it is singular and has no gender, so "it" is used
- ♦ **Daniela and Juan** planned a fabulous trip to the beach because *their* vacation times coincided this year.
  - ♦ "Daniela" and "Juan" are the antecedent; they are plural and mixed gender, so "their" is used
- ♦ **Stephen** was born in Ohio, but *he* grew up in the Midwest.
  - ♦ "Stephen" is the antecedent; he is singular and masculine, so "he" is used.

> **Think Write! Tip**
>
> Sometimes making corrections to pronoun-antecedent agreement can cause errors in subject-verb agreement. When this occurs, be sure to make corrections to subjects and verbs, as well.

Read Write! Activity 21.2

Correct errors to pronoun-antecedent agreement in the sentences below. Be aware that changes may need to be made to the verbs to make sure they agree, as well.

1. Lasagna is one of my favorite dishes, and they are what I always bring to pot luck dinners.
2. The kittens chased after the laser, clearly enjoying its time outdoors.
3. Chris stared up at the cherubs; its angelic faces made him smile.
4. Vincent submitted their letter of resignation.
5. Uber drivers get excited when conventions come to its town.

Common Problems with Pronouns and Pronoun-Antecedent Agreement

One problem with pronoun-antecedent agreement occurs when the gender of a singular antecedent is not known. For example, "a student" as an antecedent has no clear gender. However, it is singular. Therefore, it is necessary to choose "he/she," "his/her," or "him/her" as the pronoun to replace it.

Examples:

♦ A **student** has brought **his/her** essay to the office for grading.
♦ A **child** played by **himself/herself** with an imaginary friend.
♦ The **professor** made the test from **his/her** memory.

Because all of the examples have singular antecedents but unknown genders, the pronouns for both genders must be used. If they are plural, it makes it easier; just use "they," "them," or "their."

Read Write! Activity 21.3

Correct errors to pronoun-antecedent agreement with unknown gender in singular and plural below.

1. Our supervisor is never in their office when we need to speak with them.
2. The medical residents were excited when his/her residencies were finally approved.
3. Two art students will have his/her work judged by professionals.
4. The student submitted their work early to be able to enjoy Spring Break.
5. All the retiring fire fighters and police officers will receive medals from the mayor for his/her service to the city.

Indefinite pronouns also cause problems in pronoun-antecedent agreement because it is not always clear if they are singular or plural. While some are always singular or plural, others can be both.

These four indefinite pronouns are always plural. Therefore, they will always match to a plural antecedent or pronoun and take a plural verb.

Both	Few	Many	Several

Examples:

- **Both** of the police officers ate **their** lunch in the squad car.
- **Several** of the students brought **their** favorite books to class to share.

These 16 indefinite pronouns are always singular. Therefore, they will always match to a singular antecedent or pronoun and take a singular verb.

Everyone	Anyone	Someone	No one
Everybody	Anybody	Somebody	Nobody
Everything	Anything	Something	Nothing
Each	Either	Neither	One

Examples:

- **Everyone** in the room can bring **his/her** laptop tomorrow.
- **One** of the children forgot **his/her** lunch.

These five indefinite pronouns can be singular or plural. You have to check the context of the sentence to make sure you are using them correctly.

All	Any	Most	None	Some

Examples:

- **All** of the *chairs* had **their** seats broken.
  - In this sentence, we know that "all" is plural because of "chairs," so we use "their" instead of "its."
- **Some** of the *cake* was eaten, and later **it** was all gone.
  - In this sentence, we know that "some" is singular because of "cake," so we use "it" instead of "they."

Read Write! Activity 21.4

Make corrections to pronoun-antecedent errors involving indefinite pronouns in the sentences below. Remember that changes to the verbs may need to be made as well. Each sentence has two errors.

1. Each of the students need to have their parents' permission to attend the field trip.
2. All of the soldiers wore his/her medals; his/her families were so proud of them.

3. Any contractor found cutting corners on the city project will be fired on site; they will be charged with fraud, and the state will fine them.
4. Most of the cupcakes Leo baked for the party were gobbled up as soon as it was set on the table.
5. Several of the employees wrote a letter complaining about his/her supervisor Martin, who refuses to give them time off to attend his/her children's school or sporting events.

Read Write! Activity 21.5

Make corrections to pronoun-antecedent agreement errors in the paragraph below. There are five errors.

Ready, Set, Hike

The hikers met at the designated spot at 6 a.m.; he/she wanted to get an early start. Each hiker was responsible for carrying their own food and water. The small group consisted of three males and two female hikers. He/she agreed to hike for four hours, and then it would rest and eat breakfast before turning around and heading back home. Hiking is great exercise; it allows the participants to enjoy his/her time outdoors exploring nature.

Chapter 22

Commas

Key Terms

commas, restrictive, nonrestrictive, appositives, interchangeable adjectives

COMMAS

Commas, which are used to separate sentence elements, give students trouble because they have not truly mastered the comma rules. After completing this chapter, you will have a thorough understanding of commas and will no longer have to fear these pesky punctuation marks.

Commas in a Series

Commas should be inserted with items in a series of three or more things.

- Words in a series: The locker room at the recreation center was hot, crowded, and smelly.
- Phrases in a series: Maria enjoys playing the piano, shopping for antiques, and volunteering at her daughter's school.
- Clauses in a series: Jasmine is in charge of ticket sells, Ricardo is handling publicity, and Tarik is supervising the volunteers.

Read Write! Activity 22.1

Add commas after the items in a series.

1. Jose is president of the student government vice-president of the chess club and treasurer of the male initiative.
2. The mega-nut cookie recipe called for pecans walnuts almonds pistachios and cashews.
3. Chance the Rapper is a Chicago native an independent artist and a Grammy award winner.
4. Victoria goes by Vickie Lawrence goes by Larry and Gabrielle goes by Gabby.
5. Salmon catfish and shrimp are David's favorite seafood.

Commas with Coordinating Conjunctions (FANBOYS)

Commas should be inserted when there is a complete sentence on BOTH sides of the FANBOYS.

, for , and , nor , but , or , yet , so

The comma goes in front of the conjunction and follows this pattern:

a complete sentence + a comma and one of the FANBOYS + a complete sentence

♦ The baseball team won twelve games in a row, so they will definitely be in the playoffs.
♦ Jada went to the grocery store, but she left her list at home.

Read Write! Activity 22.2

Underline the FANBOYS in the following sentences. Only insert a comma if there is a complete sentence on BOTH sides of the FANBOYS. Five sentences are correct.

1. Ben is a vegetarian so he does not eat meat.
2. He became a vegetarian when he was nineteen and he encourages others to consider giving up meat.
3. Renee has stopped eating pork after talking to Ben but she is struggling with giving up beef.
4. She eats hamburgers on Tuesdays and a T-bone steak every Sunday.
5. Melissa is considering becoming a vegetarian or a vegan.
6. Melissa may become a vegetarian or she may become a vegan.
7. Vegans do not eat meat and any products that are derived from animals.
8. Some vegans also do not wear or use any products made from animals.
9. Some people become vegetarians or vegans for ethical reasons and others change their eating habits for health reasons.
10. Some individuals are concerned about how animals are treated and that they stay in small pens and cages from the time they are born until the day they are slaughtered.

Commas with Introductory Words, Phrases, and Clauses

Introductory Words: Commas should be inserted after introductory words when they are the first words of the sentence.

Common Introductory Words

First,	Then,	Also,	Therefore,	For example,
Secondly,	Next,	In addition,	Consequently,	For instance,
Finally,	Lastly,	Furthermore,	However,	On the other hand,

Introductory Phrases: Commas should be used after introductory phrases.

♦ In lieu of wedding gifts, guests were asked to give donations to the couple's favorite charities.
♦ To save money, Michael brings his lunch to work three times a week.
♦ Listening closely, Christina was able to eavesdrop on several private conversations.

Introductory Clauses: Commas should be used after introductory clauses that begin with subordinating conjunctions.

♦ Because my watch stopped working, I was late to class.
♦ If the Los Angeles Lakers win another championship, I will become a fan.
♦ Although Professor Martinez is very strict, students enjoy being in her class.

Read Write! Activity 22.3

Insert commas after the introductory words, phrases, and clauses.

1. When Cynthia was twelve years old her parents divorced.
2. To help her adjust she went to counseling.
3. During her counseling sessions Cynthia expressed her emotions.
4. For example she expressed her sadness and her anger about the situation.
5. Because she went to counseling she now feels better.

> **Read Write! Tip**

As you write sentences, you will find that you use commas in a sentence for more than one reason. For example, you may write a sentence that contains an introductory word AND items in a series of three or more things. Therefore, you must analyze your sentences looking for multiple reasons for inserting commas instead of just one.

Read Write! Activity 22.4

Add any necessary commas based on the three comma rules discussed so far:

♦ Commas with items in a series of three or more things
♦ Commas with FANBOYS when there is a complete sentence on both sides
♦ Commas after introductory words, phrases, and clauses

Hint: The sentences may require commas for more than one reason.

1. While dogs are considered man's best friend some people consider their dogs as their children so they take them everywhere with them.
2. Because Sue waited until the last minute to do her project she felt anxious pressured and frustrated.
3. On Sunday Pedro watches sporting events and he takes his children to the park.

4. After Marie decided to start her own business she talked to entrepreneurs enrolled in a business course and sought out business investors.
5. Also Marie read numerous books on how to succeed in business and she looked for a successful helpful and experienced businesswoman to be her mentor.

Restrictive and Nonrestrictive Information

Commas with Which and That: Always use commas with the word *Which* to set off information because the information is extra or not needed. In other words, the information is **nonrestrictive** or not essential. Never use commas with the word *That* to set off information because the information is needed to make the sentence's meaning clear. In other words, the information is **restrictive** or essential.

♦ The English classes, which were overloaded by three students, were packed.
♦ The English classes that were overloaded by three students were packed.

While the two sentences above are almost identical, their meanings are completely different. The sentence that contains the *which* clause set off with commas means that ALL of the English classes were packed because all of them had three extra students in them. On the other hand, the sentence that contains the word *that* not set off with commas means only some of the English classes were packed. To help make it clearer which classes were packed the *that* clause is added. This information is necessary or essential to know to help your readers understand the sentence or in this case to know that only the English classes that were overloaded were packed.

Who Clauses: Clauses that begin with *who* can be either nonrestrictive or restrictive; therefore, you must know when to use commas and when not to use commas.

Use commas when someone's specific name comes before the word *who*.

♦ Jason, who is very smart, tutors his classmates after class.
♦ Dr. Naim Lee, who served in the military for fifteen years, is very knowledgeable about the latest laser surgical procedures.

Do not use commas when a common noun comes before the word *who*.

♦ The student who has agreed to tutor his classmates after class is very smart.
♦ The doctor who served in the military for fifteen years is very knowledgeable about the latest surgical procedures.

EXCEPTION: If possessive pronouns, such as *my* or *our*, come before the common noun, then commas are needed.

♦ My oldest sister, who is a lawyer, volunteers at a free legal clinic on Thursday nights.

Appositives: Appositives, which are nonrestrictive, provide additional and nonessential information about a noun or pronoun. Therefore, you set appositives off with commas.

♦ Lucy, the star of the *I Love Lucy* show, makes me laugh even before she says anything.
♦ My favorite group is Maze, led by Frankie Beverly.
♦ Eastfield College, one of the seven campuses of the DCCCD, is located in Mesquite, a suburban area near Dallas.

Appositives contain information that could easily follow *who* or *which* as long as a verb, such as *is* or *are*, is added. Although these words are not used, commas are still needed because the information is nonessential to making it clear who or what is being discussed. In other words, the information set off by commas is extra. The three example sentences that contain appositives have been rewritten, turning them into who and which clauses to clarify why commas are needed with appositives.

♦ Lucy, who is the star of the *I Love Lucy* show, makes me laugh even before she says anything.
♦ My favorite musical group is Maze, which is led by Frankie Beverly.
♦ Eastfield College, which is one of the seven campuses of the DCCCD, is located in Mesquite, which is a suburban area near Dallas.

Read Write! Activity 22.5

Add commas as needed. Two sentences are correct.

1. Walmart which is my favorite store is always crowded on Saturdays.
2. Lee who is from Georgia does not like living in Texas.
3. The boy who sits behind me in my English class is a really good writer.
4. Lin Woo the fastest runner in our school received a track scholarship.
5. That movie that I watched yesterday was not nearly as good as the movie I saw last week.

Lead-ins for Lists

When the words *such as, especially, including,* and *like* are used, it usually means that some nonrestrictive information has been included; therefore, it is set off with a comma because it is not essential to the sentence. A comma comes before these words. However, no comma goes after them unless the nonrestrictive information appears towards the beginning of the sentence.

Examples:

♦ Veronica needs to buy some furniture for her bedroom, such as a dresser and two night stands.
♦ I love all flavors of ice cream, especially chocolate, vanilla, and strawberry.
♦ Everyone must get involved in stopping bullying, including students.
♦ Apostrophes, like commas, are pesky punctuation marks.

Read Write! Activity 22.6

Add commas as needed.

1. I am trying to add positive activities into my life such as exercise and yoga.
2. My cell phone bill is $40 a month including taxes.
3. Animals like people need love.
4. My nephew is really cute especially when he is wearing his sailor suit.
5. There will be 50 people at Billy's eighth birthday party including children, their parents, and special guests.

Interchangeable Adjectives: This rule is a little tricky because you have learned to put commas with items in a series of *three* or more things; however, this is the exception to that rule. A comma is used to separate two adjectives if the following conditions are met: the adjectives can be switched AND the word *and* can be inserted between them.

- ♦ The refreshing, cool water was appreciated after the six-mile hike.
   The refreshing and cool water was appreciated after the six-mile hike.
   The cool and refreshing water was appreciated after the six-mile hike.
- ♦ The light green suit is ugly.
   The light and green suit is ugly. These cannot be switched
   The green and light suit is ugly. Light must come before green.

Read Write! Activity 22.7

Add commas as needed. One sentence is correct.

1. The dark gloomy sky suddenly became filled with light when the sun came out.
2. I only date honest caring people.
3. We laughed when we saw the clown doing silly childish antics.
4. The light blue sky did not have any clouds in it.
5. Everyone was shocked when the arrogant selfish man gave a large donation to the charity.

Direct Quotations

Commas with Direct Quotations to Set Off the Speaker

"I am so happy to have Ms. Rodriquez as my instructor," said Michael.

Michael said, "I am so happy to have Ms. Rodriquez as my instructor."

"I am so happy," Michael said, "to have Ms. Rodriquez as my instructor."

Read Write! Activity 22.8

Add commas as needed.

1. "I can help do the dishes" offered Lisa.
2. Mario asked "Will you marry me?"
3. "As soon as you get home from school" said Roberto's mother "do your homework."
4. Billy shouted "Fire! Everyone get out!"
5. "I love you" said Enrique to Isabella.

Commas with Names When Speaking Directly to the Person

♦ Mary, where have you been?
♦ Where have you been, Mary?

Do not confuse speaking directly to the person with the person being the subject of the sentence or the direct object of the sentence.

Mary is very friendly and smart.
Mary is the subject of the sentence; no one is speaking directly to her.
We should ask Mary for help.
Mary is the direct object of the sentence; no one is speaking directly to her.

Read Write! Activity 22.9

Add commas as needed. One sentence is correct.

1. Lulu why are you laughing?
2. Why are you laughing Lulu?
3. Lulu was laughing because she thought the joke was funny.

Commas with Addresses and Dates

Addresses: Use commas with addresses to separate the items listed: the street address from the city and the city from the state or the country.

♦ Geraldo lives at 2357 Elm St., Fort Worth, Texas 76116.
♦ Mary used to live at 43 Seine Way, Paris, France, before moving back to the United States.

Dates: Use commas with dates to separate the items listed: the day of the week from the month and the day of the month from the year. If a sentence that includes commas in the address or date continues on, insert a comma after the state or country or after the month or year.

Read Write! Activity 22.10

Insert commas as needed.

1. The party will be held at 3334 Rochester Lane Kalamazoo Michigan on Tuesday March 30.
2. The 2016 Summer Olympics were held in Rio de Janeiro Brazil.
3. On July 14 2017 my government class toured the state capitol building in Austin Texas.

Read Write! Activity 22.11

Add 25 commas using all of the comma rules in this chapter.

The Pros and Cons of Adopting a Dog

"I'm thinking about getting a dog" said Jill to her friends Betty Juan and Steve. Her friend Betty who has a German shepherd expressed her concerns that there are many expenses associated with having a dog such as the cost of food veterinary services and doggy daycare. When Betty finished speaking Juan expressed his opinion. He said "I agree with you Betty. Dogs are expensive and they need a great deal of care. For example you must feed walk and play with them every day." After hearing these comments Jill was starting to reconsider getting a dog. However Steve's comments made her think that getting a dog may not be a bad idea after all. Steve said "Jill what Betty and Juan have said is true. However dogs also bring a great deal of joy. The best day of my life was June 1 2013; that was the day I adopted Max a loving happy bull terrier. I adopted him from

the Pasadena Humane Society which is located in Pasadena California."

Even though all of her friends gave their opinion Jill knew that the decision

was hers to make.

Chapter 23
Apostrophes

Key Terms

contractions, irregular plurals

APOSTROPHES

Apostrophes, like commas, sometimes get sprinkled in students' writing in places where they are not supposed to be. Therefore, you must look out for apostrophes and know when to use them and when not to use them. Basically, apostrophes are used two ways: to form contractions and to show ownership.

Apostrophes in Contractions

A **contraction** is a word that is formed by joining two words into one with an apostrophe. The apostrophe takes the place of the missing letter or letters.

Chart of Commonly Used Contractions

I am	I'm
Do not	Don't
Cannot	Can't
Could not	Couldn't
It is, it has	It's
There is, there was	There's
Are not	Aren't
Is not	Isn't
will not	Won't

It's versus Its

Sometimes the contraction it's gives students problems because it is confused with the possessive pronoun its. Here is a tip to help you not confuse the two words. It's is the contraction form of it is or it has. As you analyze a sentence to determine whether you need an apostrophe with its, mentally put one in and then reread the sentence inserting "it is" or "it has" in place of its. If either spelled out form of the contraction makes sense, then you know that you need it's. However, if neither spelled out form makes perfect sense, then you need to use its.

Examples:

The dog chased its tail.   Insert <u>it is</u> or <u>it has</u>: The dog chased <u>it is</u> tail. The dog chased <u>it has</u> tail. Neither it is nor it has makes sense, so *its* is correct.

It's hot in here.   Insert it is or it has. It <u>is hot</u> in here. <u>It has</u> hot in here. *It is* makes sense, so *it's* is correct.

Note that its' is not a word; therefore, it should never be used.

> ➤ **Read Write! Tip**
>
> In formal academic writing, most of your instructors do not allow students to use contractions unless they are writing dialogue or an informal assignment. Check with your instructors regarding their policy regarding contractions.

Read Write! Activity 23.1

Add apostrophes to form contractions.

1. I dont mean to stare, but arent you Bruno Mars?
2. Theres nothing like a three-day weekend.
3. Its so good to see you; I cant believe its been three years since we last saw each other.
4. The plane couldnt take off since its wings were icy.

Singular Possessive

To show ownership or possession of singular nouns or indefinite pronouns, add an apostrophe and an s.

Examples:

The little girl's bedroom is pink.
Malik's bicycle has a flat tire.
Anyone's ideas regarding the party will be appreciated.
Saturday's events include a hot dog eating contest.

If the singular word ends in an s, add an apostrophe and an s or just an apostrophe.

Examples:

Douglas's glasses are missing. Or Douglas' glasses are missing.

Read Write! Activity 23.2

Add apostrophes as needed to form singular possessives.

1. Everyones opinion is important.
2. Julias mothers name is Julia, also.
3. Larrys essay must be submitted by Fridays deadline.
4. The professors rules are strict but fair.
5. Tom Bradys jersey went missing after the Super Bowl.

Plural Possessive

To show ownership or possession of plural nouns that end in an s, simply add an apostrophe.

Plural Possessive	Singular Possessive
The players' victory was a surprise for them.	The player's victory was a surprise for her.
The students' essays are due on Thursday.	The student's essay is due on Thursday.
Her parents' motor home is enormous.	Her father's motor home is enormous
The soldiers' guns are shiny.	The soldier's guns are shiny.
The Thompsons' house is blue.	Mr. Thompson's house is blue.
The cities' zoning laws are confusing.	The city's zoning laws are confusing.
I am taking two weeks' vacation in June.	One week's vacation is not long enough.
My two sister-in-laws' houses are ginormous.	My sister-in-law's house is ginormous.

Read Write! Activity 23.3

Insert apostrophes as needed to form plural possessives. One sentence is correct.

1. The three background singers threats to quit were ignored.
2. I am taking two weeks vacation in July to San Juan.
3. Management refused to consider any of its employees needs.
4. The strikers were forced to return to work or risk being fired by their supervisors.
5. After 2,000 physicians registered for the conference, the doctors conference had to move to a larger location.

Irregular Plurals

While most nouns become plural by adding an s, **irregular plurals** change their spelling. For these words, you must add an apostrophe and an s to show ownership or possession.

Singular Possessive		Plural Possessive	Incorrect /Never Use
the child's bike	the child's bikes	the children's bikes	childrens'
the man's hat	the man's hats	the men's hats	mens'
the lady's purse	the lady's purses	the ladies' purses	ladie's
The woman's gun	the woman's guns	the women's guns	womens'

Read Write! Activity 23.4

Add apostrophes as needed.

1. The mans cashmere coat is very warm.
2. The mens soccer team challenged the womens team to a match.
3. The childrens parents are donating their kids old bikes to charity.
4. The line to the ladies restroom is always four times longer than the line to the mens restroom.
5. The womens book club is reading *Gone Girl* by Gillian Flynn.

Possessive Compound Nouns

Place an apostrophe and an "s" ('s) after the second name when two people jointly own something; place an apostrophe and an "s" ('s) after each name when they have separate ownership.

Leonardo and Gina's car wash is very successful. (Leonardo and Gina jointly own the car wash.)

Leonardo's and Gina's secretaries are throwing a surprise party for the company. (Leonardo and Gina both have their own secretaries; they do not share one secretary.)

Possessive Pronouns

Do not use an apostrophe with possessive pronouns; they already show ownership. Possessive pronouns include the following: *his, hers, its, mine, ours theirs,* and *yours*.

Possessive vs. Simply Plural Nouns

Just because a word ends in an s does not mean you should automatically add an apostrophe. The word could simply be in its plural form, showing more than one and not ownership or possession.

Example:

The sisters are identical twins, so only their parents can tell them apart.

The words *sisters, twins,* and *parents* are simply in their plural form; none of these words are showing possession, so no apostrophes are needed.

Two Common Apostrophe Mistakes: Verbs and Numerals

Do not use apostrophes with any verbs, including ones that end in s.

Wrong: Lisa **want's** to win the lottery; she **hope's** to win soon.
Correct: Lisa wants to win the lottery; she hopes to win soon.

Also, avoid using apostrophes when writing numerals in general or when writing numerals of a decade or century.

Wrong: William's **3's** look like **5's**.   William's **three's** look like **five's**.
Correct: William's 3s look like 5s.   William's threes look like fives.
Wrong: During the **1970's**, disco music was popular.
Correct: During the 1970s, disco music was popular.

Read Write! Activity 23.5

Remove any unnecessary apostrophes.

1. During the 1990's, Nelson Mandela was freed from prison and elected South Africa's first black president.
2. Kim's mother want's her to be a doctor.
3. The brothers' are going to their family's farm to celebrate their grandfather's birthday.
4. James' and Lucy's son is named James, Jr.
5. The musicans' put on a great concert for fans of their's.

Read Write! 23.6

Correct the ten apostrophe mistakes in the following paragraph.

Communication 101

Betty always thought she was a good communicator until she went to a communication workshop that was sponsored by her schools communication department. The workshops title was Common Communication Mistakes. One of Bettys main communication errors was interrupting. Betty used to frequently interrupt when it was her husbands turn to speak, but thanks to the workshop, she now let's him finish his thoughts when its his turn. She also used to shout when she got angry at her husbands' mistakes. Now she controls her volume and refrain's from raising her voice. The third mistake Betty used to make involved name calling. However, since completing this workshop, shes learned that name calling is a form of verbal abuse. Because Betty has apologized to her husband and is now communicating better, she and her husbands marriage is much stronger.

PART V
Further Readings

This section of *Read Write! Breaking down a Text and Building up an Essay* contains supplementary readings. They are arranged in no specific order but represent several different rhetorical modes and organizational patterns. You should use PAUSE on each passage to actively engage with it and keep track of new vocabulary words in your vocabulary journal. It is a good idea to try to find at least three new vocabulary words in each text. Some passages have prereading questions; however, reading comprehension and writing questions follow every reading.

Prereading Questions for "Learning to Read and Write"

1. What background knowledge do you have of Frederick Douglas?
2. What is something that you are willing to risk your live for to achieve it?

Frederick Douglass (1818-1895) was an American author, speaker, statesman, and abolitionist. Born in slavery, Douglass escaped in 1838 and went on to become a prominent leader of the abolitionist movement. The passage below is an excerpt from his autobiography, *Narrative of the Life of Frederick Douglass, an American Slave*.

Learning to Read and Write

by Frederick Douglass

1   I lived in Master Hugh's family about seven years. During this time, I succeeded in learning to read and write. In accomplishing this, I was compelled to resort to various stratagems. I had no regular teacher. My mistress, who had kindly commenced to instruct me, had, in compliance with the advice and direction of her husband, not only ceased to instruct, but had set her face against my being instructed by any one else. It is due, however, to my mistress to say of her, that she did not adopt this course of treatment immediately. She at first lacked the depravity indispensable to shutting me up in mental darkness. It was at least necessary for her to have some training in the exercise of irresponsible power, to make her equal to the task of treating me as though I were a brute.

2   My mistress was, as I have said, a kind and tender-hearted woman; and in the simplicity of her soul she commenced, when I first went to live with her, to treat me as she supposed one human being ought to treat another. In entering upon the duties of a slaveholder, she did not seem to perceive that I sustained to her the relation of a mere chattel, and that for her to treat me

as a human being was not only wrong, but dangerously so. Slavery proved as injurious to her as it did to me. When I went there, she was a pious, warm, and tender-hearted woman. There was no sorrow or suffering for which she had not a tear. She had bread for the hungry, clothes for the naked, and comfort for every mourner that came within her reach. Slavery soon proved its ability to divest her of these heavenly qualities. Under its influence, the tender heart became stone, and the lamblike disposition gave way to one of tiger-like fierceness. The first step in her downward course was in her ceasing to instruct me. She now commenced to practise her husband's precepts. She finally became even more violent in her opposition than her husband himself. She was not satisfied with simply doing as well as he had commanded; she seemed anxious to do better. Nothing seemed to make her more angry than to see me with a newspaper. She seemed to think that here lay the danger. I have had her rush at me with a face made all up of fury, and snatch from me a newspaper, in a manner that fully revealed her apprehension. She was an apt woman; and a little experience soon demonstrated, to her satisfaction, that education and slavery were incompatible with each other.

3   From this time I was most narrowly watched. If I was in a separate room any considerable length of time, I was sure to be suspected of having a book, and was at once called to give an account of myself. All this, however, was too late. The first step had been taken. Mistress, in teaching me the alphabet, had given me the *inch,* and no precaution could prevent me from taking the *ell.*

4   The plan which I adopted, and the one by which I was most successful, was that of making friends of all the little white boys whom I met in the street. As many of these as I could, I converted into teachers. With their kindly aid, obtained at different times and in different places, I finally succeeded in learning to read. When I was sent of errands, I always took my book with me, and by going one part of my errand quickly, I found time to get a lesson before my return. I used also to carry bread with me, enough of which was always in the house, and to which I was always welcome; for I was much better off in this regard than many of the poor white children in our neighborhood. This bread I used to bestow upon the hungry little urchins, who, in return, would give me that more valuable bread of knowledge. I am strongly tempted to give the names of two or three of those little boys, as a testimonial of the gratitude and affection I bear them; but prudence forbids;—not that it would injure me, but it might embarrass them; for it is almost an unpardonable offence to teach slaves to read in this Christian country. It is enough to say of the dear little fellows, that they lived on Philpot Street, very near Durgin and Bailey's ship-yard. I used to talk this matter of slavery over with them. I would sometimes say to them, I wished I could be as free as they would be when they got to be men. "You will be free as soon as you are twenty-one, *but I am a slave for life!* Have not I as good a right to be free as you have?" These words used to trouble them; they would express for me the liveliest sympathy, and console me with the hope that something would occur by which I might be free.

5   I was now about twelve years old, and the thought of being *a slave for life* began to bear heavily upon my heart. Just about this time, I got hold of a book entitled "The Columbian Orator." Every opportunity I got, I used to read this book. Among much of other interesting matter, I found in it a dialogue between a master and his slave. The slave was represented as having run away from his master three times. The dialogue represented the conversation which took place between them, when the slave was retaken the third time. In this dialogue, the whole argument in behalf of slavery was brought forward by the master, all of which was disposed of by the slave. The slave was made to say some very smart as well as impressive things in reply to his master—things which had the desired though unexpected effect; for the conversation resulted in the voluntary emancipation of the slave on the part of the master.

6   In the same book, I met with one of Sheridan's mighty speeches on and in behalf of Catholic emancipation. These were choice documents to me. I read them over and over again with unabated interest. They gave tongue to interesting thoughts of my own soul, which had frequently flashed through my mind, and died away for want of utterance. The moral which I gained from the dialogue was the power of truth over the conscience of even a slaveholder. What I got from Sheridan was a bold denunciation of slavery, and a powerful vindication of human rights. The reading of these documents enabled me to utter my thoughts, and to meet the arguments brought forward to sustain slavery; but while they relieved me of one difficulty, they brought on another even more painful than

the one of which I was relieved. The more I read, the more I was led to abhor and detest my enslavers. I could regard them in no other light than a band of successful robbers, who had left their homes, and gone to Africa, and stolen us from our homes, and in a strange land reduced us to slavery. I loathed them as being the meanest as well as the most wicked of men. As I read and contemplated the subject, behold! that very discontentment which Master Hugh had predicted would follow my learning to read had already come, to torment and sting my soul to unutterable anguish. As I writhed under it, I would at times feel that learning to read had been a curse rather than a blessing. It had given me a view of my wretched condition, without the remedy. It opened my eyes to the horrible pit, but to no ladder upon which to get out. In moments of agony, I envied my fellow-slaves for their stupidity. I have often wished myself a beast. I preferred the condition of the meanest reptile to my own. Any thing, no matter what, to get rid of thinking! It was this everlasting thinking of my condition that tormented me. There was no getting rid of it. It was pressed upon me by every object within sight or hearing, animate or inanimate. The silver trump of freedom had roused my soul to eternal wakefulness. Freedom now appeared, to disappear no more forever. It was heard in every sound, and seen in every thing. It was ever present to torment me with a sense of my wretched condition. I saw nothing without seeing it, I heard nothing without hearing it, and felt nothing without feeling it. It looked from every star, it smiled in every calm, breathed in every wind, and moved in every storm.

7   I often found myself regretting my own existence, and wishing myself dead; and but for the hope of being free, I have no doubt but that I should have killed myself, or done something for which I should have been killed. While in this state of mind, I was eager to hear any one speak of slavery. I was a ready listener. Every little while, I could hear something about the abolitionists. It was some time before I found what the word meant. It was always used in such connections as to make it an interesting word to me. If a slave ran away and succeeded in getting clear, or if a slave killed his master, set fire to a barn, or did any thing very wrong in the mind of a slaveholder, it was spoken of as the fruit of *abolition.* Hearing the word in this connection very often, I set about learning what it meant. The dictionary afforded me little or no help. I found it was "the act of abolishing;" but then I did not know what was to be abolished. Here I was perplexed. I did not dare to ask any one about its meaning, for I was satisfied that it was something they wanted me to know very little about. After a patient waiting, I got one of our city papers, containing an account of the number of petitions from the north, praying for the abolition of slavery in the District of Columbia, and of the slave trade between the States. From this time I understood the words *abolition* and *abolitionist,* and always drew near when that word was spoken, expecting to hear something of importance to myself and fellow-slaves. The light broke in upon me by degrees. I went one day down on the wharf of Mr. Waters; and seeing two Irishmen unloading a scow of stone, I

went, unasked, and helped them. When we had finished, one of them came to me and asked me if I were a slave. I told him I was. He asked, "Are ye a slave for life?" I told him that I was. The good Irishman seemed to be deeply affected by the statement. He said to the other that it was a pity so fine a little fellow as myself should be a slave for life. He said it was a shame to hold me. They both advised me to run away to the north; that I should find friends there, and that I should be free. I pretended not to be interested in what they said, and treated them as if I did not understand them; for I feared they might be treacherous. White men have been known to encourage slaves to escape, and then, to get the reward, catch them and return them to their masters. I was afraid that these seemingly good men might use me so; but I nevertheless remembered their advice, and from that time I resolved to run away. I looked forward to a time at which it would be safe for me to escape. I was too young to think of doing so immediately; besides, I wished to learn how to write, as I might have occasion to write my own pass. I consoled myself with the hope that I should one day find a good chance. Meanwhile, I would learn to write.

8   The idea as to how I might learn to write was suggested to me by being in Durgin and Bailey's ship-yard, and frequently seeing the ship carpenters, after hewing, and getting a piece of timber ready for use, write on the timber the name of that part of the ship for which it was intended. When a piece of timber was intended for the larboard side, it would be marked thus— "L."

When a piece was for the starboard side, it would be marked thus— "S." A piece for the larboard side forward, would be marked thus— "L. F." When a piece was for starboard side forward, it would be marked thus— "S. F." For larboard aft, it would be marked thus— "L. A." For starboard aft, it would be marked thus— "S. A." I soon learned the names of these letters, and for what they were intended when placed upon a piece of timber in the ship-yard. I immediately commenced copying them, and in a short time was able to make the four letters named. After that, when I met with any boy who I knew could write, I would tell him I could write as well as he. The next word would be, "I don't believe you. Let me see you try it." I would then make the letters which I had been so fortunate as to learn, and ask him to beat that. In this way I got a good many lessons in writing, which it is quite possible I should never have gotten in any other way. During this time, my copy-book was the board fence, brick wall, and pavement; my pen and ink was a lump of chalk. With these, I learned mainly how to write. I then commenced and continued copying the Italics in Webster's Spelling Book, until I could make them all without looking on the book. By this time, my little Master Thomas had gone to school, and learned how to write, and had written over a number of copy-books. These had been brought home, and shown to some of our near neighbors, and then laid aside. My mistress used to go to class meeting at the Wilk Street meetinghouse every Monday afternoon, and leave me to take care of the house. When left thus, I used to spend the time in writing in the spaces left in Master Thomas's copy-book, copying what he had written. I continued to do this until I could write a hand very similar to that of Master Thomas. Thus, after a long, tedious effort for years, I finally succeeded in learning how to write.

Read Write! Comprehension and Writing Questions

1. What can you infer about the title?

2. What does the author mean when he speaks of the mistress treating him as a human was dangerous?

3. Why did the mistress believe education and slavery were incompatible?

4. How did the author learn to read?

5. The author speaks of "bread" in paragraph 5. What bread was more important to the author? Explain your answer.

6. What is the difference between an enslaver and a slave master?

7. After reading the essay, what can you add to your previous inferences about the title?

8. Writing prompt: Imagine that you are a slave. Write a letter to your slave master arguing three reasons you should be emancipated.

9. Discussion prompt: Around age 12 or 13 in many cultures, boys are considered men. Why do you think the author feels so hopeless?

Prereading Questions for "Take the Time to Manage Your Time"

1. What do you spend most of your time doing?
2. How often do you access social networking sites?

When this was published, David Ramirez was a student journalist at Eastfield College in Mesquite, TX. The passage below first appeared as a column in Eastfield College's newspaper, *The EtCetera*, in Volume 45, Issue 9, in March 2014. He graduated in May 2014.

Take the Time to Manage Your Time

by David Ramirez

1   College students, especially new ones, are learning something you can't learn in a classroom: time management.

2   When full-time students juggle classes and a job, it can be quite difficult.

3   As a student with a 4.0 GPA, I wanted to challenge myself beyond this semester. I'm taking six college courses and working two jobs, which makes time management very important.

4   When I tell my classmates about my situation, they ask me how I do it. I always respond with, "That's easy; I just gave up my free time."

5   Students are often distracted by things other than school, such as social networking, video games, and procrastination. I used to spend most of my time on social networking sites, such as Facebook or Instagram, but now I rarely have time for those activities.

6   I use a planner to assist me with my time management. Seeing your time on paper or through an app on a smartphone can give you a better idea of what

free time you have. I love having a planner app on my phone. It's always easy to access my schedule because it's always at my fingertips. I have alarms set up for certain tasks to remind myself what I should be doing at what specific time.

7   Setting deadlines is helpful. Breaking down everything step by step is a sure way to conquer time. Although I sometimes feel like stress will overtake me, I always try to think positively because I believe thinking positively helps students perform better at work and on tests.

8   Prioritizing tasks is also very important. Worry about the most important items on your list first before tackling smaller tasks.

9   Sometimes, situations can pop out of nowhere. In those circumstances, all I can do is work through it efficiently. Since I use a planner, I can adjust my time as needed.

10   I always stay busy, but I simply love it because I know I'm completing many goals while earning money. I get a great sense of accomplishment knowing that I can achieve many objectives simultaneously.

11   I honestly didn't mind giving up all of my free time because I would rather do something productive than just sit around.

12   If I can do it, you can do it, as well.

13   To reach your full potential in life, you must overcome many challenges. So put down the remote control or your smartphone and ask yourself what you should really be doing right now.

Read Write! Reading Comprehension and Writing Questions

1. What is the main idea of the passage?

2. Who is the author's primary audience?

3. How does the author prove he is credible to write about time management?

4. In order to manage his time, the author had to give up accessing social networking sites. Write a paragraph about some of the things you would have to give up to manage your time more wisely.

5. Write a comparison-contrast essay using this piece and the piece by Frederick Douglass. Compare and/or contrast the sacrifices each made to get what he wanted.

The Cost of Plagiarism

1   Plagiarism is the unacknowledged incorporation of another's words into your own written work. Essentially, it means you have stolen someone's words and called them your own. What most students do not realize is that plagiarism is expensive. It can cost you in more ways than you realize.

2   The cheapest price you will pay for plagiarism is a failing grade on the assignment in question. However, this may not end up being cheap. Sometimes that one zero can push you over the edge, taking you from an A to a B, a B to a C, a C to a D, or worst of all, a D to an F. The cost of plagiarism rises if your instructor's academic dishonesty policy is to fail the offending student for the semester. This would mean that plagiarism has cost you the entire course. That is a hefty price indeed. It gets worse, though. Some instructors consider plagiarism so serious (and it *is* serious) that they choose to report you to the dean, which may result in your suspension from the college. This is a very high price to pay for academic dishonesty. Can you afford it?

3   The steepest price you pay when committing plagiarism is the fact that you are cheating yourself out of valuable learning. The point of your coursework is for you to acquire and apply knowledge, eventually creating your own work to show competency in a subject. If you steal someone else's work or you let a friend or family member do the work for you, what have you gotten out of it? If you get caught, all you have gotten is a failing grade. If you did not get

caught, perhaps you got a good grade. However, you have lost the chance to learn valuable knowledge or a new skill. Sometimes this new knowledge is foundational or scaffolded, which means you need it to learn the next concept. Now you are missing a step—you are behind because you did not do your own work. Suddenly college has become that much more difficult, and we all know college is not easy to begin with. Is this a price you are willing to pay?

4   Moreover, it is much easier today for professors to catch plagiarism than it was in the past. They have access to programs like turnitin.com and SafeAssign. Such programs run students' writing through a database to check for plagiarism, and most professors, in particular composition professors, use such programs to effectively eradicate plagiarism from their classrooms. If your instructor uses a plagiarism checker, it exponentially increases the chances that you will get caught, even if you attempt to pull single lines from multiple sources and reword them in an attempt to hide your tracks.

5   Plagiarism is too expensive a cost for any student. You can end up failing an assignment or course or being suspended from your college. You also lose the chance to acquire valuable information and gain a better understanding of larger concepts and the world around you. In fact, today you have more of a chance of getting caught than in any other time period. Thus, plagiarism should be avoided at all costs.

Read Write! Comprehension and Writing Questions

1. What is the main idea of this passage?

2. How is plagiarism defined?

3. What are some of the supporting details for the main idea of this passage?

4. What does "scaffolded" mean in the context of this essay?

5. Write a reading response to this passage, including more types of academic dishonesty, as well, such as cheating and collusion.

Stephen M. Kintner is a math educator at the secondary level. He has taught mathematics for eight years, including the subjects of geometry, algebra II, pre-calculus, and calculus. He enjoys watching college football, playing video games, and spending time with his wife, daughter, and pets.

Practical Mathematics

by Stephen M. Kintner

1   For many people, the study of mathematics can be frustrating. The formulas and all the rules can be difficult to keep straight. However, math is a skill. It is more about training your mind to think logically and build your reasoning skills to come to an accurate conclusion than about memorizing the quadratic formula. But, like most skills, it requires persistence and practice. Unless you become a math teacher, I doubt you will have a job that will require you to solve for a mysterious "x". However, there are a great many jobs in the workforce today that want people who can solve problems – to analyze a situation and to make an appropriate deduction about how to solve the situation. An employee that is able to understand a situation and be insightful is incredibly valuable. In fact, having strong math skills has been a useful skill throughout the ages, from using trigonometry to design a chair or building that won't collapse, calculating trajectories for a course of travel (or even ballistics), to programming your computer or smartphone, running your car, and many important medical advances. The world you experience today would not be possible without mathematics.

2   The most common field of mathematics that people are familiar with is statistics. An argument backed with facts is significantly stronger when attempting to prove a point. A person who can give a position and say "my position is better" will not sound as strong as someone stating that their position is 50 percent better due to reasons x, y, and z. Tune in to a sports talk channel. There are always arguments and discussions about who the best player is and which team is the best – and all will be argued passionately with the statistics to back it up. However, statistics is not limited to sports. A strong business position can be created to help sell your product if you are able to create a positive image for yourself (or a negative image for a competitor!). This product could even be your services to a potential employer or maybe even your current boss. Why do you deserve the job? You can use statistics to show you are the best choice because you are better than the competition. What about that promotion you want? You can use statistics to show your productivity or how efficient you are compared to others. Backing up something with statistics strengthens an argument, no matter what the argument is about.

3   Another field of mathematics that is frequently studied is geometry. Geometry is another sort of subject that many people wonder about. Geometry as experienced by many students is a study of shapes, distances, angles and a lot of theorems. Some may even remember the dreaded "proofs". However, the shapes that are studied are more about creating logical conclusions based on observations that arise in the world around us. Shapes and lines have many

repetitive patterns and natures that can be easily recognized and applied to help build our reasoning skills. If you can logically think through a situation based on past experiences, it is more likely you can come to a reasonable conclusion about the outcome. Geometry uses these principles all the time, and so do you.

4   Next, trigonometry is an incredible study of mathematics that has developed all across the world. Foundations of trigonometry can be traced back 2000 years to the Middle East, China, Europe, and India. Trigonometry was originally developed to help track the position of stars in the sky and other distances in the real world and very quickly was applied to determining the course of a journey – simple knowledge would help determine if a path was in the right direction. Many people have seen the use of a spyglass followed by the use of a compass (or other object with two pointed ends, almost like an upside down "V") in a movie that a ship's captain is using to march across a map. What is never mentioned is that the ship's captain is actually doing trigonometry to verify the ship's course or estimate the amount of time to the planned destination. Trigonometry is also frequently used in carpentry – verifying the lengths of beams without formal measurements and also determining a maximum load that could be held. It would not be very useful to make a chair that would not hold someone up. Trigonometry has also been used on battlefields for centuries to determine how to fire weapons, from the catapults of ancient Greece and Rome to the rockets used during World War II. In fact, during World War II, there were strategic outposts dedicated to determining what angle to fire artillery at to hit

a location. Trigonometry is exceptionally useful when discussing anything that can be recognized as a repeated pattern, and today it is used frequently when working with digital signals. Many people have seen a .wav file for a computer, especially for an MP3 or a video. These are trigonometric patterns used to tell the computer what to do. Trigonometry is much like geometry in that it is based on observations and our determination to understand more of how the world works around us.

5   On the other hand, calculus is a subject of mathematics that has a certain stigma about it – being the final destination of many people's mathematics education (or even above it). Outside of some movie references, many do not know what calculus is other than "hard math". Calculus, however, is very often seen in real life. If stripped down to the bare essence, calculus would be a discussion of how a rate of change affects our lives. Many of the foundations of calculus can be credited to Sir Isaac Newton – the same man that originated many principles of modern day physics. Calculus was originally how Newton explained his physics equations. How does acceleration change an object's velocity? How does a velocity changing affect an object's current position? If you've ever completed a physics equation involving these items, you've done some rudimentary calculus. However, calculus is not limited to only acceleration, velocity, and position of an object. How does an interest rate affect a loan, or what do you do when creating a budget—especially if the household expenses increase or decrease? How can you determine how far your

gas tank will go if you continue on your current usage? In the end, calculus is about using a situation to make an accurate prediction of what will happen in the future and how that can be applied to an incredible number of situations.

6   Math's real world applications are plentiful. It may seem as though it is all about solving for that mysterious "x" or graphing, but in reality, people use math constantly in the form of basic problem solving skills. Moreover, mathematics helps to build the world around us. Even when you move into more traditional sounding mathematical subjects, like geometry or calculus, the principle remains the same: mathematics is critical thinking, and you do it every day.

Read Write! Comprehension and Writing Questions

1. What is the main idea of this passage?

2. What rhetorical mode does this passage fall under?

3. What can be inferred about the author's attitude toward math?

4. The author suggests math is everywhere, and we use it every day. List at least two specific examples from the passage that support the author's opinion about math.

5. Write a reading response about how you feel about mathematics. Did this passage give you any new insights as to how mathematics is used? Did it change how you feel about math?

Prereading Questions for "Choose Wisely"

1. When you were a child, what is an activity or an event that you saved your money for that you looked forward to being able to do or attend?
2. Recall an event that you looked forward to attending when you were a child that did not turn out like you expected. What happened?
3. Do you participate in certain activities with certain people? How do you go about determining which of your friends you will include when you want to attend a particular function or event?

Michelle Stewart-Thomas is a sociology professor who specializes in helping people improve and enjoy healthy relationships with themselves, with others, and with the Lord. She has a Ph.D. in sociology from the University of Southern California, an M.S. in sociology from Purdue University and two degrees from Fuller Theological Seminary—an M.A. in theology and an M.S. in marriage and family therapy. Besides being a professor, she is also the executive director of the Relationship Repair and Care Center; the passage "Choose Wisely" is a post from the center's website, which means it does not fall into a traditional essay format but rather combines several rhetorical modes.

Choose Wisely

by Michelle Stewart-Thomas

1   For an adult, choosing the right partner to accompany you for the rest of your life in the bond of marriage is as important as it is for a child to choose the right friend to accompany him or her to a fun-filled day at Six Flags Amusement Park. In both cases, choosing the wrong partner can have disastrous effects.

A Fun Day at Six Flags?

2   When I was younger, going to Six Flags was one of the momentous events of the summer. I would save my allowance diligently—Six Flags was not cheap—and I planned to get my money's worth by staying all day. But in order for the day to be truly rewarding, I had to be careful to choose the right companion. I never again wanted to make the mistake of inviting someone like my friend Maria to go to Six Flags with me.

3   The summer I turned eleven, my older sister agreed to chaperone Maria and me at Six Flags. Maria and I were excited the whole way to Six Flags, happily anticipating all the fun we'd have. I could hardly wait to get inside the gates and ride the first roller coaster I saw. Once inside the gates, I started dashing toward the Shockwave, the scariest of all the rides. Maria held back, however, and said, "I don't like roller coasters."

4   I couldn't believe it! Who in their right mind would spend all that money to come to Six Flags and not ride the roller coasters? I looked to my sister for assistance, but she betrayed me.

5   "If Maria doesn't like roller coasters," she said, "we'd better find something you both can enjoy. After all, it wouldn't be fair to make her stand in those long, hot lines for nothing."

6   Fair? Of course it wasn't fair—to me! I tried to protest, but my sister said I was being selfish and threatened to take us home.

7   Not wanting the day to be a total loss, I suggested we ride the parachute ride, but Maria was afraid of heights. Next, I suggested the boat ride, but Maria didn't want to get her hair wet.

8   Exasperated, I shouted, "Why do you come to Six Flags?"

9   Her answer was simple, "For the shows."

10   The next thing you know we were waiting for the Chevy Show, and then the Gun Fight Show, and finally the Dolphin Show. Unhappily I sat in show after show wondering what happened to my sister's idea of doing something

we both liked. I guess the problem was that although Maria and I both liked Six Flags, we liked it for different reasons.

11   Finally, the disastrous day ended with me not having ridden a single roller coaster ride. I was completely devastated, but I learned my lesson. Never again would I invite someone to spend the day with me at Six Flags without first making sure our objectives were the same—to ride as many roller coasters as possible.

A Roller Coaster Ride of Misery!

12   Too often people begin marriages in the same manner that Maria and I began our day at Six Flags. They know that they want to be married, and because they care for each other in a special way, they decide to enter marriage together. They realize the cost of marriage is high, but they believe they are willing to pay the price because each partner anticipates having an over-all positive experience. Unfortunately, because they do not thoroughly determine before marriage their likes and dislikes, their goals and expectations, and the way in which they plan to meet their individual and joint needs, they often end up feeling disillusioned and cheated. This feeling can be especially frustrating when it seems as though one partner is getting his or her "way" most of the time. Sometimes people clearly know that their partners' needs, desires, personality, and values are incongruent with their own, but because they want the relationship so much, they are

willing to short-change themselves and compromise who they are. But when you short-change yourself, you only end of short-changing the marriage, and then no one is happy.

13   Picking a marriage partner and then staying with that partner is never easy. However, the more information you have about yourself and your potential mate before you make a commitment, the greater chance you have of creating a marriage that will last a lifetime without being a roller coaster ride of misery.

Read Write! Comprehension and Writing Questions

1. What is the main idea of the passage?

2. What rhetorical modes have been combined in this piece?

3. According to the author, what should individuals fully know about each other before agreeing to get married? Why is this important?

4. If you were to rewrite this piece, how would you organize it based on what you have learned from this textbook about the rhetorical modes and essay format?

5. What is a childhood lesson you have learned that serves you well as an adult? Write a response about your experience.

Jane Stanford is a travel enthusiast. She has traveled to four out of the seven continents and visited such places as Paris, France; Riga, Latvia; Marrakech, Morocco; Pula, Croatia; and Buenos Aires, Argentina. She also enjoys traveling in the US and has lived both here and abroad in Great Britain and the Netherlands. "Learning to Queue" recounts some of Stanford's experiences studying abroad in Brighton, England, for her master's degree.

Learning to Queue

by Jane Stanford

1   I was sobbing when I had to leave England. I was crying so much the security guard took a step back as I approached the gate. He glanced at my passport and waved me through, eager for me to be as far away from him as possible. It did make me laugh that even hardened airport security guards are scared of crying girls. I had been studying abroad in England, and it was the best year of my life. . .I wasn't ready for it to be over.

2   A year before, I had just finished my bachelor's degree, but I hadn't been interested in entering the working world yet, so I applied for graduate school. I knew I wanted something completely different, so I only applied to two schools in England. One didn't accept me, but the other did. Suddenly, I was planning a new life on the south coast of England in a city I had never been to: Brighton. From the day I arrived, I fell in love with Brighton and with England. I loved the adventure and fully embraced all England had to offer me. I made myself go with the way of life there and not constantly compare it to the U.S. I let myself become British and do things that I never would have done before. That was the best thing about living abroad—not just learning about other countries and cultures, but learning about myself.

3   Acting like a Brit was a lot of fun. My day didn't begin until I had a cup of tea with milk, and the day didn't end until I had a cup of tea with milk, usually with a biscuit (cookie in American) on the side. I lived in a house with other international students, and we spent many evenings comparing languages and trying to decipher England English. I had it easier than others, but some words still always tripped me up. I had lots of "mates" in my course, I crossed the street on "zebras," and "queued" for everything. That was survival in England—queue and move to the left. Anything else they could overlook, but if you jumped the line and moved to the right, they let you know you were in the wrong. But it wasn't just learning Brit-speak and watching football (American soccer), and it certainly wasn't just learning about international law in my classes: it was about learning about me. Studying abroad opens up your eyes and makes you grow.

4   Living abroad you're away from everything that you have known: your family and friends, TV channels, even something as basic as knowing how to navigate a grocery store. Frequently, you're dropped in a country where you don't speak the language. Even though most students study the language before they leave, studying it in a class with an English-speaking teacher and trying to navigate the train station in a foreign city are two completely different things. You learn that you can find the right train, get off the bus at the right stop, and buy the right ticket to get to the university. You might end up in the wrong city a couple of times, or get kicked off for having the wrong

ticket, but eventually you figure it out, and then you're navigating the public transportation like a native.

5   Being in a country by yourself forces you to become more outgoing and social. If you are a shy person, you have no choice but to overcome it and talk to new people even though it may feel like the longest and worst experience of your life. It's either that or be friendless and alone for the next year. I became much more outgoing and confident after living abroad. Starting conversations with strangers and walking into a group of people for the first time isn't as scary as it was before. It taught me the art of small talk and how to make friends with complete strangers. You also learn how to admit when you are completely lost or don't understand something; it's a skill you need to learn early when living abroad—how to swallow your pride. It's hard at first, but like everything else, you learn from it. When you realize you don't really know everything in the world, it's kind of a relaxing feeling.

6   Living abroad was a wonderful experience because I learned about England and learned things about other cultures that I had no idea existed before I lived abroad. I became friends with people from all around the world and traveled to amazing countries, some of which I never would have considered before living in Europe. But most importantly, I learned about myself and everything that I could do. After navigating through customs by myself and stumbling through requests for directions and butchering the language, I realized that I would survive . . . and that it was actually fun! There were hard times and great

times, and I learned from all of them. I went as a college student and came

back as an adult. I'm more confident, more outgoing, have no fears traveling to

new places, and have a love for biscuits and football—and a love for queuing.

Because, after everything, that was still the key to survival in England.

Read Write! Comprehension and Writing Questions

1. What is the main idea of the passage?

2. What are some things the author learned while in England?

3. List some ways the author gives for survival while studying abroad.

4. Search online for what a "zebra" is in England. Using context clues to determine which words you should plug into the search engine besides "zebra" and "England." What is a "zebra"?

5. Write a narrative essay about a time you experienced a new culture. What did you learn from the experience?

Prereading Questions for "The Girl behind the Scarf"
1. Were you picked on or teased as a child? How did it make you feel?
2. Do you display any outward expression of your religion? If so, what? If not, why not?

Tasneem Basha is a student at Eastfield College in Mesquite, TX. This piece originally appeared in Eastfield's student literary magazine, *The Alternative*, in the spring 2013 edition.

The Girl behind the Scarf

by Tasneem Basha

1   Growing up, I always wanted to be just like my mother and sisters. That is, after all, how most girls feel when they are young. I am a Muslim American. Living in Texas all of my life put my mind at ease when it came to applying my religious requirements to my everyday life. In my religion of Islam, all females must wear a headscarf once they reach puberty. I was certain that transitioning into a teenager would be the best time of my life, or so I thought.

2   "You are still too young for it," my mother sighed while I stood in front of the mirror with a scarf wrapped around my head one summer day in 2006. Islam requires that a woman wear a headscarf and clothing long enough to cover her flesh. Sacrificing beauty for God is a major belief in Islam. "No, Mom, I am twelve!" I exclaimed. I was excited to finally wear a scarf.

3   Summertime was drawing to an end, and middle school was about to begin. After my parents dropped me off at school, I began walking to the front door of my new school. Everything felt the same until I opened the door. I had never felt as nervous and sweaty as I did that first day of the seventh grade.

4   "What is that rag on your head?" a young classmate yelled, breaking the silence. Soon after, others began mumbling the same questions, some with rude remarks. None of my friends recognized the new me. I walked to first period quietly and with my head down. So many thoughts began to race through my mind. How can this transition that felt like an honor just an hour ago at home feel like such an embarrassment now?

5   Mrs. Smith, my first period English teacher, helped relax my mind with one simple question. "Where did you get this beautiful scarf from?" she asked. This question, as common as it was, helped me realize I was still the same me. There was no reason to feel ashamed.

6   I realized I was just letting a few people's rude remarks get the best of me. I explained to Mrs. Smith that I found my scarf at a vintage shop in the mall. She kindly asked me why I wore it in front of all of my classmates. I realized this was a great opportunity to educate my peers on why I wear the scarf and a little about my religion. I was surprised to find that my teacher and classmates were astonished by the uniqueness of my culture and religion.

7   During lunch, many of my friends asked similar questions. I had accepted the fact that just as this was hard and awkward for me, my friends felt the same way. It was not their fault that they did not understand the sudden change in my wardrobe. As the days passed, I began to feel more and more comfortable with myself at school.

8   Even though the majority of my peers respected my decision to pursue my religious beliefs, I still experienced some ongoing prejudice from an ignorant few. Hurtful comments, such as "rag head" and "towel head," were thrown my way. The fact that those bullies did what they did made it more important that I stood up for my beliefs. I pride myself in being a unique, self-respecting person.

9   I am proud to have pursued my goal to lead a religious life in a diverse environment. I learned to respect myself and always defend my decisions. This change helped me realize that educating others around me is the key to a successful lifestyle. I also found myself wanting to learn about other religions and cultures and expand my knowledge of all people around me. I do not let rude remarks anger me. Instead, I see them as an opportunity to teach others about myself and my religion.

Read Write! Reading Comprehension and Writing Questions

1. What is the theme of this passage?

2. What rite of passage did the author encounter as she made the transition from elementary school to middle school?

3. What rhetorical mode is this piece?

4. What literary device is the last sentence of the first paragraph an example of?

5. Write a reading response about other rites of passage you are aware of or have participated in.

Prereading Question for "What Did You Steal This Time?"

1. Have you ever been judged or judged someone by the way he/she is dressed or by his/her race?

Kenny Wiley is a youth minister in Denver, Colorado. He enjoys working with young people and reading and writing about race, gender, and class issues in America. He originally posted the passage below on Facebook on July 3, 2012.

What Did You Steal This Time?

by Kenny Wiley

1   There's an old joke that isn't really very funny at all.

2   *What do you call a black man in a suit?*

3   This past Sunday night, I was running down a street near Harvard Yard, trying to get to Harvard Sq. Station in time to catch a bus. I was wearing, backwards, my Houston Texans hat, a "Cosby Show" T-shirt, tennis shoes, and khaki shorts. I had my Mizzou "Summer Welcome 2010" bag over my shoulder. I wasn't sprinting, but I was moving pretty quickly (for me, anyway). I passed a group of four people, strangers who looked somewhere between 17 and 21—two women and two guys.

4   As I ran by, one of the guys, a white guy, yelled out, "Hey, bro, you running from the cops or something?" One of the women quickly added, "What'd you steal this time?"

5   Surely, I didn't hear correctly. I stopped and turned around. "Are you kidding me?" I asked. The group looked a) tipsy, and b) unapologetic. "We're just messing around, man," one said. "Hey, we saw a black guy running at night, so why wouldn't we say that?" said another, indifferently.

6   The exchange quickly grew heated, with me trying to explain to them why their comments were inappropriate. They weren't having any of it. They refused to understand why them suggesting that a young black man running down the street must be evading the cops was a problem. They told me I needed to lighten up, learn to take a joke, and "get over" myself. Rather than start a physical confrontation, I decided to walk on to the station.

7   The whole episode took maybe sixty seconds.

8   To me, the analysis of what happened is simple and straightforward. Four people, none of whom were black, saw a young black guy running down the street late at night. Because they were in a group, or they'd been drinking, or whatever, they decided to say some dumb things.

9   But discussing *anything* about race in the 21st century is rarely simple and straightforward. The people didn't call me the N-word, or darkie, or any other slur. They probably all have at least a handful of black friends. Indeed, one of the guys looked Latino. They didn't try to beat me up. There are other possible explanations: maybe it was my age, or my hat being on backwards. Maybe it was how fast I was running. Maybe if one of my white peers was dressed the same way with the same bag, the group says exactly the same things.

10   Maybe.

11   But probably not.

12   It wasn't easy to write about the incident. It was hard for two reasons: One, do I really have anything to complain about? Was it really that bad? Two,

other black and brown folks have it much worse than I do. I am a 24-year-old black male who attends graduate school at Harvard, one of the best schools in the world. My father is a lawyer, as was my mother. I had most everything I wanted growing up. I come home to a comfortable living situation and as much food as I want, assuming I can figure out how to cook it. In short, this is, for some, the best time in U.S. history to have dark skin.

13   *For some.*

14   The reason Sunday night's incident matters is because to the group of four who yelled those things at me, it didn't matter that I'm student body president-elect at Harvard Divinity School. It didn't matter that I'm the soon-to-be Ministerial Intern at a largely white church less than a mile from where we stood. It didn't matter how many degrees my parents earned. None of it mattered. All that mattered was my skin color, that it was night, and that I was running. And for black and brown men and women who are targeted throughout our country, sometimes that's all that matters for them, too.

15   Oh, the joke. *What do you call a black man in a suit?*

16   If you don't know, look it up. It's a word I don't say.

17   My Unitarian Universalist faith teaches me that every person has inherent worth and dignity. Every person matters, and every person has some good in them. I don't hate those four strangers who loudly suggested that I must be a

criminal, "joking" or not. I don't suddenly hate white people because of the actions of a few. Going after a whole group because of the actions of some is exactly what I'm trying to stop. My faith teaches me that nobody is beyond reconciliation, beyond redemption. I do not hate them.

18   What I want is for us to stop pretending. I want us to stop pretending that racism is over. If it were, tipsy strangers wouldn't have heckled me. I want us to stop pretending that it's not harder to be female than male. That it's not harder to be gay than straight. I want us to stop pretending that we live in an equal society. We don't. It isn't one person's fault, or one group's fault. Instead of blaming or evading, we can encourage and confront, *together.* Instead of pretending that all these 'isms' are over, we can say *"Things are better than they've ever been, and there's so much more to be done."* I don't think that's so bad.

19   Why not now?

20   Since Sunday night's incident, I've been listening a lot to Keb' Mo's version of *America the Beautiful.* Keb' Mo is black, and clearly loves this country. I know I do. But three days before America's birthday, I was made to feel like I didn't really belong, albeit briefly. I know better. Keb' Mo helped me remember. How many people with darker skin are made to feel as I felt? I don't know. But I think we can all do something about it.

21   May *God shed his grace on thee.*

Read Write! Reading Comprehension and Writing Questions

1. What is the main idea of the passage?

2. Is this passage one rhetorical mode or a combination? Can you name them?

3. Why do you think the author refers to the old joke before he writes about the incident and then brings it up again when he finishes?

4. Make an inference about why the author purposefully mentions that this incident took place three days before "America's birthday." Think between the lines.

5. What connections can you draw between "The Girl behind the Scarf" and "What Did You Steal This Time?"

6. Write about a time you experienced prejudice.

7. Write a reading response about whether or not you believe America is a nation that truly accepts all people.

Kerry L. Stanford is a mechanical and forensic engineer by day and an artist by night. His preferred art medium is drawing, and he creates and sells both pencil and pen and ink sketches. Stanford sketches from photographs and favors historical subjects, particularly in regards to World Wars I and II and the American West.

A Few Comments on the Benefits of Letting Go

by Kerry L. Stanford

1   I have recently been perusing John M. Pirsig's philosophical work *Zen and the Art of Motorcycle Maintenance*. I say perusing rather than reading because that is exactly what I've been doing; not reading straight through the book, but rather going through a few pages at a time and actually absorbing the information, or trying to. Often I would read a passage or passages more than once, in rather leisurely fashion, and just as often I had to stop and mentally mark the relationship and similarities of the material in the book to my own life and experiences.

2   *Zen and the Art of Motorcycle Maintenance* as a literary work has been around for a while, having first been published in 1974, and I've meant to read it for many years. It was published while I was in college, where I was simulating the study of fine art and engineering. For quite some time it was *the* modern philosophical book to read, at least for college students. I am, however, a lazy sort, and I had some trouble convincing myself to wade through it. Perhaps that was a good thing.

3   I'm glad the book was never part of an assigned reading list, as I would almost certainly have just read it, and not absorbed it.

4   The title is intriguing though, and I often wondered how well it paralleled my own thinking on such things, especially in more recent years, that is, since I am older.

5   Not long ago I came across a used paperback copy in a thrift store. The price was only fifty cents, so I added it to my library of things to read. I then took the nearly unprecedented step of adding the book to my stack of reading material beside the bath tub, so I *would* read it. A sense of duty impelled me, or so I suppose. (I own an embarrassingly large number of unread books.)

6   It occurred to me as I was trying to absorb and consider the content, that this is not really a book for traditional college students. For me, at least, a considerable amount of life's experiences must be attained before the content can properly enter one's mind and have an effect on one's thinking. A varied set of mental parallels is required, and my guess is that the traditional college student does not have enough life experiences to have these parallels readily at hand.

7   To get to the heart of the matter, Pirsig deeply explores the relationship between what he calls classical and romantic views of technology and art, and, realistically, just about anything else as well. The author expresses his philosophical viewpoint through an idea he calls *Quality*; basically the concept that an engineering design, a work of art, or maintenance of one's motorcycle, is an effort well done and satisfying, an effort that is *good,* and appropriate

to the situation. At least it *can* be good, if you have the right state of mind while doing it.

8   Pirsig also notes a conflicting duality between the classical and romantic views of such things.

9   On the one hand, the classical view is the one most often found in science and engineering, i.e., a direct attention to the collected data, the design, the expectation of result. All well and good, but lacking in Quality because it does not necessarily concern itself with the romantic aspect as described below, and it has little concern for the creative requirements.

10   The romantic aspect is the one that admires the work of art for its beauty or effect, but doesn't necessarily understand what impelled the artist to create the work. This aspect also admires the engineering design for its cleverness and accomplishment. Again, all well and good, but this viewpoint lacks Quality as well because it has little understanding of the underlying technical or artistically-driven principals involved. Like the classical view, the self-awareness and creative aspect are also short-changed.

11   According to Pirsig, both of the above viewpoints share critical lacks; small understanding of the *time-dependent* aspects of the creative flow of the human mind, that is, little grasp of the *here and now* as it applies to such things, and little appreciation for the *requirement, the need,* to understand these things as they apply to Quality. Both viewpoints lack an understanding of the creative state of mind, and how creative effort flows time-wise. This time-dependent

self-awareness during the creation of anything, or simply a job well done, is one and the same for the attitude most often needed, and most often lacking, in both types of endeavor, be they classically or romantically viewed.

12   This duality creates two camps of thought, two camps of attitude, and the camps do not mix well. The inherent conflicting duality drove Pirsig into an asylum.

13   Those from the classical side often have little appreciation for fine art, and small patience for those who do not understand the technicalities of what they are doing. They most often do not sense the *Elegance* of their own effort, the *Quality* to be found in the scientific endeavor, the *Elegance* of an engineering design, or that to be had from viewing a fine piece of art. They have little or no sense of creative time flow for the moment. They are, in effect, nuts-and-bolts types.

14   Those from the romantic side of things most often do not understand the technical principals involved with an effort by the classical side, and so they also lack an appreciation of the Quality of the effort. While they may well have a greater appreciation for a work of art, to Pirsig's mind, the appreciation is typically somewhat artificial and shallow, because these people don't necessarily have a good grasp of what was actually involved in the art's creation. They see only the beauty or the symmetry or the colors, the surface of the work, if you will, not the underlying thrust of the creative flow required. They do not see, or feel, the Quality. They are merely observers.

15   In fact, both camps are all too often merely observers.

16   Pirsig states that this duality for both sides creates a mental blockage. Classical types may wonder at a public passion for an artwork, a movie, a ballet. There is a good chance that it makes little sense to them. On the other hand, romantic types may well find their ignorance of the technical aspects of modern life hanging over them like a dark cloud. They can use their computer, but they do not understand it. They can drive their car, but they do not understand its inner workings.

17   As an example or three, perhaps you enjoy working on your vehicle. A good many men, and some women, find this activity relaxing, and they enjoy the feeling of a job well done afterward. They may not have a complete understanding of the vehicle and its systems, but they know enough to be basically knowledgeable, and they are not afraid to at least partially disassemble their vehicle and repair it. They are not dissuaded by a lack of understanding hanging over their heads like the proverbial dark cloud.

18   On the other hand, most people are frozen and bereft if their "check engine" light comes on.

19   A good many men and women enjoy various forms of the creation of art; sketching, scrap-booking, writing, choreography, whatever it may be, and at whatever level. Again they find the effort relaxing and satisfying, and enjoy the fact that they have carried it out. There is no "I can't even draw a straight line" attitude. They just do it.

20   Others feel they have no talent for any such thing and don't even try, or even flat-out refuse to try.

21   Some mathematicians talk about the *Elegance* of the study of numbers. You might be one of those people who hates math, claims to not understand it, and is thoroughly turned off by it. As far as you are concerned, there is no elegance involved. Please believe me when I say that mathematical elegance certainly exists, and in a very pure form, even when it begins to verge into the philosophical, perhaps especially then. I believe that mathematicians who express such feelings at least partially understand the concept expressed here. They understand there is a certain *Quality,* an *Elegance,* to what they are doing, as do the mechanics and artists mentioned above.

22   The same can be said for a good carpenter. Even if he or she is merely completing the simplest of joints, with a good carpenter there is often an appreciation for the *Quality* of the work. I'm not just talking about the strength of the joint, nor just its appearance, but the effort that went into it, the design, the selection of materials, the satisfaction of knowing the completed effort is *right,* is *good,* the *why* of its need for creation, the simple fact that the joint has been *created* in a Quality way. The carpenter relaxed and enjoyed himself while doing it, and was quietly satisfied with his effort. The same applies to needlework, sketching, plumbing, or maintaining your motorcycle.

23   I had a few engineering professors (not many) who talked about the Elegance of an aircraft design, the Elegance of a gas dynamic study, the Elegance of the

way these things were sometimes done. A similar viewpoint occasionally came across from a few of my art professors, though typically in a more esoteric fashion. Both were, of course, talking about the same thing in different ways. In both cases they were trying to present a mental handle on the Quality of the endeavor for us dumb-ass students. I'm not sure it took, at least with me. Perhaps it has, finally.

24   Most people do not have this understanding of Quality, in their jobs, in their hobbies, whatever they may be doing. Pirsig believes this lack of understanding is based upon their being firmly in either the romantic or classical camps, with its resultant blockage, and in their not being in the here and now, in their *focus*, in their *self-awareness* during the flow of the effort, at the moments of creation.

25   Pirsig, at least to my way of thinking, defines this self-awareness as being at one with the flow of time during these efforts, or the appreciation thereof. There are a number of corny colloquial descriptions for this mental state, being "in the groove", having "perfect focus" or being "in the now". All mean the same thing. You are actively involved in the *here and now* of the creative moment, in the *here and now* of fixing your motorcycle. You are not ahead of it, and you are not behind it. You are *there,* and fully aware you are *there.*

26   Have you ever had one of those very rare times when you've gone into a bar and played eight-ball on the pool table most of the evening, wherein you simply could not lose? Perhaps you felt an odd, relaxed peacefulness settle over your

mind. What must be done with each shot was utterly obvious, and you knew exactly where and how hard to hit the cue ball. You may unconsciously have been playing several shots ahead as a strategy. There was no frustration with hitting a bad shot, because they were few and far between. You simply lined up and took each shot, and your actions were as natural and instinctive to you as breathing. It may be that while you were playing, the noisy bar simply faded away. There was no distraction to your effort. You simply flowed along with it, in the moment, in each moment. Every shot, even the most difficult of distant cuts, was simple and completely apparent. The pool table was your world, and nothing else. You could not, and did not, lose. Your concentration, your focus, was perfect.

27   This has happened to me a few times while playing pool. It has also happened while playing chess, or cards, or even pin-ball. The type of effort does not matter, only the *self-awareness* matters, the *focus,* the *state of mind,* being *in the moment.*

28   Sometimes, when I sketch, the drawing flows out of the pencil or pen like veritable magic. It is almost as though I am creating the work without effort, without angst, and quite quickly, with a sureness that defies any mistake. If a mistake does occur, particularly with ink, it quickly becomes a part of the drawing, as though it was meant to be there. The model flows into my eyes, into my brain, down to my hand, and on to the paper with such deft ease. I am *in the moment.*

29   Other times, trying to draw is like pulling my own teeth.

30   With no sure memory of exactly *how* it was done, I can simply take a look at my assorted works and readily tell you which is which. I was either pulling teeth, or simply flowing merrily along.

31   How do you get *in the moment*, and how do you get it back next time? I don't actually know.

32   As an interesting side note, you may remember the movie *The Legend of Bagger Vance*. In the film, Will Smith plays a caddie who appears from nowhere to help exceptional golfer Matt Damon not only get his swing back, but recapture his whole mental attitude about the game from the horrific stress of combat in the trenches of World War One.

33   Bagger said that golf is a game that cannot be won, only played. The parallel here is obvious enough, but he also refers to the whole effort of playing quality golf as "seeing the field". For this exceptional level of play, the player has to *let go*, quit thinking, "see the field", and just go with the flow. This is an exact parallel to my few exceptional games on the pool table, or my moments of flowing, artistic sketching. You *must* be *in the moment* to have an exceptional round of golf, or an exceptional game of pool. You must let go and "see the field". By exactly the same token, you must "see the model" when you are sketching and simply let the artwork flow and happen. If you can do so, it will.

34   Pirsig defines this sort of thing as the *Quality* of the moment, the *Quality* of the effort, the *Quality* of the result. You cannot fully appreciate it, much

less do anything very well, unless you have that flowing, *in the moment,* state of mind. He feels creativity, or any effort, is much enhanced if you can get to this "see the field" mental state of perfect focus. Angst has no place.

35   I agree. Being the dummy that I am though, what I don't know is how to get there on a reliable basis.

36   A realization of the *Quality* of all types of effort is an underlying human capability, or perhaps a need, that Pirsig points out repeatedly. This understanding of the *Quality,* the *Goodness,* of an endeavor is all too often lacking. It doesn't matter what the endeavor is; carpentry, drawing, machining, plumbing, scientific research, painting, designing an engine, or pursuit of a mathematical proof. It runs the gamut of things humans do. All of these efforts have a *Quality* associated with them, an *Elegance,* that needs to be realized from both the classical and the romantic viewpoints. The bridge must be crossed for full appreciation and success, and you have to be *in the moment* to walk across.

37   Here is where the Zen part comes in. You have to let go, and you have to just flow with it to get *in the moment.* Occasionally, I can.

38   Sometimes, I sits and thinks . . . and sometimes, I just sits.

Read Write! Reading Comprehension and Writing Questions

1. What is the main idea of the passage?

2. What other piece of written work is referenced throughout?

3. What rhetorical modes have been combined in this piece?

4. The author describes people from different sides. What are the names of the sides and what do they not appreciate?

5. What does "esoteric" mean in paragraph 23?

6. Why do you think the author purposefully misuses subject-verb agreement in paragraph 38? What is he trying to convey to the reader?

7. What does the author mean when he refers to Quality and Elegance? What are some benefits of incorporating Quality and Elegance into your work?

8. Write a short response explaining the side you believe the author is on: Classical or Romantic. Defend your answer.

9. Write a formal summary of this passage.

10. Write a reading response to this passage regarding a skill, talent, or hobby you have that sometimes "flows" and sometimes is like "pulling teeth."

Nelda Contreras is a developmental writing and English professor at Brookhaven College in Farmer's Branch, TX. She enjoys reading and traveling and is currently working on a book about marriage. The passage below is an excerpt from this book. It describes how she met her husband.

An excerpt from *My Marriage with Him*

by Nelda Contreras

1   I knew this trip would change my life, but I never expected what would happen to me in Africa. The fact that I was going on this journey in itself was a miracle. If it were not for a scholarship I received, there was no way I could have afforded it. Before I ever left the ground in Dallas, I felt there was a reason that I was going to Africa beyond just work. God wanted me on that plane; I just was not sure why. This would launch a perpetual questioning about Makhtar that still echoes today. It's been ten years since I met him. Why did I go? Why didn't we break up? How have we survived this marriage for eight years?

2   When I stepped off the plane in Senegal, the first thing I noticed was the distinct smell. The air seemed uninviting with its heavy and unpleasant odor. The international airport did not live up to its name. It is a forced structure erected without much thought about organization or traffic. The lack of city planning is true for most of Senegal. My travel companions and I huddled together waiting in a crowded room while our bags were being opened and searched. The men had no regard that their owners were standing by watching.

3   The quaint hotel where we stayed in Dakar was run by a French couple. Our meals were delicious, and the rooms were comfortable. The roof was the

best place to put on my headphones, listen to my favorite Chomsky CD, and write about my experiences in my journal. The breeze there was refreshing, and I had a view of the entire neighborhood. I could see the delivery van full of baked bread across the street. There were women sitting on the corner in their traditional dresses gossiping about the day while the street vendors forced their items on anyone walking by. I was so far from home, but there was also something comfortable and familiar about Dakar. I now know it's because this is Makhtar's home.

4   I fell in love with him the first time I heard his voice. I tell people it was love at first sight, but really it was love at first voice. He managed the front desk at the hotel where we were staying. I had never seen his face before that day. One of the women from our trip was at the front counter talking to him. I was looking at some postcards, not really paying attention to anything in particular. Our group was gathering in the front lobby to go to the local market, so we were waiting for everyone to arrive.

5   "Why do you not have a girlfriend?" the woman asked the guy at the front counter.

6   "There are so many beautiful women in Senegal," Makhtar answered. "There are many beautiful women in Senegal, but she must also have a good heart."

7   His response jolted me out of boredom. His voice was deep, and he had a strong accent. He spoke his answer with pure sincerity, and I immediately asked myself why I did not know him. From that moment, I wanted to find out more about the mysterious man behind the counter.

8   I moved away from the postcards and invited myself in to the conversation. I heard the stranger addressed as Makhtar. He went around the group of us and made sure he had all of our names straight. We would be staying in the hotel for a while, and he wanted to make sure he addressed us properly. I was sure this was something that he was trained to do and not because he had any interest in knowing any of us.

9   During one of the times in the hotel, it was quiet, and I found Makhtar sitting on one of the couches by himself. I learned so much about him that day. He spoke five languages: English, Spanish, French, Wolof, and Serer. He graduated from the local university with a degree in foreign languages. He was Muslim, and his father was a polygamist who had three wives and a lot of children. He told me he suffered a lot emotionally because of his extended family. There were lots of jealousy and rivalry between wives. He also told me he never wanted to have more than one wife. He never wanted to have children with more than one woman. He had seen all the pain it caused in his own family, and he did not want that for his children.

10   I was fascinated with him. He was so different from me. I am Hispanic and Catholic. I grew up in a traditional family, and we are all extremely close. My parents have been married forever. They had four kids, and we never wanted for anything, emotionally or otherwise.

11   As our trip neared its end, I never thought I would see him again. My life was on the other side of the world, and I was headed home. I remember

hoping that our group would leave before I saw him. It was going to be hard.

I could easily love him. We were so different on the outside, but we thought

the same way. We had the same strong belief in family and how we wanted to

raise children. Education was extremely important. We had our differences

in religion, but we also respected each other's beliefs. I wondered why I had

met him. He was wonderful, and now I was leaving.

12   I took in everything that morning. My thought was that Senegal was not

finished with me. I did not understand why, but I was not done there.

Read Write! Reading Comprehension and Writing Questions

1. Search online for more information about Senegal. What did you find? Read the excerpt a second time. Do you feel this new knowledge contributed to your second reading?

2. What about the author's future husband originally attracted her to him?

3. Why do the author and her husband go so well together despite their differences?

4. What connections can you draw between the piece "Choose Wisely" and this excerpt?

5. Write a hypothetical ending to this excerpt. What do you believe happens between the author and her future husband when she tries to leave Senegal?

Malik Alexander is a sophomore at the University of Alabama studying business. He is a member of the Honors College and the Alpha Phi Beta Lambda business fraternity. He is an award winning poet who enjoys reading, playing video games, and playing basketball.

The Hero Shot

by Malik Alexander

I back em down

I post em up

I watch the ball

It's going up

I shoot the three   5

I make the shot

Watch out now

I'm getting hot

Through my legs

Behind my back   10

I crossed him over

I made him sit down flat

Down by two

We gotta win

I try the hero shot   15

Nothing but rim

Then I hear the buzzer go off

And I know that we lost

Because I took the hero shot

In the locker room I get yelled at 20

They told me that I should've passed

Next game I start to pass

And we start to win

Game after game we get closer

To playing that team again 25

Finally we get there

To the final game

Right before the tipoff

I know it won't be the same

We play great 30

But it must be fate

Because at the end

It's time for the hero shot again

But this time I pass

And the guy makes the three 35

Though the points go to him

The assist goes to me

Read Write! Reading Comprehension and Writing Questions

1. What is the theme of the poem?

2. Make an inference about which sport this poem is about.

3. Make an inference about what "the hero shot" is.

4. Write a response to this poem about a time you had to work with others to achieve something great.

5. Write about a time you had to swallow your pride for the greater good.

Edgar Allan Poe (1809-1849) was a 19th century American author and poet. Many of his works were originally published in newspapers, and though not all of his writing was popular during his lifetime, many, such as the poem The Raven, were quite well received. Today Poe is most well-known for his horror, but he also wrote comedy and detective stories. *Annabel Lee,* which was published posthumously in 1849, is the last complete poem written before Poe's death.

Annabel Lee

by Edgar Allan Poe

It was many and many a year ago,

In a kingdom by the sea,

That a maiden there lived whom you may know

By the name of Annabel Lee;

And this maiden she lived with no other thought   5

Than to love and be loved by me.

I was a child and *she* was a child,

In this kingdom by the sea:

But we loved with a love that was more than love—

I and my Annabel Lee;   10

With a love that the winged seraphs of heaven

Coveted her and me.

And this was the reason that, long ago,

In this kingdom by the sea,

A wind blew out of a cloud, chilling   15

My beautiful Annabel Lee;

So that her highborn kinsman came

And bore her away from me,

To shut her up in a sepulchre

In this kingdom by the sea.   20

The angels, not half so happy in heaven,

Went envying her and me—

Yes!—that was the reason (as all men know,

In this kingdom by the sea)

That the wind came out of the cloud by night,   25

Chilling and killing my Annabel Lee.

But our love it was stronger by far than the love

Of those who were older than we—

Of many far wiser than we—

And neither the angels in heaven above,   30

Nor the demons down under the sea,

Can ever dissever my soul from the soul

Of the beautiful Annabel Lee:

For the moon never beams, without bringing me dreams

Of the beautiful Annabel Lee;   35

And the stars never rise, but I feel the bright eyes

Of the beautiful Annabel Lee;

And so, all the night-tide, I lie down by the side

Of my darling—my darling—my life and my bride,

In her sepulchre there by the sea,   40

In her tomb by the sounding sea.

Read Write! Reading Comprehension and Writing Questions

1. Circle any words you do not recognize and then define them using context clues and/or a dictionary.

2. Highlight any descriptive language you see.

3. What can you infer happened to Annabel Lee?

4. What kind of imagery do you see within the poem? What do you think Poe's purpose is in using this imagery?

5. What is the tone of the passage?

6. What is the mood of the passage?

Appendix

OUTLINE TEMPLATE

Thesis Statement: _____

_____

Topic Sentence Body Paragraph 1:

I. _____

a. _____

b. _____

c. _____

Topic Sentence Body Paragraph 2:

II. _____

a. _____

b. _____

c. _____

Topic Sentence Body Paragraph 3:

III. _____

a. _____

b. _____

c. _____

Conclusion paragraph:

_____

_____

PYRAMID TEMPLATE

Beyond the lines

Between the lines

On the lines

L What have I learned

W What do I want to know

K What do I already know

LITERARY DEVICES QUICK REFERENCE

Alliteration	The repetition of words starting with the same letter that makes the same sound, usually a consonant sound. Example: Peter Piper picked a peck of pickled peppers.
Assonance	The repetition of vowel sounds at the start of words or within words in a phrase, clause, or sentence. Example: The moon was in bloom.
Consonance	The repetition of consonant sounds at the start of words or within words in a phrase, clause, or sentence. Example: Her shoes clacked on the cracked concrete.
Foreshadowing	Hinting to the reader that something will soon happen Example: I thought I knew everything about going to Comi-Con, but I was in for a surprise.
Hyperbole	Excessive exaggeration Example: Marian has the best husband in the entire world.
Metaphor	A figure of speech that describes something by comparing it directly to something else (does not use "like" or "as") Example: The river was a snake.
Onomatopoeia	Words that sound like the words they are describing. Example: The door creaked shut.
Personification	Giving human characteristics to inanimate objects or ideas Example: The leaves danced in the wind.
Sensory imagery	Descriptions that appeal to the reader's five senses Example: The rich smelling leather was soft and supple.
Simile	A figure of speech that describes something by comparing it to something else using the words "like" or "as" Example: The boy was as mean as a snake.

COMMONLY CONFUSED WORDS QUICK REFERENCE

Word 1	Meaning	Word 2	Meaning	Example Sentences
A	Article used before words that begin with a consonant sound	An	Article used before words that begin with a vowel sound	1. Sinbad is a hilarious comedian. 2. Liza needs an X-ray taken of her foot.
Accept	To agree to receive or do	Except	Not including	1. I accept your apology. 2. I want all the clothes except the red shirt.
Advice	Recommendations about what to do	Advise	To recommend something	1. Helen gives good advice. 2. She always advises everyone to make good choices.
Affect	To change or make a difference to	Effect	A result; to bring about a result	1. The neighborhood was affected by the hurricane. 2. The special effects were poor.
Aisle	A passage between rows of seats	Isle	An island	1. Melanie walked down the aisle of the plane. 2. The Caribbean isle is lovely.
All together	All in one place, all at once	Altogether	Completely; on the whole	1. The whole family was all together in Aspen. 2. Altogether, I don't like it.
Along	Moving or extending horizontally on	A long	Referring to something of great length	1. Maribel went along with Jose. 2. It is a long road.
Aloud	Out loud	Allowed	Permitted	1. Penelope accidently said what she was thinking out loud. 2. The dog is allowed on the couch.
Altar	A sacred table in a church or religious center	Alter	To change	1. Harold worshipped at the altar. 2. Daisy altered her hair cut.
Among	Used when discussing three or more things/people	Between	Used when discussing only two things/people	1. Evelyn was chosen from among all the students to represent the school at the state speech contest. 2. The book fell between the chair and the end table.

Word 1	Meaning	Word 2	Meaning	Example Sentences
Amoral	Not concerned with right or wrong	Immoral	Not following accepted moral standards	1. Charles Manson is an amoral person. 2. Immoral people are often shunned by society.
Assent	Agreement, approval	Ascent	The action of rising or climbing up	1. Kanella assented to let the twins go to the party. 2. The ascent to the top of the mountain was difficult.
Bare	Naked; to uncover	Bear	To carry; to put up with	1. Jimmy bared his chest. 2. Angelica had to bear the weight of the guilt because she betrayed Andre.
Bazaar	A Middle Eastern market	Bizarre	Strange	1. Jane shopped at the Moroccan bazaar. 2. Bill is such a bizarre fellow.
Born	Having started life	Borne	Carried	1. Cynthia was born in May. 2. The weight of the travel pack was borne by Jorge.
Bough	A branch of a tree	Bow	To bend the head; the front of a ship	1. The tree bough broke in the storm. 2. The people bowed to the king and queen.
Brake	A device for stopping a vehicle; to stop a vehicle	Break	To separate into pieces; a pause	1. Owen pressed the brake pedal to stop the car. 2. Spring break is fun. 3. It hurts to break one's arm.
Breath	Noun form referring to the intake of air	Breathe	Verb form referring to the action of inhaling air	1. Eduardo could not catch his breath. 2. The air was smoggy, and it was hard to breathe.
Breach	To break through, or break a rule; a gap	Breech	The back part of a gun barrel	1. An iceberg breached the Titanic's hull. 2. The gun breech cracked and broke when it hit the ground.
Buy	Purchase	By	Beside; through	1. I want to buy that new video game. 2. Pratik drove by the college.

(*Continued*)

Word 1	Meaning	Word 2	Meaning	Example Sentences
Canvas	A type of strong cloth	Canvass	To seek people's votes, opinions; to find out information from others	1. The sail was made of canvas. 2. Devon canvassed the neighborhood.
Censure	To criticize strongly	Censor	To ban parts of a book or film; a person who does this	1. The FCC censured the radio station for obscene language and then fined them thousands of dollars. 2. The government censored the newspaper because of libelous statements.
Cereal	A grass producing an edible grain; a breakfast food made from grains	Serial	Happening in a series	1. Tommy eats cereal for breakfast. 2. *Smallville*, a television serial, was my favorite show.
Chord	A group of musical notes	Cord	A length of string; a cord-like body part	1. Adam played the chord on his guitar. 2. The cord of rope was very thick.
Coarse	Rough	Course	A direction; a school subject; part of a meal	1. The coarse material scratched Grant's face. 2. The developmental writing course was enlightening.
Complement	To add to so as to improve; an addition that improves something	Compliment	To praise or express approval; an admiring remark	1. The new tutoring center complemented the college's mission of excellence in teaching and learning. 2. Ricky complimented Lucy on her new haircut.
Council	A group of people who manage or advise	Counsel	Advice; to advise	1. The council passed the bill. 2. Harry counseled Urica about which college to attend.
Cue	A signal for action; a wooden rod	Queue	A line of people or vehicles	1. The lightning crash was Maria's cue to go on stage. 2. The movie theatre queue seemed a mile long.

Word 1	Meaning	Word 2	Meaning	Example Sentences
Currant	A dried grape	Current	Happening now; a flow of water, air, or electricity	1. Lyle does not like currants. 2. The river current is fast in this area.
Defuse	To make a situation less tense	Diffuse	To spread over a wide area	1. Elias defused the argument between Joe and Kasey. 2. The smell of the perfume diffused throughout the room.
Desert	A waterless, empty area; to abandon someone	Dessert	The sweet course of a meal	1. The desert can be a dangerous place. 2. Wendy's favorite dessert is pineapple upside down cake.
Discreet	Careful not to attract attention	Discrete	Separate and distinct	1. Oliver tried to sneak into work late, but he was not discreet enough. 2. The men's dressing room and the women's dressing room must be discrete in order to preserve privacy.
Disinterested	Impartial	Uninterested	Not interested	1. Roberto was disinterested in the fact that Pablo and Karen had gotten back together. 2. Many people are uninterested in politics today.
Dual	Having two parts	Duel	A fight or contest between two people	1. The developmental writing class has a dual exit exam. 2. Alexander Hamilton was killed in a duel with Aaron Burr.
Elicit	To draw out a reply or reaction	Illicit	Not allowed by law or rules	1. The reporter attempted to elicit a response from the politician. 2. Upton's illicit behavior resulted in suspension from the college.
Ensure	To make certain that something will happen	Insure	To provide compensation if a person dies or property is damaged	1. Isabelle studied to ensure a high grade in her history class. 2. Quentin insured his house against tornado damage.

(*Continued*)

Word 1	Meaning	Word 2	Meaning	Example Sentences
Envelop	To cover or surround	Envelope	A paper container for a letter	1. Rachel was enveloped in a soft blanket. 2. I mailed my bills in brown envelopes.
Farther	Use for physical distance	Further	Use for figurative distance	1. Narcedalia walked farther down the street than last week. 2. The psychology class will further one's understanding of Sigmund Freud's theories.
Feel	Touch; have emotion	Fill	To make full	1. I do not feel well. 2. I filled my belly with too much food.
Flaunt	To display ostentatiously	Flout	To disregard a rule	1. Willis flaunted his new car. 2. Tara flouted the rules by lighting a cigarette in the non-smoking section of the restaurant.
Flounder	To move clumsily; to have difficulty doing something	Founder	To fail; one who establishes something; to sink	1. Raul floundered in the shallow water of the pool. 2. The internet business foundered when the economy went into a recession.
Foreword	An introduction to a book	Forward	Onward, ahead	1. Illiana read the textbook's foreword. 2. Opal moved forward with the project.
Good	Adjective—can only describe nouns and pronouns	Well	Adverb—can only describe actions, adjectives, or other adverbs	1. Morgan did a good job on her assignment. 2. Ramon also did well.
Himself	Reflexive/intensive form of he	Hisself	Not a word—do not use	1. Jesse got himself suspended when he smoked a cigarette in the bathroom.
Imply	To suggest indirectly	Infer	To draw a conclusion	1. You do not need to say "I think" in a thesis statement; it is implied. 2. From the white paint transfer marks on my bumper, I can infer someone hit me and drove off afterward.

Word 1	Meaning	Word 2	Meaning	Example Sentences
Its	Possessive form of it	It's	Contraction of it is or it has	1. The dog chases its tail. 2. It's going to rain tomorrow.
Loath	Reluctant, unwilling	Loathe	To hate	1. I am loath to go to work today. 2. Jessica loathes tomatoes.
Loose	To unfasten; to set free	Lose	To be deprived of; to be unable to find	1. Since Lester lost weight, his pants are loose. 2. Kevin always loses his keys.
Past	Time frame that already happened; beyond	Passed	Went by	1. I walked past the church for the first time yesterday. 2. The argument is in the past. 3. Gregory passed all his classes!
Pole	A long, slender piece of wood	Poll	Voting in an election	1. The light pole was blown over in the wind. 2. The poll showed Ben would win the school election.
Pour	To flow or cause to flow	Pore	A tiny opening; to study something closely	1. Nancy poured water into a glass. 2. Alan pored over his homework.
Principal	Most important; the head of a school	Principle	A fundamental rule or belief	1. The principal is my pal. 2. The principles of writing can be mastered with practice.
Sight	The ability to see	Site	A location	1. Carson's sight was perfect after his LASIK surgery. 2. The building site was on the lakeshore.
Stationary	Not moving	Stationery	Writing materials	1. The stationary bike is an excellent exercise tool. 2. Felicia uses her personal stationery to answer correspondence.
Then	Shows time; cause and effect	Than	Makes a comparison	1. Then, Ellenore went to the movies with Neil. 2. She likes Neil better than her old boyfriend.
Tortuous	Full of twists; complex	Torturous	Full of pain or suffering	1. The maze was tortuous. 2. Roger's headache was torturous.

(Continued)

Word 1	Meaning	Word 2	Meaning	Example Sentences
Use	To put into service	Used to	Something done previously	1. On Sundays, we use the good dishes. 2. Cathy used to live in New York.
Wreath	A ring-shaped arrangement of flowers etc.	Wreathe	To surround or encircle	1. The holiday wreath on the Summers' door is lovely. 2. The religious altar was wreathed with candles.
Your	Possessive form of you	You're	Contraction of you are or you were	1. Is this your backpack? 2. You're going to get in trouble.

Below are some of the commonly confused words that have three or more confused forms of words.

Word	Meaning
Quiet	Hushed
Quit	Stop
Quite	Very

Example Sentences

1. The library is a quiet place.

2. Xander quit his job at the warehouse.

3. The weather is quite lovely today.

Word	Meaning
Their	Possessive form of they
There	In or at that place
They're	Contraction of they are or they were

Example Sentences

1. The Shepherds are a very sweet family, and their house is always clean.

2. There is one room in the house that is a mess, though: the guest room.

3. They're in the process of remodeling it.

Word	Meaning
Themselves	Reflexive/intensive pronoun form of they
Themself	Not a word
Theirself	Not a word
Theirselves	Not a word

Example Sentences

1. The students wondered to themselves if they had made good grades on their tests.

Word	Meaning
Through	In at one end and out at the other
Thorough	Extremely attentive to accuracy and detail
Threw	The past tense of throw; to propel an object

Example Sentences

The car sped through the tunnel.

The police did a thorough investigation of the stolen museum paintings.

Rhonda accidentally threw the baseball through the window while playing catch.

Word	Meaning
To	To indicate direction
Too	Also or very
Two	The number 2

Example Sentences

1. Paul is going to Palm Beach for spring break.

2. Allison is taking a ballet class, and Miriam wants to take one, too.

3. There are two windows on the side of the house that need to be cleaned.

Word	Meaning
Weather	Outdoor atmosphere including temperature, rain, sun, etc.
Whether	Two possibilities
Rather	Prefer to, instead

Example Sentences

1. The weather can quickly become dangerous in Oklahoma during spring.

2. I love cats, whether they are long haired or short haired.

3. I would rather have a short haired cat, though.

Word	Meaning
Where	Refers to place
Were	Past tense form of be in third person plural
Wear	To put on
Ware	Goods
We're	Contraction of we are or we were

Example Sentences

1. Where are the restrooms?

2. They were down the hall, but renovations caused them to be moved.

3. Cee Lo Green always seems to wear red clothes.

4. Street vendors sell their wares in parks in New York City.

5. We're going to buy knock off Prada bags from them.

PREFIX, SUFFIX, AND ROOT QUICK REFERENCE

Knowing the meaning of common prefixes, roots, and suffixes will help you figure out the meaning of unknown words.

Prefixes are at the beginning of words. They change the meaning of the root of words.

Common Prefixes

Prefix	Meaning	Example
a	not	atypical
ante	before	antebellum
anti	against	anti-itch
auto	self	autobiography
bi	two	biracial
circum	around	circumstance
co	with	coauthor
com, con	together, with	compile consider
con, contra	against	convict, contraband
de	off, away from	desegregate
dis	not	disassociate
en	put into	envelope
ex	out of, former	ex-husband
extra	beyond, more than	extraordinary
hetero	different	heterosexual
homo	same	homogenize
hyper	over, more	hypersensitive
il, im, in, ir	not, without	illiterate, impolite, incorrect, irregular
in	into	integrate
inter	between	interpersonal
intra	between	intrapersonal
macro	large	macroeconomics
meta	about	metacognition
micro	small	microscopic
mono	one	monorail

Prefix	Meaning	Example
multi	many	multimillionaire
non	not, without	nonconformist
omni	all, every	omnipresent
poly	many	polygamy
post	after	post-menopause
pre, pro	before, forward	preview, prorate
re	again	review
semi	half	semiliterate
sub	under	subordinate
syn	same time	synonym
trans	across	transfer
tri	three	tripod
un	not	unfriendly
uni	one	uni-brow

Knowing the **root** form of words will help you determine its meaning as prefixes and suffixes are added to it.

Common Roots

Root	Meaning	Example
aster, astro	star	asteroid
audi	hear	audience
bene	good	beneficial
bio	life	biography
chrono	time	chronological
cosmo	order, universe	cosmos
dict	say	edict
duc	lead, make	deduce
ego	self	egocentric

Root	Meaning	Example
fact, fac	make, do	factor
frater	brother	fraternity
gen	give birth	generation
geo	earth	geology
graph	write	autograph,
gyn	woman	gynecologist
jur, jus	law	justice
log, logue	thought	dialogue
logy	study of	psychology
luc	light	trans-lucid
manu	hand	manual
mand, mend	order	amendment
mis, mit	send	transmit
mut, muta	change	mutant
neg, negat	say no, deny	negativity
nomen, nym	name	synonym
path	feel	sympathy
philo, phil	love	philanthropy
phono	sound	phonics
photo	light	photography
port	carry	deport
pseudo	fake	pseudonym
scrib script	write	transcribe, transcript
sens, sent	feel	resent
soror	sister	sorority
tele	far off	telegram
terr	earth	terrestrial
theo	God	theology
vac	empty	vacuum
vid, vis	see	video, visual

Suffixes appear at the end of words. They are typically used to change the part of speech of a word.

Common Suffixes

Noun Suffix	Meaning	Example
acy	state or quality	bureaucracy
al	act or process of	denial
ance, ence	state or quality of	performance, permanence
dom	place or state of being	freedom
ee	one who	employee
er, or	one who	teacher, trainer
hood	being like	neighborhood
ism	doctrine, belief	socialism
ist	one who	biologist
ity, ty	quality of	tenacity
ment	condition of	agreement
ness	state of being	weariness
ship	position held	friendship
sion, tion	state of being	tension

Verb Suffixes	Meaning	Example
ate	become	terminate
en	become	enliven
ify, fy	make or become	horrify
ize, ise	become	harmonize, chastise

Adjective Suffixes	Meaning	Example
able, ible	capable of being	hospitable
al	pertaining to	sectional
esque	reminiscent of	statuesque
ful	notable for	beautiful

Adjective Suffixes	Meaning	Example
ic, ical	pertaining to	diabolic, diabolical
ious, ous	characterized by	mischievous
ish	having the quality of	impish
ive	having the nature of	suggestive
less	without	meaningless
y	characterized by	beauty

THE PARTS OF SPEECH

Below are definitions of the parts of speech in the English language. Every part of speech is used in order to help writers and speakers convey meaning in a clear way. Although not all of the parts of speech are used in every sentence, a sentence must contain at least a subject and a verb. Words are classified by their function in a sentence, not their forms. In other words, the word *cook,* for example, can function as a noun in one sentence and as a verb in another.

Articles	*A, an*, and *the* come before a noun or a noun phrase in a sentence
	The dog barked.
Nouns	A person, place, thing, or idea (nouns are the subject of every sentence you write. They state who or what the sentence is about)
	The dog barked all night long at the cat.
Pronouns	Refer to or take the place of a noun or another pronoun
	The dog owner enjoys walking her dog. She also enjoys teaching her dog tricks.
Adjectives	Describe nouns or pronouns
	The ferocious dog growled at the frightened mail carrier.
Verbs	Show action or a state of being (am, is, are, was, were, be, being, been)
	The ferocious dog growled. It was trying to bite the frightened mail carrier.
Adverbs	Describe how an action is being done or another adjective or adverb (adverbs answer how, when, why, or where)
	The dog growled very loudly at the extremely frightened mail carrier.
Conjunctions	Join words, phrases, and clauses together in a sentence (FANBOYS: for, and, nor, but, or yet, so; transitional words: therefore, however; subordinating conjunctions: because, although, if, when)
	Because the dog growled at the mail carrier, she refused to deliver mail to the dog owners' house or to their adjacent neighbors' houses.
Prepositions	Part of propositional phrases that contain a noun or pronoun (in, on, at, by, with)
	The dog growled at the mail carrier only on Tuesdays.
Interjections	Words like Wow! Oh! or Hey! used to express emotion
	Wow! I have never seen a mail carrier run so fast before.

EDITING SYMBOLS

Unclear meaning:

If there are cows, there are stars.

Add a comma:

When I went to the store it was closed.

Add a period:

I really wanted cereal

Add an apostrophe:

The students tests were graded quickly.

Spelling error:

SP
Weather or not we have storms, the soccer game will not be canceled.

Word choice error:

WC
Dropping a class is a serial choice.

Indent:

¶There is a beautiful house on the hill. It is such a lovely house that my parents decided to buy it. They put in an offer yesterday, and it was accepted. I cannot wait to move.

Capitalize a letter:

George washington was the first U.S. president.

Lowercase a letter:

Many High Schools are overcrowded.

Combine words:

Sam likes to eat ginger bread.

Sentence fragment:

frag
To become a better student. Come to every class meeting.

Comma splice:

c/s

The dog ran wildly out the door, Jerry had left it open too long.

Run-on:

r/o

The dog ran wildly out the door Jerry had left it open too long.

Subject-verb agreement error:

S-v agree

Each student in Mr. Carter's classes are passing.

Pronoun-antecedent agreement error:

p-a agree

All of the students know his/her grades.

Remove something:

Rylin sunbathed all morning. She lay in the hammock. ~~The kitchen door was open.~~

Connect to a previous paragraph:

Alex was very sleepy. He took a nap.
When he awoke, he felt refreshed.

Split in to two words:

Yoroung loves icecream.